Raising a Rare Girl

Raising a
Rare Girl

A MEMOIR

~

HEATHER LANIER

PIATKUS

PIATKUS

First published in the USA in 2020 by Penguin Press, an imprint of
Penguin Random House LLC
First published in Great Britain in 2020 by Piatkus

Portions of this book appeared in different form in *Brain, Child Magazine,
Monday Coffee, The Mighty, Salon, The Sun, Vela Magazine*, and the
author's blog starinhereye.wordpress.com.

Photograph on page 2 © Raymond Baldwin

A CIP catalogue record for this book
is available from the British Library.

ISBN: 978-0-349-42098-1

Design by Amanda Dewey

Printed and bound in Great Britain by
Clays Ltd, Elcograf S.p.A.

Papers used by Piatkus are from well-managed forests
and other responsible sources.

Piatkus
An imprint of
Little, Brown Book Group
Carmelite House
50 Victoria Embankment
London EC4Y 0DZ

An Hachette UK Company
www.hachette.co.uk

www.littlebrown.co.uk

To J, F, & P
without whom I'd be stuck
in a much smaller version of self.

First you should know that they have planets inside just as you do; rivers; acacia trees; windfall apples.

—Stephen Kuusisto
"The Souls of Disabled Folks"

Your children are not your children.
They are the sons and daughters of Life's longing for itself.

—Kahlil Gibran
The Prophet

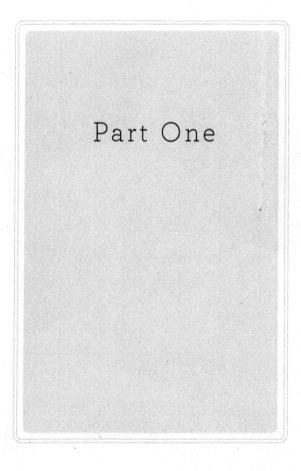

Part One

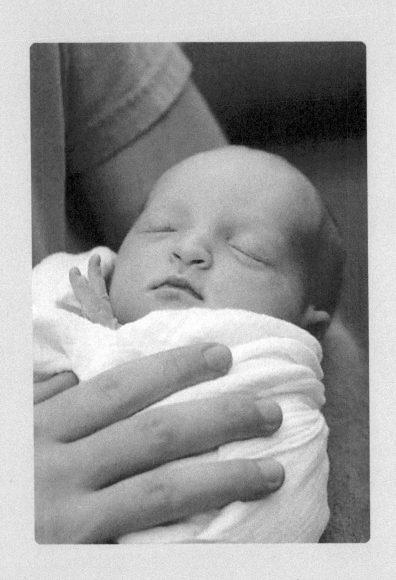

Chapter One

⌒

When I was pregnant, I tried to make a SuperBaby. I didn't realize I was doing this. I thought I'd long ago shed the theory that a body could be made perfect. But looking back, my goal was clear. I swallowed capsules of mercury-free DHA to help grow my SuperBaby's brain. I filled my grocery cart with organic fruits and veggies, letting our monthly food bill consume a quarter of our income. Of course, I followed the medical advice standard for women of my generation. I avoided soft cheeses and cold cuts, and I microwaved my smoked turkey slices so they curled into crispy-edged Frisbees. But I went above and beyond. I gave up wheat for reasons I forget. I kept my flip phone at least an arm's length away from my belly to avoid damaging my Super-Baby with electromagnetic waves. I tried not to let a kernel of GMO corn touch my estrogen-laden tongue. I spoke to my Super-Baby, welcoming it into my body so it would feel loved and supported. I avoided finding out my SuperBaby's sex so I wouldn't project gender roles onto her/him/them. I slept on my left side because I'd read it was best for my circulation, which was in turn best for Baby's. In the last months, I never once reclined on a sofa because I'd heard the position could put a baby posterior, which would dramatically increase my chances of having a C-section, which would rob my baby of certain vaginal bacteria that was beneficial for reasons cited in academic journals I couldn't explain. Instead, I always leaned forward, my elbows propped on my spread knees like I was forever on the verge of imparting a proverb.

And I prepared meticulously for an unmedicated birth. In the final months of pregnancy, I ended each hip-aching day by popping earbuds into my ears, closing my eyes, and listening to Hypnobabies, a natural-birthing program that guided me through self-hypnosis.

My baby will be born healthy and at the perfect time, a woman's voice uttered as I descended into a dreamy soup of electronica chords and affirmations.

My body is made to give birth nice and easy.

I look forward to giving birth with happiness.

*My baby is developing normally and is
healthy and strong.*

The words were supposed to lodge in my subconscious, creating the reality I wanted: a pain-free birth and a perfect child. *I focus on all going right . . .*

After thirty-six hours of labor, the last five of which can best be described as an apocalypse in my perineum, I pushed my baby out and into the warm waters of a hospital tub. For a second, she dangled before me, legs curled toward her chest. Without my glasses, my child appeared to me as a bean-shaped blur suspended in midair.

My husband, Justin, later told me that this was the point at which the nurses became palpably anxious.

"A peanut," said the midwife. "Just a wittle peanut." That was about the kindest thing a medical professional would say about my newborn's body.

Put Baby right on Momma's chest, the books had told me, because oxytocin would flow and enhance SuperBaby with strong bonding. That was in our birthing plan.

But the midwife ordered my husband: "Dad, you need to cut the cord."

"We were gonna wait until the cord stops . . . ," Justin said. *Cutting a cord prematurely,* I'd read, *could rob SuperBaby of vital nutrients and . . .*

In a voice used to direct people swiftly but without panic toward an emergency exit, she said, "No, we need to get Baby on the table now."

My husband took scissors to the cord, and just like that, the stranger who'd lived inside me for nine months was detached, then whisked from my fuzzy line of vision. Too spent from the thirty-six-hour feat, I closed my eyes and felt the weight of the nine months lift. I'd made it to the other side.

I moved to a bed. Flat on my back, waiting to deliver the

placenta, I turned my head to the nurse beside me. "Is the baby okay?" I asked. Labor thrusts a woman into the psychological stratosphere, and I was coming back down.

But the nurse didn't answer.

A few minutes later, though, the midwife returned with my new family member. "She's fine. Just small."

And there she was, my daughter, this product of wheatgrass and self-hypnosis and free-range eggs, of hope and risk and love and a maddeningly loud biological urge. She lay on my chest, perplexed and limp. Her vernix-covered head was no larger than a grapefruit. My hand cradled its entirety. Her black eyes stared up at me, alert and confused. My husband curled beside me and gazed at her in awe. Someone snapped a photo.

We named her Fiona Soen Ray. *Fiona* because I liked it. *Ray* after Justin's father. And *Soen* after Soen Nakagawa Roshi, an eccentric Zen master who played jokes on his students. We weren't trying in the least to be prophetic.

"Welcome to the world," I said. A nurse was inflating a blood pressure cuff around my arm. "Or at least, one very small corner of the world," I added.

The nurse laughed through her nose.

A baby receives her first test within sixty seconds of birth. Anesthesiologist Virginia Apgar created the Apgar assessment in 1952 to study the effects of anesthesia on newborns, but the test also proved useful in determining whether a baby needed immediate medical interventions. *Is Baby's heart beating? Is Baby breathing? Is Baby reactive?* These questions and others help a doctor, midwife, or nurse calculate a baby's immediate health post-birth, and the medical professional assigns the baby a "score" on a scale from zero to ten. Zero means the baby has no pulse, isn't moving or breathing, doesn't respond to a mild pinch, and is bluish-gray or pale. Ten means the baby is actively moving, responds strongly to a mild pinch, has a heart rate of at least 100 beats per minute, is a healthy color, and breathes robustly enough to produce a "satisfying cry," as Apgar wrote.

When I was pregnant with Fiona, I saw that women on natural birthing websites used the Apgar score as a measurement for their achievements. Within the very first minute of a newborn's life, a mother could get confirmation of her child's potential SuperBaby status. Mothers who made it through birth without any drugs sometimes bragged that their babies scored a "perfect ten." Apgar herself acknowledged that a score of ten is unusual, given that most newborns have slightly blue hands or feet immediately after birth. The phrase—*perfect ten*—always reminded me of short-haired Olympian Mary Lou Retton dismounting the gymnastics vault in her American flag leotard, arms held high. I both resisted the mothers' competitive tone and kind of bought into it.

I also figured the competition was a modern-day perversion of Apgar's purpose—a by-product of the perfectionistic pressures that middle-class women of my generation felt. But the language of competition is embedded in Virginia Apgar's own writing. In her 1953 proposal for this "new method" of testing babies, she talks about " 'grading' of [the] newborn infant" and "giving a 'score' to a patient." She writes, "It has been most gratifying to note the enthusiastic interest and competitive spirit displayed by the obstetric house staff who took great pride in a baby with a high score." In other words, striving for SuperBabies has roots almost seventy years old—and older still.

In the Dayton hospital, after Fiona was whisked away for those few minutes, the midwife was examining her body, asking questions: How was the baby breathing? How fast was her heart beating? Was her body moving? What color was her skin tone? Did she respond to stimulation? Fiona's scores at the one- and five-minute marks were a respectable eight and nine. Apgar called her "normal." It was the first and last time anyone would.

Fiona had been born in the evening, and by the next morning, a single task had been scrawled on my room's whiteboard beneath the phrase *Patient Goals*. That word was *Rest*.

In my thirty-two years, I'd never seen such a short to-do list. I'd always been an overachiever, creating long lists and measuring my worth by what I could cross off. For the past nine months, I was not only pregnant, I'd taken on a new job as a visiting professor of English, taught four courses per semester, managed chronic nausea between classes, and worked on a new poetry collection in my "spare" time. In the years before that, I'd earned a master's degree in creative writing while cobbling together a few part-time gigs, and I'd earned another master's degree in teaching while working full-time as a high school English teacher. I was used to overdoing it. For the first time, *Rest* was my sole job for the day. *Rest* was all anyone required. I'd already done both the impossible and the everyday: I'd brought a human into the world. Who needed to expect anything else from herself? I put on pajamas and ordered an omelet.

But as that first morning wore on, it became clear from the nurses and doctors that I needed to do something else. I needed to worry.

Fiona was four pounds, twelve ounces. Given the nurses' and doctors' shock when they relayed this weight to one another, I learned that four pounds, twelve ounces was an alarming size for an infant born full-term. Someone showed me a chart on which seven half-rainbows shot across graph paper. The half-rainbows began close together, at the word "birth," each somewhere between five and nine pounds. This chart illustrated the weight range of normal babies at birth and beyond. There was a handwritten X below all of them, scratched in ballpoint pen. This was Fiona, someone told me. She was in the bowels of the chart.

The nurses made clear that I had much more to do than rest. I needed to get Fiona eating. And if I wanted to breastfeed, I needed to get Fiona latching. I needed to try every two hours, and the nurses and I recorded my efforts on a feeding log: how long, which boob, whether Fiona and I were successful. We weren't. So after each attempt, I also had to pump. I attached myself to a hospital-grade breast pump that was wheeled in and out of the room and squeezed tiny drops of colostrum from me, which Justin then drop-fed into Fiona's mouth. This whole process took sometimes ninety minutes, which, when repeated every two hours, left approximately thirty minutes to obey the blessed command on my whiteboard.

. . .

Fiona had been a planned baby, an answer to a call I'd found both beautiful and bizarre. How could something so loud inside me also be so out of my control? Justin too had wanted kids. But we'd spent a solid decade together before entertaining an actual conception. We'd traveled, lived on the East Coast and the West Coast, in the Midwest and Japan, earned graduate degrees on sparse stipends, drove old beaters to avoid car loans, reveled in each other, meditated together, watched sci-fi shows together, and prioritized our not-so-lucrative passions—mine, creative writing; his, Christianity and Zen Buddhism. By the time we landed in Ohio, we both had full-time jobs (Justin was a deacon at an Episcopal church), but neither of those jobs was permanent. The day I found out I was pregnant, I pulled the ultimate backtrack.

"Did we make a good choice?" I asked my husband in the kitchen.

Accustomed to my fretting an already-made decision, my partner of ten years put a hand on my shoulder and offered what I needed: unequivocal assurance. "We made a good choice."

But would I make a good mother? Would I enjoy having a child? "People say it's hard," I told him. "What if it's too hard? What if it's so hard we hate it?"

My husband isn't prone to worry. He's prone to joy, to leaping into the next adventure, to showing up at a party in full Scottish garb, including knee-high socks and a kilt, drawing a flask of Scotch from the leather sporran tied around his waist, and offering anyone a dram. But he's also a former monk. He has lived for seasons without heat, without socks, without hot water, and he has sat in meditation for twenty-plus hours a day as the blood in his fingers crystallized into frost. He did this—as he does nearly everything—in the name of what one might call enlightenment.

"The hard things," he said on that night, "are worth doing. In my experience, the hard things are usually the most transformative ones."

I nodded in that kitchen, imagining a bead of light below my belly button, consenting to the fact that parenting, as regular parenting goes, would be both very hard and very worth it.

The morning after Fiona's birth, a pediatrician came to perform an examination. He was tall and lanky and had a gentle demeanor. I liked him. He lifted eighteen-inch Fiona in the air using a one-handed grip on her torso. Then he rotated her body 180 degrees. He ran his hand along her back—her spine, her wee ribs, her day-old skin. "She's got good tone," he said.

I had no idea what this meant, but I took faint pride. I was sitting cross-legged on my bed and filling my face with a chicken salad sandwich. (For the first time in eight months, my new hormonal state had made me not just un-nauseous but voracious.) Of course my baby had "good tone." My kid was perfect.

But the doctor's face remained pensive. He detailed the potential problems for a too-small baby: low blood sugar, trouble regulating her own body temperature. "She might need to spend time in the NICU," he said.

Something about the word "NICU" pierced my faith. My

shoulders curled toward my food tray, and I wanted to burst tears into my fruit cup. My postpartum emotions had turned on a dime.

"There must be a reason," he said. "Mom, did you gain the proper weight?"

I nodded. Each week while pregnant, I watched the scale tip up a pound or two. The week I passed one-fifty, I sat on Justin's thighs, proud of my substance. Did I feel heavier? *Oof*, he said, meaning yes, and I smiled.

The doctor took one last look into Fiona's bassinet and sighed. There was no need for the NICU, he said. "Not yet," and he left the room.

My husband had no problem taking the command on the whiteboard literally. He stretched his lean six feet on the double bed, shut his eyes, and napped.

Fiona was asleep. Alone, I fixated on her face. I scanned her pale features and tried to read them—the flat nose bridge, the centimeter slit of a mouth, the slanted, small eyes. Something about her eyes looked different to me. Maybe it was the absence of eyelashes.

"Are all babies born without eyelashes?" I asked the nurse when she came to check our vitals. Body temperature normal. Blood pressure low.

"No," the nurse answered. "*Some* don't have any." But there was suspicion in her voice. I thought she saw it too—something in Fiona's eyes. Not the color—mysteriously onyx—but the shape. I tried to read those onyx eyes the way I might read a Magic 8-Ball. *Reply hazy, try again.*

I lay down and tried to sleep.

I focus on all going right . . . , the hypnosis woman had said.

But then there was a shift change, and a new nurse entered my room, someone who *hadn't* just seen me squeeze a person from my body without medication, and she asked a question that felt like a face-slap: "Mom, did you take any drugs while pregnant?"

No, Nurse, I wanted to say. *I took superfoods. I took reiki. I took electronica chords and affirmations.*

In my first few days on the job, motherhood entailed losing things. My bra, which I hadn't worn since labor. My circadian rhythm, fractured from waking every ninety minutes to try to nurse my impossibly small baby, who wouldn't latch. My purist parenting approach, which I had to ditch when a nurse woke me in the middle of a sleep cycle and posed a theory: maybe Fiona wasn't latching because she was malnourished. Maybe if we fed her a bottle of formula, she'd have the strength to breastfeed. I recalled in a flash all those websites that warned, *Formula is poison!* I let go of them too. I watched as the nurse fed Fiona thirty cubic centimeters of something buttery yellow, and after, my baby still screamed when confronted with my boob.

Justin was accustomed to letting things go. In a photo from Fiona's second day, my husband is shirtless, sitting cross-legged on the natural birthing center's double bed. His lean upper body is sculpted and tan, the effects of his previously child-free existence. Wee Fiona, wrapped in a footprint-patterned blanket, lies on a thick white pillow that covers his lap. His left pinky's in her mouth, and his right hand rests on his knee, holding an eyedropper. He's feeding her, drop by drop. If it weren't for the baby,

Justin would look like he's meditating. His posture is near-perfect. His legs are folded in half-lotus, the meditation position he's held almost daily for over a decade. His knees touch the mattress, creating a tripod of stability with his butt. You can't see it, but under his butt is a round, black meditation cushion. It's the same kind he took to a Japanese monastery seven years before, when he trained as a Zen monk. It's the same kind he took to a Trappist monastery twelve years before, when he trained as a Catholic monk, and it's the kind he brings to that monastery when he returns for annual retreats. In less than a week, he'll be ordained as an Episcopal priest. On that cushion, and in the two traditions he's loved—contemplative Christianity and Zen Buddhism—my husband has spent tens of thousands of hours letting things go. Jesus got on a cross, and the Buddha sat beneath a tree, and in this photo, my husband creates a related icon of surrender, balancing his frighteningly small daughter on his lap. In other words, within the first day of Fiona's life, my husband has already turned parenting into a spiritual practice. He has no idea the unknown variables inside her body. But he has prepared for decades to welcome a being as uncertain as she is.

Me? I'd quit my decade-long meditation practice while pregnant. I'd taken up self-hypnosis instead.

In 1994, the March of Dimes published a poster that featured two baby footprints side by side. I saw it years after Fiona's birth. The first footprint is wide and fat. The second is skinny, emaciated, half the width and height of the first. The poster's caption reads, "Guess which baby's mother drank while she was pregnant." The second footprint looks exactly like Fiona's. The medical establishment has a history of blaming women for anomalous babies.

The staff at the hospital's natural birthing center gave me the faint impression that I'd done something wrong. Called "Family Beginnings," the birthing center only admitted "low-risk" women committed to unmedicated labor. It was a cushy place as far as hospital wings go, boasting a homelike atmosphere and offering double beds for parents, wood co-sleepers for babies, and Jacuzzis for water birthing. *We believe childbirth is a natural process*, the center's literature read, *and a spiritual journey for you and your family*. But Fiona's size had required us to stay longer than the center liked. "We usually only let mothers stay one night," a nurse told me. Another nurse said, "If we had known how small she was, we never would have let you birth here." The nurses agreed to letting us keep our room. Still, in the middle of that second night, I felt a hand on my shoulder.

"Mom," a gruff voice said from the surface of my rare, deep sleep. A middle-aged nurse with short curls knelt beside me. "We need to move you to a different room. We have a new mother coming."

The red numbers of the digital clock read 12:06. I'd only been asleep thirty minutes since the last feeding; I had only an hour until the next one. I considered refusing. But I thought about that other woman: forty-plus weeks pregnant. Belly bulging. Contractions like vise grips around her pelvis. She was about to squeeze a person out of her person, and she vowed to do it without meds. All she wanted was this semi-nice room with its double bed and Jacuzzi bathroom. All she wanted was her chance at her perfect

"Family Beginning." I couldn't be the one to rob her of that. With a tear newly sewn between my legs, I stood up and grabbed my glasses. Justin stuffed our things in a duffel bag.

The next morning, I woke in a different wing of the hospital, on a thin mattress, in a room about the size of a large closet. Justin's six feet were curled fetal on a vinyl pullout couch, covered by a single white sheet. Fiona slept in a new bassinet—Lucite, not wood. It felt like we were Adam and Eve booted from the garden, kicked out for our tiny baby and for our failure to have the "spiritual journey" the birthing center expected.

And yet we carried with us the luminous being that was our baby. Fiona had searching onyx eyes, lit with the wonder of consciousness. She pressed her right fist to her cheek and extended an inch-long finger toward the corner of her mouth like she was thinking interesting baby thoughts. She had a smushed nose and, through nostrils smaller than peas, took in air. When Justin placed his hand over her body, he covered her entire torso and then some: his fingers grazed her chin, and the heel of his hand reached her thighs. And yet, beneath that hand was every major organ she'd need: her heart, maybe the size of a strawberry; her lungs like the teeniest upside-down trees; her stomach and her liver and kidneys, all of it below the blanket of her father's hand.

She had a high forehead and light brown fuzz on her oblong head, which made her look like a miniature old man. The combination of her nearly bald head and her perfectly unwrinkled skin made her seem both vernal and ancient, like she contained everything of the past and nothing but the future. Her skin was mesmerizing in its newness, nearly seamless, untouched by sun or soil, and although I'd been a chronic skeptic for decades, practicing doubt in my life as much as faith, she looked divinely made. Humans made polyester and nail polish remover, plastic sandwich baggies and spackle. We made nothing so luminescent as this.

That next morning, with the sunlight streaming through the window of our tiny room, we needed to break free, into the greater world, which loved all babies and wouldn't harass us for making one who fell off the growth charts. The problem, we'd decided, was not Fiona's small size. It was this place and its bizarre contradictions. *Congratulations—now worry. Rest—but wake up, wake up. Birth is a spiritual journey—you've somehow fucked yours up.* We sat in that room together, taking turns holding Fiona, awaiting the discharge papers.

"The on-call pediatrician will come and do a final check," a nurse said. "Then you can go home." I relaxed at the thought of one final hurdle before our escape.

The new pediatrician was a shadow hunched over my baby. I sat cross-legged on my narrow hospital bed, wondering when I might scarf down another meal. This new pediatrician was even more suspicious than the first. He said nothing like, "She's got good tone." He made no cute coos, offered no chirpy hellos. He looked at my girl with displeasure.

"What was the placenta like?" he asked. "Anything unusual about it? Was it small?"

If you've ever seen a placenta, you know there is everything unusual about it. The one that came out of me was a red blob with a network of veins in its center like a bird claw clutching tight. It was a temporary organ my body had grown without me ever ordering it up. It was grotesque magic. I'd marveled when the midwife had shown it to me. *I made that?* But I had no idea how it compared in a lineup of other placentas.

"I don't know," I told the doctor. "She's having trouble latching. A lactation consultant thinks she's tongue-tied." One nurse felt confident that Fiona's frenulum was giving her feeding troubles and that we should have it "clipped" so she could nurse better.

The pediatrician used a gloved finger to pull down on Fiona's chin and lift her tongue. "No," he said. "Tongue's fine."

He kept looking at my baby. He kept looking at the human I'd gestated for nine months, the one who'd grown in a room of my body I'd never seen. I knew her more intimately than any other person, and yet I hardly knew her at all. She was a small sun in an air-conditioned room, a mystery to orbit eternal.

"If it's not the placenta," he said, "then it's the baby."

What was "it"? His pronoun was a stuffed suitcase, splitting at the zipper. "It" was a problem. The doctor and I were on different floors of thought, in different wings.

"You see," he said, before dropping a bomb, "it's either bad seed . . . or bad soil."

I wasn't so sleep-deprived to lose the thread of his logic.

I was the soil.

My daughter was the seed.

My newborn, according to his expert eyes, was a bad plant.

He left. I cried. A sandwich came. I tried to eat it.

. . .

With discharge papers in hand, my husband and I fled in the opposite fashion one usually flees—as slowly as possible. Justin merged onto I-75 with the gentle care of a grandpa. He drove in the right-hand lane, five miles below the speed limit. I sat in the back seat with our new family member, who was bean-shaped and nearly engulfed by her gargantuan car seat. Fiona was her name, but the word on her onesie was FRAGILE, stenciled in the font used for cargo crates. When a friend had given it to us months ago, I was dubious of its size. No way a person could be so small. But now my baby swam inside it, her lean torso lost in the white folds, her wrists poking out of the short sleeves where underarms should be. She was too small for the smallest clothes. She was too small for FRAGILE. A semi roared passed in the center lane, and I cast an arm across Fiona's car seat, feeling a flash of fury at the world's steel and speed.

Our child was a wiggling riddle. How could she be both miraculous and medically concerning? *She couldn't* was my answer. *He's wrong, that doctor,* I thought. *She's fine. She's just small.*

In one way, this was the voice of wisdom whispering truth from my gut. But I made that wisdom speak more than it could.

She'll catch up, I added. *We'll show them.*

We exited the highway slowly. We took the familiar turns to our little house in a suburb of a suburb of Cincinnati. If Fiona cried in the cab of our car, I don't remember. If the radio played, I don't remember. In my memory, there's only silence as my husband and I move forward. My arm lies across the car seat like an extra safety belt. My neck is craned so I can see between the front seats and spot any danger. My husband's hands are at 10 and 2. We are uncharacteristically cautious about a twenty-mile drive. We're driving with the quiet of a hundred unknowns, questions we know but can't answer, and questions we don't know at all.

Among the known questions: *Is something wrong with the baby?* My encounter with that second pediatrician was a bucket of ice water on my postpartum head. *Either bad seed or bad soil.* But his words were a useful forewarning, one I couldn't yet hear: *The world will not always see your beloved as good.* And because I couldn't hear the forewarning, I couldn't hear its conjoined questions, the biggest of the things I didn't know: *How will you love such a person anyway? How will you reconcile the noisy values of the culture with the bursting pangs in your chest?*

I knew this: I already loved her so much it hurt.

Chapter Two

~

As a kid trying to fall asleep at night, I used to watch a ceiling fan spin. Because it was directly above my bed, and because it spun with a clanking violence, I worried it would spiral off and cut me. I confessed my fears once to my mother and stepfather, figuring they'd reassure me that a ceiling fan would never do such a thing, that the bolts in the unit were made of X material and the fan itself was anchored with Y gadget built to withstand Z weight and centrifugal force.

My stepfather, a man who resembled Jack Nicholson without the devilishly pointy eyebrows, pressed his thin lips together in concern. My mother seemed to know what he was thinking. "You know," she said, "if you believe things badly enough, you can make them happen."

My stepfather nodded. He was a chiropractor, and my mother worked as his assistant. Although my mother had been a devout Christian, my stepfather believed more in an invisible energy that entered into each of us and extended out of all of us. He believed our thoughts affected this energy, which then responded by giving us what we thought about. Our minds could shape our realities. This was almost two decades before Rhonda Byrne's 2006 bestseller, *The Secret*, which has sold thirty million copies worldwide, but the concept was the same. My parents both sub-scribed to the philosophy that *thoughts made things*. Whatever you wanted, you could get by thinking positively. If you weren't getting what you wanted, you weren't being a good enough stew-ard of your mind.

This was not always my family's religion. In my first eight years, my mother had been married to my biological father, who drove our family of four to a Baptist church each Sunday and my sister and me to an evangelical school on weekdays. At school, a teacher told me that the dental contraption installed in my mouth to fix my rascally, spaced-out teeth was a punishment from God. For what sin? Who could keep track? We humans were incessant sinners. As fundamentalist Christians, we believed in a higher power named God the Father, who made his only son, Jesus, die for our sins. I learned that my own salvation hinged on my ability to accept this as fact, and each night I attempted to lasso Jesus into my heart with the rope of my repentance. *Come on, Jesus. Save me.* I learned too that my father was a terrifying man. I sometimes found him in my room at night, watching me undress with silent, fixed interest, his fingers meddling in the coarse hairs of his mustache. At church, I saw his face as plaster, gripped into a grin for his fellow Christians. We joined the chorus, singing praises to God the Father, the giant man in the sky who required willy-nilly suffering for our broken human souls.

My mother was a do-gooder, a silver-lining finder, and a fol-lower of rules. If someone in authority told her what to do, she was predisposed to comply. She wanted to please people, from the minister to the doctor to the grocery-store cashier, assuming politeness and pleasantries as a religious duty. She thanked you for your kindness, for your everything, and she sometimes apologized for your rudeness, finding reason to blame herself. To my childhood eyes, she was rouge-cheeked and pretty, dark-haired and smiling. As I grew older, I was baffled by how comfortable she was in the traditional roles of her gender: cleaning, keeping house, cooking, child-rearing. But when I was a little girl, she felt like my nearly angelic protector. Her bleach-smelling hands hovered above me, her skirts were knee-length for my constant tugging, and she rocked my scrawny preschool tush to Mr. Rogers each morning. When I woke from naps, the wood surfaces shined with Pledge.

My mother found joy in being a mother; she also found joy in lofting her warm, falsetto voice into the highest corners of church in praise of the Jesus she loved. But she also became depressed. Over the course of her marriage, she withdrew from church potlucks and spent chunks of time in her shared walk-in closet, knees drawn to chest, unable to stop shaking. The minister told her it was the sign of a great sin. Depression was the devil's work. It took her years to hear the voice of her inner wisdom: *You are not happy in this religion, and you are not happy in this marriage.*

I marvel that a woman so obedient to authority had the gall to leave. When she divorced both my father and our fundamentalist faith, I wanted to break from both too. I was a crappy Baptist anyway, prone to doubt, wiggly at church, and worshiping Madonna circa 1984 more than the Messiah. When my mother fell in love with my stepfather, who smoked Salem cigarettes and (gasp) drank beer and laughed hard and loved fiercely, I got on board with his religion of universal energy. I liked the idea of some mystical white ether humming through every cell. It was benevolent but also responsive. It yielded to human beings. And it was right here among us, inside us, rather than striking us with lightning from the clouds.

n 1987, the year of my mother's divorce, a New Age author named Louise Hay published a book: *Heal Your Body: The Mental Causes for Physical Illness and the Metaphysical Way to Overcome Them.* The book listed hundreds of ailments in alphabetical order. For each, it offered a "probable cause" and then gave an affirmation meant to rewrite a patient's thinking. I was nine when the book was published, and for as long as I can remember, my parents—my mother and stepfather—consulted this tiny, blue-covered volume in times of distress the way a good Christian might turn to the Bible.

> *AIDS: Probable Cause: Feeling defenseless and hopeless. . . . A strong belief in not being good enough. . . . New Thought Pattern: I am part of the Universal design. I am important, and I am loved by Life itself. . . .*
>
> *Gangrene: Mental morbidity. Drowning of joy with poisonous thoughts. New Thought Pattern: I now choose harmonious thoughts and let the joy flow freely through me.*

In author photos, Hay has bouncy white hair brushed away from her high cheekbones. "We've learned," Hay writes, "that for every effect in our lives, there's a thought pattern that precedes and maintains it."

In other words, our minds are in control of our bodies, and of our lives. My parents' belief in the mind-body connection sometimes meant that they unintentionally blamed me when I caught colds and flus. If I developed a case of sinusitis, we went to the book. *Sinus Problems: Irritation to one person, someone close.* Who was I annoyed with? I sometimes got bronchitis and had to take a week off from track practice. *Lungs: Depression. Grief. . . . Not feeling worthy of living life fully.* What was wrong? Was I depressed? If, in my mother's former fundamentalist Christianity, sin was the cause of depression, then in our New Age religion, depression caused a sin of the body: illness.

Both religions, I realize now, attempted to explain suffering by finding blame within the afflicted.

The associations were sometimes eerily on target, though. In the first weeks of college, I fell hard for a boy, had my first kiss, and thought I'd found my first boyfriend. A week later, I saw him kissing someone else. I reacted by staying up too late and sleeping too little. A few weeks later, I developed a high fever and tonsils as big as golf balls.

Mononucleosis, Louise Hay writes. *Anger at not receiving love and appreciation. No longer caring for the self.*

I read this on the same childhood bed beneath the same childhood fan that had always, with the power of negative thinking, threatened to spin off and cut me.

Sure, mononucleosis is usually caused by the Epstein-Barr virus, a physical thing about 150 nanometers in diameter and composed of a double-stranded DNA that contains eighty-five genes. But according to Hay and co., if you have mono, you don't just have the existence of a virus in your body. You have certain emotional and mental states that allow the virus to thrive.

Too ill to go back to school, I slept in my childhood bed for six weeks, trying to love myself back to health.

f you flip Hay's book to the "C" section, you will find an entry for cellulite: *stored anger and self-punishment.*

You will find entries for coughs, cramps, corns, and Crohn's.

You will not, however, find an entry for chromosomal anomalies.

was thirty-two when I had Fiona. Much of my mind-body fundamentalism had worn away, in part because just two years after my bout with mono, my beloved stepfather had gotten cancer, and his woo-woo methods of positive thinking hadn't healed him. He pursued conventional treatment for the fist-size tumor beneath his arm, but he also went to a naturopath. The naturopath's conclusion was simple. *Cancer: Deep hurt. Long-standing resentment.* My stepfather's melanoma, the naturopath said, had been caused by a deep wound he hadn't forgiven. What did he still resent?

My stepfather didn't know. Like that "great sin" a minister wanted my mom to name a decade before, my stepfather came up empty. He was diagnosed in May, and he died in October. Within months, the cancer had spread to major organs, including his stomach. He stopped eating. To stop eating was to stop living, he'd once thought. When he was a tan, hot-blooded, thick-forearmed former-Marine-turned-plumber-turned-chiropractor, he believed patients with cancer had to force themselves to eat; otherwise they were cutting themselves off from life. But with cancer, his forearms grew thin. His usually ruddy skin resembled beige clay. My mother repeated his own advice back to him. He had to make himself eat. "Hon," he said, "I was wrong."

With his death, I lost my father figure and my champion and my protector. I also lost a religion I could no longer reconcile—the second religion of my life. These bodies weren't remote-control cars we could master with switches in our hearts and minds. Believing we could shape our bodies with our thoughts and our diets was as foolhardy as believing we could guard ourselves against all pain.

But carrying a new life inside me triggered my old thinking. Twelve years after my stepfather's death, there it was, as unmistakable as my kicking fetus: the belief that I was entirely responsible for my wellness. Only now I had my baby's wellness too. With week-by-week reminders about his/her/their size (*fig! peapod! carrot! pineapple!*), my desire to shape my future child's health clutched me as tightly as that claw-like artery in the placenta.

I suspect my old views were activated largely by the culture of pregnancy itself. Once our pee contains enough human chorionic gonadotropin to mark a plus sign on a stick, women are advised on every single lifestyle choice. How much we should exercise. *Too little won't be effective; too much can be debilitating.* How we should position our bodies. *Try not to stand for long periods. But sitting for long periods can be bad for your back.* How often we should do Kegels. *Daily. Doing them faithfully may help you avoid an episiotomy or a bad tear.* What we should avoid: *caffeine, deli meat, ibuprofen, alcohol, hot dogs, shark meat, swordfish, king mackerel, tilefish, cookie dough, cake batter, Brie, raw sprouts, fresh-squeezed orange juice.* How we should feel. *Learn to relax. Many problems are aggravated by stress.*

Pregnancy advice books abounded, and I was surprised that reading them made me feel less like I was sitting down with a helpful friend over coffee and more like I was propped on a paper-covered examining table, receiving perky but condescending commands to do X, Y, and Z or else I'd fuck up my kid. I watched many mothers around me strain equally hard for perfect pregnancies. People took up new exercise regimens, fretted the radiation exposure of airline travel. During a trip to Berkeley, California, I stayed at the apartment of married friends who were out of town. Upon entering their home, I saw a note on the table, written by the husband. *Please take your shoes off whenever you enter the door. Heavy metals found outside aren't good for our developing baby's brain.*

To what extent was this a white, middle-class phenomenon? Trying to make a SuperBaby is certainly a privileged endeavor, and I had privilege in spades, not only from my race, class, and ability but from my willing co-parent. In her ethnographic research of American mothers, however, anthropology professor Gail Heidi Landsman finds that the pressure to make a "perfect" child cuts at least across class lines. For her book, *Reconstructing Motherhood and Disability in the Age of "Perfect" Babies*, she interviews sixty American women. Most of them are white, perhaps a product of her focus in upstate New York. Yet they range in age from teens to late thirties, and in level of education, from women without high school diplomas to women with graduate degrees. All sixty women had children with disabilities, and nearly all of them felt in some way responsible for their failure to make a "perfect" child. Most of them commented that they'd done "everything right," meaning that they'd followed the meticulous advice of the medical world. Many still speculated about how they might be at fault. "By far," Landsman writes, "the most common feature of mothers' narratives about their pregnancies is women's sense of responsibility for controlling fetal development through diet."

The pressure on women to make perfect children also appears to have global reach. In her research on child-rearing in China, anthropology professor Teresa Kuan cites "excellent birth" campaigns of the 1980s, in which mothers were encouraged to minimize "defective" births and maximize intelligence. One strategy: play different classical songs to fetuses during different trimesters. Journalist Celia Dodd noted a British trend of SuperBaby-making back in 1997: "It is not simply a question of creating a superbaby," she writes. "The new fundamentalist reasoning insists that if women don't follow the rules, they risk damaging not only their children's health but that of future generations." The future of the human race, in other words, rested on our shoulders—or, more specifically, in our uteruses. And in the most unabashed promotion of SuperBaby-striving, in 2015, the India branch of Nestlé released an animated video campaign of dancing infants who literally call themselves "SuperBabies," wear superhero capes, and rap about the benefits of mother's milk. The company boasted that it had reached twenty million mothers globally. So while the flavor of my SuperBaby-striving certainly manifested in an unmistakably white, liberal, middle-class, American, organic-food-obsessed way, I suspect it's not the only flavor.

What I found in pregnancy culture, however, wasn't just the message that I was responsible for my baby's wellness through my physical choices. I was responsible through my emotional choices too. What was once a fringe theory in my youth became, now that I was pregnant, a mainstream principle. Article after online article declared what my parents had taught me in my teens: emotions can shape your health—or, in this case, the health of your baby. The popular and pithy online reporting most pregnant women consulted—including me—vaguely mentioned "scientific studies" that proved stress, anxiety, and depression in pregnant women increased the chances of stillbirth, premature birth, low birth weight, and behavior problems. In 2010, the UK's *Daily Mail* published an article titled "Why Pregnant Film Fans Should Stick to Happy Movies." The article cites a Japanese study that fetuses were more animated when their mothers watched a happy film clip, but when their moms watched a sad one, they became quiet and still.

Smile, women hear from male strangers randomly—when we're walking down a hall or working a retail register or otherwise going about our day. Feminists like me critique the command, noting that men are rarely ordered by strangers to display a cheerier disposition. But from August 2010 to June 2011, I belonged to a cohort of pregnant women, and it felt a bit like having the whole world, including scientists in white lab coats and nurses in scrubs, order us all to smile or else we'd put our beloved children—and humanity—at risk.

I now feel inner peace and serenity, the hypnosis woman had said.

It seemed that, once pregnant, we were supposed to become conduits of total joy and safety.

I will give birth easily, comfortably, and without complications.

The voices of culture implied that we should become carriers of life that will not experience what life inevitably feels—pain.

I tell my feelings what to feel, and they do, and they feel very calm, confident, and at ease.

We are urged to stop the growing body inside us from having what all bodies inherently have: vulnerability, that crack of a doorway through which our suffering creeps.

During my nine months of pregnancy, the culture of mother-hood had been clear about one thing, which midwives and pamphlets delivered in a three-word declaration: *Breast is best.* Breast milk was the perfect cocktail of essential nutrients and antibodies that would not only sustain my baby but reduce her risk of viruses, diabetes, Crohn's, cancer, sudden infant death syndrome, obesity, tragedy, heartbreak, and not really those last two, but all the others and more. On the online forums I fre-quented, the same women who bragged about their babies' "per-fect ten" Apgar scores also described near-mystical moments when first nursing their infants. The standard victory story went something like this: Immediately after birth, Midwife lays New-born on Mother's bare chest. Newborn, covered in white vernix that resembles cottage cheese, gums around Mother's boob a few moments. Newborn squirms toward boob's center with an innate wisdom that's proof of Newborn's destiny. Newborn finds nipple, creates perfect, painless seal, and sucks. Colostrum flows—that early yellow super-fluid chock-full of antibodies. Love hormone oxytocin courses through everyone's bloodstream. Angels sing from above. SuperBaby status confirmed. All is love.

Fiona's feeding ritual went like this: She wails with the pitch of a cat. I strap a shelf-like pillow to my waist and retrieve a cone-shaped silicon nipple shield from a dish beside me. I finagle my nipple into the shield, despite the fact that no nipple should ever have to be *finagled* into anything, let alone a cone-shaped silicon something. I lift wailing Fiona onto the foam pillow and bring her gummy-red mouth to the cone. She screams. She screams at my encased nipple as though it's some one-eyed evil Tolkien deity intent on destroying hobbits and babies and other well-meaning creatures.

Distraught that I'm failing at this most basic of "natural" mothering moves, I say to my husband, "I'm done." He's seated beside me, trying to figure out how to help with his flat, tiny nipples and milkless chest. He gets the drop feeder and the pumped milk from the kitchen. He lays Fiona on his lap, fills the drop feeder with milk, slips a pinky finger into her mouth, and lets her suck on skin while he squeezes milk past her lips. The nurses at the hospital have taught us this pre-breastfeeding method, which is meant to fake my kid into believing that she's only getting fed because she's sucking on someone's skin. In this rare instance, loving requires lying.

Meanwhile, I get the breast pump.

"We could just feed her formula?" Justin offers, because he means well and is starting to believe my methods are akin to torture. I give him a cold side-eye. He shuts up.

I place plastic trumpets over my boobs, align my nipples with the shafts of the trumpets, attach those trumpets to bottles and then to a machine that sucks my nipples through the trumpets' shafts. I watch the slightest drops of milk creep across the trumpets' shafts. I'm doing another version of lying: tricking my body into believing a baby's mouth is on the other end of that draw. This way, my supply will continue and my milk won't *dry up*, as they say, a phrase that always conjures in my mind a desert inside a woman's boob, with cacti and tumbleweeds rolling across her mammography.

I pump for thirty minutes. I yield two ounces per side. My husband dutifully drop-feeds.

When we're done, one of us gets up to wash all the parts. The whole process takes over an hour. An hour later, we'll start again. *Rinse, wash, repeat.* Or, in this case, *nipple shield, pump, drop-feed, repeat.* We must feed her every two hours to help her "catch up." We do this night and day. The feeding logs from those early weeks reveal valiant, dogged, futile efforts at getting our baby onto the growth chart.

When I was pregnant, Justin and I knew our baby would most likely arrive days before his ordination to the priesthood in the Episcopal Church. This was not ideal timing.

The road to Justin's ordination had been long. He entered the Trappist monastery at age twenty-one. There, he encountered devout Roman Catholic monks who chanted psalms and bowed to a crucifix, but they also "cross-trained," as he called it, studying Buddhism, Sufism, and Taoism. They regularly invited swamis,

Zen masters, rabbis, and medicine men to lead trainings and retreats. It was the abbot there who had encouraged Justin to cross-train in a Rinzai Zen monastery. My future husband left the Trappist monastery believing he'd someday return. Then he fell in love with me, which ruled out his former plan. He wondered if Buddhism might be his vocational home and spent several months in a Rinzai Zen monastery in Japan, but the words of Jesus still bubbled up from inside him. And he loved the sacraments. He eventually met some Episcopal priests. Their church was both progressive and traditional. It ordained women, married gay couples, didn't require celibacy, and yet celebrated in all catholic glory the Eucharist. On an adjunct's teaching wages, I got him through three years of seminary in impossibly expensive Berkeley, California. He spent a year as a transitional deacon. And here we were now: globe-shaped wife ready to burst, husband about to be ordained a priest. We joked that he'd become "father" twice in one week. Father to the second power.

Before I had Fiona, I figured the collision of major life events would work out. I imagined the ordination ceremony going something like this: As Justin bows to a bishop and makes his lifelong vows wearing fancy vestments, I sway back and forth while wearing a peacefully soothed baby in a cotton wrap. Or if Baby becomes fussy, I step out of the church sanctuary for ten minutes and place her to my breast, and this phrase—*place her to my breast*—sufficiently describes all that I'll need to do to feed my new love.

But at under five pounds, Fiona didn't qualify to fit inside the great symbol of natural mothering, the cotton wrap, a fact that felt like a metaphor in itself. And now that feeding my child required not only the shields but the nursing pillow and the drop feeder and the pump and the pumped milk (refrigerated) and even a sink to wash all the parts afterward, I essentially needed everything and the kitchen sink to attend my husband's ordination. Also, the doctor told me not to go. My baby was too small for the public, he said. So even though it had taken Justin over ten years to arrive at this moment, I couldn't bear witness to it. I hadn't been through one week of mothering yet, and one early parenting lesson had become clear: this four-pound, twelve-ounce human demanded nearly everything.

When Justin stepped into the Episcopal church in an Ohio suburb, he was alone, carrying his black meditation cushion. He found himself exhausted in a way that his body found familiar. He'd slept less than ten hours in three days. There was a fire in his eyes from the fatigue. His mind was quiet. The hour-by-hour necessities of baby-tending had interrupted all his natural states—sleeping, eating, bathroom-using. And all of this, he would later tell me, reminded him of how he felt as a Zen monk in Kyoto, Japan, particularly during the most grueling week of the year: *rohatsu*.

During the weeklong intensive training session of *rohatsu*, the monks at Tofukuji monastery didn't speak. They barely slept. They never lay down, and they meditated through the night. When they weren't meditating on cushions, they were meditating while walking or while doing rote work, like washing their bowls. Now a father, Justin found that parenting a newborn was surprisingly similar to Zen monastic life. Hour by hour, very little was yours. You postponed your natural rhythms. You barely slept, and you ate but not quite enough, and you turned all your energy and attention toward one thing, one central, precious thing. For the monk, that thing is enlightenment—the bright dawning of a new way of seeing all of creation. For a new parent, that thing is creation itself—the new life in your arms, the squirming and sucking and sleeping and breathing, totally vulnerable, fully conscious being in a tiny bundle.

So when Justin plopped down his cushion in the Ohio church and nestled his butt onto it and placed his hands in his lap, he felt like he'd already spent days on an intensive retreat—only one that included diapers and breast-pump parts. Years had passed since his Zen training, and he'd since committed himself to a form of Christian meditation called Centering Prayer. If he had a thought, he let it be. If he became gripped by a thought, he released it. For ninety minutes before his ordination, he did this again and again, constantly opening a metaphorical hand to free whatever it clutched, constantly surrendering to something larger than himself.

It's almost the opposite of what my parents had taught. I was taught that people could control reality with their minds. Justin was taught to let go of what his mind clung to and open to reality as it was.

The ordination began, and I missed my husband's procession down the church aisle. I missed whatever sermon the bishop gave, and I missed seeing that whoever carried the incense placed it right beneath the church's smoke detector. So I also missed the fire alarm, which interrupted the praying and chanting and wouldn't stop. I missed sitting for five minutes in the pews while the alarm blared and some folks grimaced and others, including my husband, snickered. The fire department eventually came to turn it off. But even if I'd been in attendance, I wouldn't have been able to see what is now my favorite detail about the ceremony.

Midway through the service, the ordinands, as the soon-to-be priests are called, lie belly down and touch their foreheads to the ground in full prostration. It's an act of total surrender. The future priests are giving everything they have—their bodies, their minds, their hearts, their souls—to God. Versions of these deep bows appear in several religions; Justin had made similar prostrations in the Zen monastery. So there he was, lying facedown on the floor of a church after days of sleep deprivation. The choir was singing an ancient hymn. The bishop would soon put his hands on my husband's head and consecrate his priesthood. For a few short minutes on that church floor, my husband got to take a break. So he closed his eyes and, as he told me hours later, "took a little nap."

I laughed. "You didn't!"

"I wasn't fully asleep," he said. He insisted he was always partly conscious, able to hear what was happening around him. But he said he'd entered the kind of half-sleep he'd learned in Tofukuji.

The ordinands were supposed to get as low as possible, as close to the dust of the earth as they could. *You come from dust, and to dust you shall return*, reads a prayer from both Ash Wednesday and the Episcopal funeral rite. Every new beginning involves a dying of something, and every death precedes a birth. A friend of ours, a priest and a meditator, told us that after the birth of his first child, it took him months to let go of his old life and surrender to the demands of parenting. He struggled to ride the swells of the baby's needs. He wanted the baby to sleep longer, to require less holding, to need less burping. He wanted parts of his old life back. He wanted to be less tethered, and instead the baby required a full-body prostration. My friend said he didn't enjoy parenting until months into the gig, when he finally let go.

A full prostration is a total relinquishing. *Let the whole world see and know,* prayed the bishop at the start of my husband's ordination, *that things which were cast down are being raised up, and things which had grown old are being made new.*

I didn't hear the prayer. I didn't know that, in becoming a mother, my old worldview would get cast down, that much of what I thought mattered in life would grow old. I didn't know just how profoundly my life would be made new from this baby, and not in the usual "a baby changes everything" way. No, in a way that would toss my deepest hidden values upside-down, like once-revered bronze statues flung onto their heads, sunken into the sand, feet skyward.

n a photo taken a day or two after returning home from the hospital, I'm in the living room holding Fiona up against my chest. I'm looking over my shoulder at the camera so that Justin, who's taking the picture, can capture her sleeping face. Her little mouth is slack, gaping open. Curled against my chest, she measures shorter than a foot. I'm wearing a yellow floral tank top and a self-assured smirk.

The woman in this photo is not entirely me anymore. She has the same curly, reddish-brown hair. She has the same brown eyes, the same narrow mouth. But she's something of another person. She's holding that tiny baby against her chest because the baby curls easily there, and because it feels good, but also because those attachment parenting experts told her to keep Baby close. She's holding that baby against her chest because it seems like something a good mother would do. *Hold Baby to body. Look over shoulder. Smile.*

Right now, she's sleep-deprived only a few days. Right now, she's not even sporting bags under her eyes. And her smile is confident because beneath her feet is a ground built by a series of unshakable beliefs.

She believes her baby will catch up in weight.

She believes her baby will eventually develop according to her generation's parenting bible, a nearly eight-hundred-page tome called *The Baby Book*, which she always keeps an arm's reach from the couch. (It has four giant, naked babies on the cover, all different skin tones but precisely the same size, doing precisely the same thing—sitting bare-bottomed and looking leftward and up. *We are racially diverse,* the cover implies, *but we behave the same way.*)

She believes in what the experts say. She believes if she keeps wrangling the four-pound-something baby to her breast, if she keeps writing down every feeding attempt, which she has recorded in a notebook called "Log," and if the intervals between feedings never exceed two hours, then the giant worry that is the baby's weight will lift. This is just another bold-printed task on her to-do list. If she busts her ass hard enough, she can bend reality to her desire. She can make things "right."

And right is average or exceptional. Right is normal or superior. Right is the way all those varicolored babies on the cover do precisely the same thing. Right is racially diverse but developmentally identical. And right is measured by the yardstick stored in someone else's closet.

She will love her baby out of the *wrong* category—what the doctors call *abnormal*. She believes in normal, and she believes she and her child will reach it.

Chapter Three

⌒

By the time Fiona reached one month old, she'd figured out that nipple shields were her friends, and we no longer needed to drop-feed her. She filled that FRAGILE onesie a bit more, but she was still nowhere near fitting into newborn clothes. "Don't even bother buying newborn diapers," my sister had told me when I was pregnant. She encouraged me to stock up on "size ones," for eight- to fourteen-pound babies. Her newborns were average size and breastfed easily and grew quickly into gargantuan babies. A month into Fiona's life, Justin and I were still pulling the sticky tabs of newborn diapers so far across our baby's body that they didn't just overlap—they surpassed each other. From waist to crotch, those diapers were just shy of five inches, and we rolled the waists down more than an inch.

My stepfather once told me that fear was the opposite of love. He'd learned this, I think, from one of his favorite spiritual teachers: Oprah. As a teenager, I was suspicious. No way fear and love were opposed. They were on totally different trajectories. Now as a new mother, I felt my body's chemical contrast illustrate his belief: the panicky edge of cortisol clashed with the warm flush of oxytocin. It was like pacing between two rooms, one made of steel, another of cotton. Love and fear, I understood, weren't opposites in the way vectors can head toward each other in a collision. They were headed away from each other. And they tore me in two. The result was a shaky motherhood, literally. Nervous fingers as I fastened her onesie snaps. A tense, wrinkled eleven between my eyebrows as I rocked her car seat with my foot.

At Fiona's one-month checkup, I held my breath while a nurse put my baby on a scale. I was hoping my body and its milk and my dutiful commitment to every-two-hour feedings had somehow made Fiona's body closer to normal.

The nurse announced the results. Six pounds.

My shoulders fell.

"That's great," the doctor said. "She's growing!"

Our family doctor was a rugged guy in his thirties who looked like he might head to a campsite immediately after office hours. He wore hiking boots, jeans, plaid flannels. He decorated his office in old-fashioned medical equipment: steel tabletop scales and brown-tinted Rx bottles. When we'd first met with him, he'd told me that he didn't believe in parenting books. "You know what to do," he'd said from a low stool. "All those books do is take away your instincts." When he saw Fiona at a week old, he didn't obsess over her smallness like the hospital docs. He said, "She's the most alert newborn I've ever seen." I loved him.

Still, on this day, I gave him a worried look. Six pounds? I knew this wouldn't dig my one-month-old out of the growth-chart bowels.

"She's perfect," he insisted. "She's the perfect size for her!"

The nurse agreed.

We switched to more mundane parenting concerns—poop color and eye goop and the fact that I'd recently committed the inevitable parenting sin: I'd cut my baby's fingertip while trimming her paper-thin nails. The doctor examined the finger.

"This happened two days ago?" he asked.

"Yeah," I said, and waited for him to scold me for failing to apply some kind of necessary ointment. New mothers excel at guilt, and I was no exception.

"See, look at that," he said, holding the finger toward Justin, who was closest. "It's almost totally healed. Isn't that amazing?" He looked at me. "She'll heal so much faster than you and me. Because babies are constantly growing. They're constantly regenerating cells!"

I loved this doctor. He wasn't focused on righting any wrong, on edging my kid toward "perfect." The perfection he sought was already inside my baby. She got hurt; she healed. It reminded me of my stepfather's religion—a divine, beautiful something already pulsed through you. All you had to do was let it do its thing.

She's perfect. I carried those words home. I tried to cultivate more wonder. I snoozed on my back with the small flour sack of her body against my breast. I finally put her in that cotton wrap, and Justin and I took her for a walk in the woods. Mid-July, I sweated sheer through the multilayers of jersey cotton, but by God, I was out in the world with my baby.

Today, I thank God for that doctor's words—were they wisdom or cluelessness? I'm convinced they were the meat of wisdom wrapped in a burrito of cluelessness. Not every parent gets this, but every parent deserves this: medical professionals who see their kid not as a series of pathologies to address but as *just right*. In those words from the doctor—*she's perfect*—I found a strange truth, not quite the whole picture, but not any less true.

As a visiting professor, I had an unpaid summer off with Fiona. And thanks to the progressive and generous parenting leave of the Episcopal Church, Justin had six paid weeks. Together we learned how to be parents.

Justin's favorite parenting pastime was dancing with Fiona to the reggae hit "City Too Hot," by Lee "Scratch" Perry. He cradled her head in his hand and aligned her body down his forearm like a football. Then he gently bounced her while bopping to the upbeat. Lee Perry's reedy, meandering, sometimes off-key vibrato sang on the stereo. Justin crooned along, gazing down at Fiona, and she looked up at him, her onyx eyes transfixed. The two of them could commune like this for a full hour. Fiona sometimes pursed her lips like she wanted a kiss.

Eleven years before, I first kissed Justin in a tiny room he rented, on a twin bed pressed against the wall. He was only a few months out of a Catholic monastery—a few years away from heading to a Zen one—and his room resembled a monk's cell. The bed, desk, dresser, and meditation cushions left barely enough carpet for his six-foot frame to lie down flat. Back then he was infatuated with not reggae but blues. John Lee Hooker. Muddy Waters. Foot-tapping downbeats, coffee-rich vocals, and slide guitar. This was the soundtrack to our falling in love. But because he was only a few months out of a monastery, he also loved the psalms. And silence. I once awoke at six a.m. to find him facing a blank white wall. Above him was a cross. On the other side of the room was a Buddha. There was a *both/and* quality about Justin's vision that I immediately adored, a way of saying yes to everything—or everything that mattered.

I'd known Justin in college when we'd found ourselves taking the same courses on Eastern religions—Hinduism, Buddhism. We'd studied things like "the concept of no-self" and "the interconnectedness of everything." He was playful and goofy, sprung kangaroo-like down the dormitory hallway, and wore his scraggly blond curls to his chin, with a single dreadlock in the back. It shocked the hell out of me that he'd decided to spend his senior year in a Catholic monastery. When he came out, his hair was buzzed short, and he possessed a new gravity. He could meditate for two hours straight, and then blast his beloved Muddy Waters. He could make a joke about bodily fluids one minute, quote some Christian mystic the next. It wasn't the esoteric interests that gave him gravity—it was something in his being. When we started dating, I spent much of the time hugging his chest, my face pressed into a threadbare cotton T-shirt he'd lifted from the monastery's communal clothing pile. Around him, my jittery, anxious, future-worrying and past-pining self dropped into deep ease.

My husband was a believer in the lighthearted not because he dismissed the world's pain. As a Zen monk, he'd spent a whole winter without heat, without shoes or gloves or even a head of hair. He'd watched the purple lattice of frostbite form on his fingers, noted with Zen-like indifference the spots that had turned black and died. But even without a good grasp of Japanese, and even while living under strict guidelines that prohibited casual conversation, monk-Justin used to crack nonverbal jokes with his

Japanese monastic brothers. He feigned violent offense after sniffing their straw sandals. He acted out the short-armed screech of a Tyrannosaurus rex when he was supposed to be sweeping in meditative silence. He even paraded naked before the entire monastery on the only day monks could cut loose—winter solstice—holding a bamboo trash bucket in front of himself. Years later, I'd listen to priest-Justin give a sermon about the power of humor not just to "lighten the mood" but to help a person transcend what Christian contemplatives call their "small self." For an instant, a laughing person could let themselves go like a helium balloon, find themselves in the unfathomably spacious blue sky. I'd always been more serious, more insistent on getting things right, but in our eleven years together, Justin had taught me again and again that laughter was a spiritual practice.

So in the unscheduled, soupy postpartum days, I made my own joke—easy to do when one has to use a breast pump on the regular. I donned my pumping bra, a tight band of cotton-Lycra that has holes precisely where a woman does not want holes in a bra to be. Through those holes, I aligned my nipples and then aligned the plastic trumpets that attached to the pump. I screwed the necks of the trumpets to the bottles, then hooked the whole thing up to the pump, which plugged into a wall. I could now be electronically "milked," hands free. The contraption was a perverse version of Madonna's breast cones circa 1990. I stood up, jutted my chin high into the air, and posed. "Look," I said to Justin. I framed my face with my hands. "Vogue, vogue," I said. Then I framed the plastic trumpets. "I'm Madonna with an udder."

In our first years together, Justin and I spent a lot of time laughing in bed, drinking green tea, and flipping through books on mysticism while the smoke of sandalwood incense filigreed past. He once told me a story about one of his favorite Zen masters, Soen Nakagawa Roshi, famous for transmitting enlightenment through trickster ways. One day a student came to meet Soen Roshi in the sacred *dokusan* room, the place where a Zen master tests a student's insights. Usually the master is seated on meditation cushions, awaiting the student. The student enters, performs a series of intricate bows, and sits opposite the teacher. But on this day, the student didn't find his master. He found a large pumpkin. It sat fat on the cushions where Soen should have been. Flummoxed, the student proceeded as usual, bowing multiple times to the gourd, then sitting down. He awaited spiritual inquiry from a squash. Soen supposedly snickered from the sidelines.

A decade later, when we gave our daughter the middle name of Soen, I didn't realize how badly I would need the story's message:

We don't have to take our lives so seriously.

Also: our teachers of transcendence can be anything. A squash. A joke. A baby. Anything.

Another month passed. Fiona still wasn't making visible gains in weight. In a few weeks, I was headed back to the classroom to teach. I'd soon have to juggle parenting and employment. A friend slipped me a pediatrician's business card unsolicited and urged me to call. The gesture felt both presumptuous and prudent. We needed a second opinion.

. . .

Weight: *seven pounds. Age: three months.* These were the facts a new nurse wrote on a whiteboard nailed to our examining room door. I knew those facts announced an anomaly. Fiona's blue-and-brown-striped onesie had its own message— HANDSOME LIKE DADDY—a nod to my prenatal belief that my child's biggest threat would be the tyranny of gender conformity.

The new doctor entered with a look of concern. In the few seconds that had passed between reading the door's sign and meeting us, she probably hypothesized a malnourished and neglected infant. Her first line of inquiry was about nutrition.

"How often are you feeding her?"

I was nursing Fiona that very minute. "Every two hours," I said.

"And through the night too?"

"Yes," Justin said.

"Just breast milk, or formula too?" She was jotting down notes.

"Just breast milk," I said.

"How long does each feeding take?"

"An hour," I said.

The doctor looked up from her notes. "She nurses like that for an hour?"

I nodded. Fiona lay on the nursing pillow facing my left boob, and a stream of milk trailed out of her mouth. I'd gotten so accustomed to this stream that I always put a hand towel over the pillow.

"That's not normal," she said, pointing to the towel. "She's an inefficient nurser. She doesn't have a strong seal or suck."

I mentioned the nipple shields. "A nurse at the hospital thought she might have a tongue-tie."

"That could be," the doctor conceded with a side nod.

We'd obviously left behind the celebratory lens of Dr. Campsite. When she was done asking questions, the new doctor paused, mouth half open. Thus far she had been measured with her words, halting after each phrase, but the next sentence spilled out of her: "I mean, she's three months old and the size of a newborn!"

She said this as though we didn't know, and she raised her hands up like she was catching rain, and I said, "I know."

I pried Fiona off my boob. The doctor looked at my daughter's face. "Her eyes are wide-set," she said.

She listened to Fiona's chest with a stethoscope. "She has a heart murmur."

She peeled back the tape on Fiona's teensy newborn diaper. "She has a Y-shaped butt crease."

When she handed Fiona back to me, the doctor said, "I suspect she has a syndrome of some kind."

In the next second, something happened. Something frightening and fast: my heart went ever so briefly in the opposite direction. It had been moving in the direction of ragged love: dragged up from sleep to answer every cry, drawn away from my own needs so I could fulfill the hunger pangs of another. My husband and I had been changing every diaper, burping every gas bubble, snapping every tiny button on every onesie. For the past few months, our lives had revolved around the tiny mystery of our girl. Our hearts pumped every second for her, and her, and her.

But when the doctor said *syndrome of some kind* and placed my daughter's seven pounds back into my arms, I had a brief, basal urge to extend my arms back to the doc and say, *No. Here.* For a painful nanosecond that felt like free-falling, I wanted to hand my child to someone else.

A mother is not supposed to have this thought. A lizard, maybe, but not a mom. The urge to hand my baby back was primal and prerational and brief. When Fiona was returned to me, she was nearly weightless, and yet I now held the weight of the world.

My glass-half-full husband was in a different place. In response to the doctor's idea that our daughter had *a syndrome of some kind*, he replied, "You mean like Lincoln?"

I looked at him, perplexed.

He turned his head toward me. "Lincoln had a syndrome." He shared a theory I'd never known—modern-day physicians sometimes cite the former president's exceptional tallness and thinness as evidence that maybe he had Marfan syndrome. The pediatrician nodded, but more as concession than confirmation. As in, *Okay, sure. I'll give you Lincoln.* My panic was somewhat assuaged. Syndromes were so common, I thought, that they lived inside the bodies of American presidents.

But when the doctor looked down again at our baby, our very small, very thin baby, I followed her gaze. Fiona's cries were so meek they sounded like a cat's. We did not appear to be looking at another Lincoln.

．　．　．

We strapped our girl into her car seat and headed home. We didn't have time to think about syndromes. In less than an hour, my teaching colleague and her family were coming over for dinner to celebrate the beginning of the semester. I vacuumed the carpet. Justin sautéed meat and chopped veggies.

I answered the door with Fiona in my arms.

"I forgot how small they are," my coworker Jane said. She stretched out her arms. I placed Fiona into them. Jane lifted her arms an inch and raised her eyebrows in amazement. "How much does she weigh?"

I told her.

Jane's husband mentioned a kid they knew who was also small. Doctors threw the parents into a tailspin of worry, but everything had turned out fine. "They love to worry you."

"They do!" I said.

Jane's youngest, almost one, clutched our coffee table and sidestepped along its length. When she belly-laughed—a gorgeous golden burst—envy turned my stomach like a doorknob.

"When do they laugh like that?" I asked.

Four months? Six? Eight? To this day, I don't remember Jane's answer. What I remember is my longing. I longed for the contented smile on my coworker's face as she watched her kid laugh and toddle and learn. I longed for the certainty she had—her child was sidestepping expectantly toward a healthy future. Her oldest, three years old, was buzzing around the room, speaking in choppy, confident sentences, and his dad was responding. *That's a fireplace, buddy. That's a ficus. No, don't pull on the leaves.* They were a family of four, a solid unit sighing at the struggles of sippy cups and sleep, but otherwise at ease. Both of their children seemed to be known fixtures of their family. I'm pretty sure they never had a strange if brief urge to hand one over to a pediatrician.

My baby was flimsy, literally—she could not hold her head up. She'd still felt to me like a visitor. Now, after the latest doctor's appointment, she seemed like a stranger. She asked of me everything and offered only unknowns.

had two families as a child. The first ended when I was eight, the second when I was twenty.

In the first, I didn't feel safe at home. I didn't sense love between the two adults, who were bound less by affection than by the *Lord Our God*. I sensed danger from my father and fear from my mother. Our suburban Philly home was huge—four bedrooms, three bathrooms—and at night, when my father watched me undress, I imagined leaping out the window. I wondered if the bushes would catch my two-story fall. I was five, six, seven. He was a devout Baptist, stern sometimes and guffawing at other times, but he was to me mostly a shadowy presence I wanted to escape.

My mother was part champion: she allowed me to head to my Jesus-centered school in hot pink pleather jeans. They were lined with black fleece, and I wore them even in the June heat. I paired them with Madonna-inspired tops and fluorescent bangle bracelets that clanked against the desk when I did math. This at a school that thought pop culture was the product of the devil. My mother, who loved dainty flats and dresses, skirts and heels, was raising a rascally, pop-star-loving tomboy in a fundamentalist Baptist church. As much as she believed in Jesus, she also believed in the innate wisdom of children. An elementary-school teacher by trade, she dissented against common parenting concepts like "the terrible twos." She thought no child should receive a condemning adjective, *terrible*, for an entire year of life. She never made me finish my plate at dinner because she felt she could trust my appetite. I'd eat if I was hungry; I'd stop when I was full. She believed I possessed an internal compass, and she placed her trust in it.

This put her at odds with my Christian school. At a parent-teacher conference one day, my mother listened as the teacher expressed a concern: I held my pencil incorrectly.

My mother asked the teacher to explain.

The teacher said I placed the shaft of my pencil between my middle and ring fingers. "It's a sign of mental retardation," she warned.

My conflict-adverse mom picked up a pen. She let her hand assume her natural writing grip. "You mean like this?" There was a callus on her ring finger where the pen rested, made from years of scribbling *thank-you*s and grocery lists. "This is how I hold my pen. Is *this* a sign of mental retardation?"

The teacher didn't dare say yes.

A year later, my mother filed for divorce, left her fundamentalist church, and allowed my sister and me to choose between our Christian school and the public one. We chose public. It was the summer of 1986 when my father left the house. That was the end of my first family.

I was eleven when my second family began. My mother married my chiropractor stepfather, and his love was like a Sunday buffet—a feast spread in excess. He loved giant meals of rib eyes and white rolls, gravy and mashed potatoes. He loved excess—packaged chocolate cupcakes eaten several at a time, Breyers ice cream served in a bowl meant to contain an entire family's dinner vegetable. He eschewed portion control, and this philosophy extended to realms of the heart. Because I wasn't his biological child, I felt I'd done nothing to deserve his huge hugs and track-meet cheer, his fury over a fifth-grade boy who bullied me, and his tears when I went off to college. He called me "luvvie" and loved me fiercely. It was the ultimate gift.

He was wary, though, of outsiders. Around his bountiful table were a dozen stop signs directed outward at anyone who might cause harm. He didn't trust the government. He didn't trust medical doctors. He often worried that people were out to screw the ones he loved. This was another way he loved me: By worrying. By believing I'd get hurt if I stayed out past eleven, or thought negative thoughts about ceiling fans, or ever kissed a boy.

What hurt most came from him. He died when I was twenty, and the grief was atrocious. It was also nonnegotiable. There was no getting out of it because there was no getting him back.

Two years later I fell for Justin.

Ten years after that, I found out I was pregnant. It was some blue hour just before dawn, in a bathroom in Ohio. I peed on a stick and saw the mark. I stared out the window. The neighbor's lights were off, and the roof was a dark, squat angle against indigo air. I felt like the only soul awake, holding a secret. My third family began in that early hour, with the spark of conception folded into an unseen room of me. My third family began with Fiona.

And in that dark September morning, I proceeded while holding something fairly silly. I believed the difficult years were behind me. I believed that, from here on out, my life would be relatively simple. I believed in a higher power, and I believed this power kept a scorecard. I believed he/she/they were done divvying out hard lessons.

I know this is the foolish assumption of the privileged. I'd been through no civil war. I'd never fled my country in order to keep my life. I'd never gone to bed hungry. I'd never needed anyone to explain to me how to stay alive around a cop. My class and skin color afforded me loads of privileges that were not entirely lost on me. Still, when I began my third family, I figured the hard years were behind me. My third family would not undo me, I thought. I was done being undone. I was, for the most part, made.

On that September morning, I curled back into bed and woke Justin with a whisper. *I'm pregnant.*

Hours after the appointment with the pediatrician, I did exactly what one shouldn't do when one possesses just enough information to land in Internet black holes. I googled.

I typed search terms like "wide-set eyes" and "heart murmur." I combined them with "Y-shaped butt crevice."

I unearthed from the viscera of the Internet rare conditions like Turner syndrome and Noonan syndrome. I was convinced my child had this chromosomal disorder or that, and I read forums from parents on this chromosomal disorder and that.

I learned that their kids had digestive issues or gums that bled excessively or struggles with math class, but that they were otherwise doing fine. They were at such-and-such university.

And so I envisioned this future for my daughter: tummy troubles, bloody visits to the dentist, long nights at the kitchen table hunched over word problems. But also college. A backpack and a first day of classes and a new crush spotted across the lawn.

Yet when I closed the lid on the laptop, I was in as much darkness as the night sky beyond the window. The Internet had done what it does best: stirred my fears into such a strange froth that I no longer knew which way was up and which fact was truth.

I climbed the stairs that night, reached the bedroom, and saw my family asleep. My husband was a blanketed log in a queen-size bed. Fiona was a swaddled bundle in a beige co-sleeper, which jutted off the bed like an annex. The Arm's Reach Co-Sleeper was a rectangular bassinet meant to line up against a bed so a parent could touch the baby at any hour. In advertisements, babies slept peacefully beside their mothers' torsos. But because I was feeling nearly claustrophobic from the relentless round-the-clock-ness of motherhood, I kept that co-sleeper near the bottom half of our mattress. My daughter snoozed nightly beside my knees.

On this night, though, I made a change. I pushed the co-sleeper three feet toward my pillow. Her heart would now beat all night next to mine. She'd stay within breath's reach. If she weren't so small, I would have brought her into bed with me, tucked her beneath my armpit, and curled around her. If it were physically possible, I would have enfolded her murmuring heart into the very beating of mine.

And there it is, the strange tension of parenting: even as I wanted the uncertainty of our lives batted straight out of my life, I also wanted the reason for that uncertainty—my daughter—so close I could take her back into me.

Chapter Four

⁓

Fiona offered her first giggles on September 11, 2011. They were faint, like bubbles from the tiniest fish.

A week or two later, I was bustling around the house, stuffing last-minute things into a suitcase, trying to prep us for a flight to see family in Baltimore. The phone rang. Justin answered. I paused to eavesdrop. When he talked, his voice was serious and smooth. I walked away from the half-zipped luggage and headed his way.

I knew what this meant. The blood work had come back, and the results were not a sigh of relief. Our baby *had* something. Of course she did. Every time I looked into her eyes, I saw the face of someone who breathed with an answer I didn't have, for a question I didn't want to ask.

Justin went back and forth with the nurse on the phone. "What about the heart murmur?" He wrote down a note. "So we should just keep an eye out for blue lips?" He paused. "Is it okay to fly with her?"

I widened my eyes. Our plane took off in three hours.

He nodded at me.

Once off the phone, he told me: Our daughter was missing some genetic material on the short arm of the fourth chromosome.

I fell into a chair and cried.

"It's going to be okay," he said.

I didn't even know what it meant: missing genetic material on the short arm of the fourth chromosome. But what I'd heard was that my baby, my first child, my gargantuan love in a seven-pound package, was broken. That was not true, but that was what I heard, and it was enough to take me off my feet.

Justin looked at his notes and shared what he'd learned: This chromosomal thing was called Wolf-Hirschhorn syndrome. It caused small growth, and it explained the heart murmur.

"But it's the short arm?" I asked.

"Yeah, the short arm. Of the fourth chromosome."

The short arm sounded trivial. Who needed all of their short arm?

"And they said we could fly with her?"

"Yes," Justin said. "We just need to watch for blue lips. The nurse was mostly concerned about the heart murmur. She wasn't even concerned about the chromosomes."

Okay, I thought. *So chromosomes don't matter. Blue lips on a plane do.* We could watch for that. We could be very astute to the lip tints of our three-month-old.

We finished zipping up bags and drove to the Cincinnati airport.

Hours later, in Baltimore, from the back seat of a car, we told our daughter's grandparents that we'd gotten a diagnosis. We said this diagnosis explained Fiona's small size. We said it might pose other health concerns. We said we'd say more later when we knew.

"As long as she has ten fingers and ten toes," Justin's dad said.

In the dark of the back seat, I said nothing. I suspected we should cultivate okay-ness with things like nine toes, eleven fingers—with the body in whatever way it came.

We didn't yet know that Wolf-Hirschhorn syndrome occurs in one in fifty thousand births. Your odds of becoming a pro athlete are twice as good as your odds of having Wolf-Hirschhorn syndrome. A rare disease is one that affects fewer than five out of ten thousand people; Wolf-Hirschhorn syndrome is ultra-rare.

After we returned to Ohio, I did the inevitable: tapped my fingers on a keyboard and googled. *Wolf-Hirschhorn.* The Internet dealt me its cold, clinical blows.

> *Mental retardation ranges from mild to severe. . . .*
> *Most of the patients do not develop active speech. . . .*
> *Seizures occur in over 90% of children. . . .*
> *Some do learn to walk. . . .*
> *About 30% of children reach some autonomy with eating. . . .*
> *10% achieve sphincter control by day. . . .*
> *Mortality rate is estimated at 34% in the first 2 years of life. . . .*
> *There is no specific treatment.*

The windows were black, and the ground cracked beneath me, and the Internet glowed alien blue with its surreal news. When I looked up from the computer screen, I was not sitting on a gray couch in the beige living room of an Ohio house. I was free-falling.

I went to the kitchen. Justin was cleaning. I sobbed into his T-shirt. My sadness was no longer the selfish reaction that my baby wasn't, would not be "perfect," but that we could lose her.

I told Justin the most gutting statistic. I told him only two out of three kids with her syndrome live past the age of two.

I pushed my face back into his T-shirt and kept crying. It wasn't a worried weeping, wasn't a fretting bawl. Both of those still cling to something—the belief that a situation might still bend toward one's dreams. My cry was an emptying. My mind wasn't spinning stories that maybe the diagnosis was wrong, or maybe our child wouldn't fall into the worst of those statistics. The statistics were already clear enough. *Your child will be significantly disabled. If she lives at all.* My cry was a collapse.

He held me and didn't speak.

I've seen Justin pivot in minutes when he hasn't gotten something he's wanted. He can go quickly from slumped shoulders to the words "You know, this is a good thing because . . . ," and then he'll etch gleaming futures with the scraps of a silver lining. But as a priest, he's also sat beside people after cancer diagnoses, during divorces, in hospices. He's prayed over people taking their last breaths. He's blessed their papery skin with holy water, hugged their sobbing children. As my crying waned, I didn't know which version of him would respond: *This-is-a-good-thing* Justin, or the Justin whose job it is to sit with pain. I felt the jersey of his T-shirt on my cheek and waited.

When he finally spoke, it was soft and slow. "If our time with her is limited," he said, and I could hear that the grief of the news had pierced him, "then I'm just gonna make sure I love her. The best I can, every day."

I n our second year together, I joked that if I were ever to write a memoir about Justin and me, I'd call it *Red Wine and Green Tea*. I was full of passion and romance and fury, my emotions all up front, my hair (back then) a decibel closer to sunset red. He had half the feelings and a third the need to express them. About once a year, I got mad enough to throw a small object—a pillow, a tape dispenser—although never *at* him, I was quick to say. When he felt irritated or overwhelmed, he took a walk or medi-tated. On his cushions, the silhouette of his bald head stayed as still as a moon. When he skipped off on retreat, I sniffed his empty sleeves and pined. I made him mixtapes, left him love notes, and on our one-year anniversary, I bound him a book of 365 memories I'd culled from my romantic brain. He replied by hiding short, simple notes around the apartment. (*Bet you didn't think you'd find an "I Love You" here.*)

In that second year together, we lived in a crappy basement apartment in Baltimore with grates on the windows, and we fur-nished the place cheaply with musty hand-me-down couches, but our green tea leaves were the finest grade of Japanese *sencha*. Silky moss-colored slivers in a special canister. First thing each morning, Justin went through the dull ritual of tea-brewing with total absorption. It took him ten minutes, bringing the water to boil, heating both the cast-iron teapot and the porcelain cups, waiting until the water was just the right temperature (refusing to add cold water), then steeping the leaves a perfect forty-five seconds. During gaps of waiting, he did nothing. He didn't also cook an egg. He didn't also wash a dish. He didn't juggle at least three other tasks like I did and then offer up a cup of what we called "multitask tea," the results of which were always too hot or too bitter, the *sencha* scalded or over-steeped. He did only the one thing, which was brew the tea.

When he served me a cup, I sipped the fern-green liquid. It gave me nothing of the punchy pow of coffee. It was grounding, steadying, focusing.

Then he went into our apartment's bare second bedroom, sat cross-legged on his cushions, and adjusted his legs into half-lotus. He lit a stick of incense, closed his eyes, and was unavailable for an hour.

I both revered and resented my husband's spiritual practice, which at the time was *zazen*—literally meaning "sitting Zen." I loved that Justin aspired to things greater than power or money or fame. I loved that he sought the impossible-sounding *enlightenment*, the elusive-seeming *God*. But I wasn't sure that his spiritual pursuits wouldn't take him away from me, with all his talk of "non-attachment." I sometimes saw his meditation as an affront to my emotional life. I should be more serene, I thought. Less feeling, less attached to this world and all it offered us to love or loathe. I should meditate too.

I outright refused.

I remembered my mother's and stepfather's failed first marriages, the way their exes tried to sculpt or scold them into being something other than who they were. I remembered my squirming in a church pew as my father wrinkled his forehead at me and a pastor preached that, in order to receive God's love, I had to accept Jesus as my savior. I rejected the notion that love was transactional. In love, I took my cues from my second set of parents—my stepfather and my mother. They fought openly and cried unreluctantly. They laughed largely and would not separate their hand-holding at the mall, even for a kid in their path, even as my sister and I snickered and teased them from behind. I admired how they felt the tumult of their feelings in front of each other, and I learned that love came in finding someone who just let you be yourself.

In our decade-plus together, Justin and I had mostly figured out how to do this. He let me be messy and emotional and stubborn. I let him be sage-wise and sassy and chronically late.

And gradually, after I'd thoroughly ridden the wave of my resistance, we met beside each other on those meditation cushions, where I learned something: meditation didn't make me less of myself. It didn't take away my one thousand and one feelings. But it did offer me a buffer so I could step a meter outside of them. All of this would prove useful in parenting, not because I meditated much as a new mother—I couldn't yet find the time. But I did have a reservoir of space inside me, built up from the years sitting beside my husband.

"Aren't you scared?" I asked him on the way to the first geneticist's appointment. I was in the back seat with our baby, whose car seat was an upholstered green mouth nearly swallowing her whole. Fiona was now the object of our budding work of acceptance. We had to love her as she was, not as how we'd wanted her to be.

"No," he said, his hands on the wheel, his eyes on the interstate. "I'm curious. I want to learn more about her. I want to understand who she is. So I can love her better."

I stared out the window, watching billboards pass, choking on a lump of tears.

"Anything we learn today," he said, "will just help us love her better."

The resident at Cincinnati Children's Hospital's genetics department was a guy our age, a thirty-something redhead with a slight belly and a cherubic face. He smiled kindly when he entered the examining room and greeted us in a nasal voice. "Hello, Fiona," he said with the extra tablespoon of cheer people use to greet a baby.

The cherubic redhead opened a binder and showed Justin and me a picture of twenty-three sets of chromosomes. They looked like broken bits of ramen noodles. They'd been magnified one thousand times. Twenty-two pairs were numbered. The twenty-third pair had an X and a Y beneath each chromosome. The resident pointed to a ramen noodle in the fourth pair. It had a white, rounded tip.

"You see that top part there?" he asked in his kind voice. "That cotton-ball top?"

I nodded.

"Fiona's missing some genetic material on that cotton-ball top."

I'd never seen the fourth chromosome. I'd never heard its end described benignly as a cotton ball. It was like a cloud or the tail of a rabbit. Fluffy, harmless. All of this mattered—this cotton ball mattered, and how the resident chose his words mattered, and everything tiny was now huge. The world teetered on microscopic ramen. And if the world could teeter on ramen, if something so big could hinge on something so inconsequential, then I had a strange, shaky sense that maybe the big things—walking, talking, earning college degrees—were not so consequential.

The resident called this a "genetic deletion" and told us that the bit of genetic material had been missing in either the sperm or the egg that conceived Fiona. In other words, the missing bit had existed before her conception. It had existed prior to my DHA pills and hypnosis birthing tracks and organic grocery bills. It had existed before the dawn of her creation. If it had come from my egg, it had even existed before my own birth.

The resident continued. "We know this genetic anomaly occurs in one out of fifty thousand births. And it appears at the same rate across cultures. So it's nothing environmental. Okay? There's nothing you could have done differently. It just happens."

His remark was both a relief and a riddle. *Really?* I could have done *nothing?* I could not have to-do-listed my way out of this? I couldn't have reversed this fortune with positive thinking or potent herbs? Even a doctor's words couldn't rewrite years of training.

"Is this your first?" he asked.

We nodded.

"Congratulations!" he said heartily.

Justin laid Fiona on the paper-covered table, and the resident examined her movements. Her onyx eyes gazed up at him. In terms of interaction, though, that was about all Fiona offered. *Your four-month-old will make* ah *and* oh *sounds,* said the baby books. Fiona lay quiet, mouth closed. *Your baby's head should no longer be wobbly. You can sit her up with support.* Fiona lay supine on the paper. When we tried to sit her up, her head rolled to one side and her trunk caved in on itself. *At four months old, your baby will now laugh at things she finds entertaining.* Fiona looked up at the world with the stoic calm of someone constantly in meditation. Her dad's disposition or a developmental delay? She was alert but not easily stirred beyond the faintest giggles. *Zen baby,* a guy at Justin's church called her. He didn't know yet about her anomalous chromosomes.

A nurse was looking at Fiona over the resident's shoulder. "Is there a spectrum with this syndrome?"

"A spectrum?" I asked.

"Does it cause different levels of severity? Because she looks great."

"She does look great," the resident said, but more as fact than surprise.

About Fiona's condition, the geneticist told us what I'd already read on the Internet. He described the facial features characteristic of people with her syndrome: high forehead, small chin, wide-set eyes. He listed the possible medical complications but said we could dismiss certain concerns right off the bat, like a cleft lip or palate, and probably vision and hearing impairments. He mentioned the oral aversions and difficulties in feeding. I nodded emphatically.

"She'll probably always be small," he said. "No matter how many calories you give her. Okay? They've done studies where they've given people with Wolf-Hirschhorn syndrome hundreds of extra calories, and it didn't make them grow."

I filed his words for later, predicting we'd need them to stem off nagging relatives or nutritionists who might surmise our kid was calorie-deficient.

"And she probably won't learn to crawl or walk when other kids do. Okay?"

I nodded. I was trying to let each word settle into the various cracks inside me—the ones that held my aches and hopes and fears.

Then he said, "Most people with Wolf-Hirschhorn syndrome have intellectual disabilities to some degree."

It was the fall of 2011, two years before the *Diagnostic and Statistical Manual of Mental Disorders* replaced "mental retardation" with "intellectual developmental disorder." Our cherubic resident could have just as easily used *mental retardation*. But he didn't. And I noted the effect inside me. *Mental retardation* would have conjured images of my childhood elementary school, designed as a series of separate circular buildings. Long hallways connected each circle, and the kids who used wheelchairs or walked staggeringly or slurred when they spoke or didn't speak at all— they were taught in a different circle. We typical kids almost never saw them, but we learned, through the architecture of the school and the design of the school day, that we had no reason to interact with them. That disability was for separate, closed-off spaces. That the kids who learned in those spaces were other, were incapable of relationships with us. And their invisibility led to the mythology that they were broken. Because they sometimes made sounds that resembled moans, I thought they were suffering. We called them "mentally retarded."

Had the doctor said *mentally retarded*, I would have envisioned this isolated circle, an ostracized future for Fiona. But *intellectual* brought to mind a monocle. A *New Yorker* article. Attending a Gloria Steinem lecture. And *disability* could mean: an impairment that limits activity. So this is what I immediately grasped about the supine and onyx-eyed four-month-old who was still waking me three-plus times a night: attending a Gloria Steinem lecture while wearing a monocle and holding this week's *New Yorker* might pose a challenge for her. I could live with that.

I'd always been intellectually inclined. Part of my job as a writing professor was to teach students to analyze everything—from commercials to flyers to the layout of a room. I reveled in comparing Eastern religions, and I read poetry for fun. But my kid didn't need to spend her high school Friday nights reading feminist perspectives on the Beat generation or imitating Leonard Cohen's rhymed quatrains. She could opt for other interests.

Looking back, I see the brilliance of the resident's language. "A genetic deletion," he called it, rather than "a genetic defect." A deletion was descriptive, something I did in a Word document daily, rather than "defect," which called to mind a broken part on a factory line. And he'd said "genetic anomaly" rather than "abnormality." An anomaly was a rarity, an outlier. In simulations of the universe, a planet like Earth is a statistical anomaly, and look at all the life it sustains.

This is when I first experienced disability as a flexible reality, bent and twisted by our notions of the body, and by our assumptions about which bodies are worthy of life.

When Gail Landsman observed 130 evaluation sessions between doctors and children, she found that new mothers often pushed back against the initial diagnosis of their child, not because they didn't trust doctors but because the notion of disability is culturally associated with what Landsman calls "diminished personhood." Diagnosing doctors were essentially asking women "to apply to one body two seemingly incompatible concepts: their loved child and a diagnosis culturally associated with less than full personhood." How can the human you love be less-than? Words like "abnormal" and "mentally retarded" take on the stink of this dehumanizing view. When my mother challenged my grade-school teacher's assessment that I might be "mentally retarded" because of my grip, she was pushing back against all that phrase connoted—that I was damaged, wrong.

But on this afternoon, the geneticist's language offered the not-so-common impression that my kid could be both significantly disabled and 100 percent right. This is not a standard view from the medical world. Among my fellow Wolf-Hirschhorn syndrome parents, I've heard horror stories. One woman received her daughter's diagnosis in utero and was told by her OB that she "should" terminate. At twenty-six-weeks pregnant, she was given three out-of-state locations to call immediately. (She never did.) Another mother, also pregnant, met with a geneticist who repeatedly used the word "burden," explaining that her daughter would not only be a burden to the family but to society. "They basically made us feel like crap for *not* wanting to terminate," the mother told me. Plenty of parents recalled a diagnosing doctor using the words "vegetable" and "low quality of life." In one of the more disturbing stories, one mother, only days after giving birth, was shown a handout about the syndrome that featured a picture of a dead fetus. In the soupy, soft, tender postpartum hours, I cannot fathom processing such a message. She was told that her son would probably be "vegetative" and have "little to no personality." The doctor handed her and her husband information about a home for medically fragile children and said that they could leave their son at the hospital.

There is no good scientific reason for a doctor to be so absolute. He had access to the same 2008 peer-reviewed article I'd found online, which stated that *Intent to communicate appears to be present in most individuals with WHS* and *Slow but constant improvement has been observed over time in all individuals with WHS.* Nine years later, the mother shares a video online of her kid clapping and writes, "Here's my supposedly 'vegetative' child dancing at his school performance last week." But nine years before, the message she received was that, regardless of whether her boy lived or not, he would not really be alive. "It was a horrible time in my life," the mother wrote.

In the poker game of doctors' words, we were dealt aces.

"We won't put limits on her, okay?" the resident said. "We'll help her be all that she can be."

The resident did a powerful thing that day: through language and framing, he took my daughter's life back from a culture that might label her as less-than, and he returned that life to us. The person with the final word would be Fiona, who was lying in a onesie on the examining table, mesmerized, like most babies, by the ceiling lights.

But there was still a giant, unspoken question in the room. Maybe because of his line of work—getting calls from hospitals, rushing out the door with sacred oil and the words of last rites— Justin could broach the subject I could not.

"What about," he said, "her chances of dying early? We'd read a statistic. One out of three kids dying before age two."

The resident tipped his head sideways an inch in concession. It was true, he said, that the symptoms of Wolf-Hirschhorn syndrome could shorten life expectancies. "But the syndrome itself doesn't predict her life. And she's looking great so far. Aren't you, Fiona? She's alert. She's eating orally. Her heart condition is mild." We'd already had an echocardiogram and learned that her murmur was due to a small hole in her heart that might close over time. "People with Wolf-Hirschhorn syndrome can certainly live well into middle age."

I looked at my little girl, whose onyx eyes were still as black as Magic 8-Balls. The worst of the news we'd heard today was "intellectual disabilities," and in those words, my daughter's condition seemed manageable. After all, the intellect could not feel a ray of sunshine. It could not giggle. It would not delight over farts. The intellect performed the sterile dissection of thoughts with its sharpened scalpel. I appreciated my own intellect, with its ability to analyze a TV show and parse a sentence, to write essays and books and teach undergraduates how to do the same. But the intellect wasn't everything.

Then the lead doctor entered the room, and the power dynamic shifted. He was a thin, brown-haired man with a serious face. Our wingless cherubic resident explained what we'd covered so far, and the lead geneticist nodded in approval.

"The most common causes of mortality in Wolf-Hirschhorn syndrome," he said, and started counting on his fingers, "are seizures, kidney failure, and aspiration. She hasn't had any seizures yet, right?"

"Not that we know of," Justin said.

"We'll need to assess her kidney function and her swallow function right away." He sat slumped on a wheelie stool, his hands in an upside-down prayer position between his knees, like he offered benedictions of practicality to the linoleum floor. "She appears to be handling her saliva just fine. But kids with Wolf-Hirschhorn syndrome can have what we call silent aspiration, where saliva creeps down their lungs without anyone knowing." He reported this with the flat delivery of a person accustomed to describing flesh-eating infections. "This can go on for years, and over time it damages their lungs, causing irreparable harm."

Then the geneticist explained something dazzling: swallowing, he said, was a complex thing. The mouth has to push food forward in one way and backward another, all the while guarding the airway. This, he said, was a difficult cognitive skill.

Was it a miracle that all those Cincinnatians this morning, standing at intersections near the hospital and looking down at their phones and waiting for traffic lights, were also swallowing? Was it a miracle that they were also handling their own spit without dying? Were we all kinesthetic geniuses unpraised?

"Kidney failure," he went on in his deadpan voice, "could

strike later in life, but we should start monitoring her kidneys now. And see if she has any reflux." He looked at the resident. "Any history of UTIs?"

"Not that the family reported." The resident looked at the folder in his lap.

"No," I said.

"Good," the geneticist said, unsmiling. "Hopefully it will stay that way. Now there's an eighty-five percent chance that Fiona's deletion was de novo, meaning it occurred spontaneously. But there's a fifteen percent chance that one of you is a carrier. So if you want, while you're here"—he paused, his voice upturned in an uncharacteristic ounce of perkiness at the convenience—"you could each get a blood test!"

Justin and I agreed.

We carried Fiona out of the genetics wing. If I had feelings about the possibility of silent aspiration or kidney failure, I didn't know exactly what they were. I was numb in a way I would know plenty in the years to come, experiencing a kind of hospital fatigue brought on by receiving huge news with the emotionally tempered focus of an astronaut mid-flight. I had a job to do. I had to hear things clearly, had to wear all my antennae on high alert. My feelings were somewhere on a shelf.

Justin and I took Fiona into a family-style bathroom, marked on the door by a blue sign with a stick-figure woman, a stick-figure man, and a stick-figure wheelchair guy. Against one wall was an adult-size changing table, padded and covered in vinyl. Once an otherworldly object, it represented the kind of life that

America sometimes tucks into its excluded confines, like the unseen disabled kids in my elementary school. But this adult-size changing table could now become an object of my future. As in, *Oh, thank God, I can change my adult kid's diaper here!*

My husband had his eye on something else. Against another wall, a floor-length mirror was warped so badly it could have competed with a funhouse mirror. He stared into it, grinning. "Look at this," he said.

I stood beside him and peered into the mirror. Justin's forehead was an inch longer than usual, and his chin was smaller and narrower at the bottom. Top-heavy, his face resembled the images of kids with our daughter's syndrome.

I turned my gaze on myself. I was his reverse. My forehead was compressed up top; my mouth was stretched into a plate with teeth. The two of us bent our knees to shorten ourselves, then stretched our bodies tall, watching as we morphed. We giggled. We got ourselves closer to our genetically anomalous daughter. We said, "Check this one out." We laughed at the spontaneity of difference. We delighted over the flimsiness of normal.

In the face of doctors who used words like "vegetable" or urged a mother to leave her baby at the hospital, I know I would have been crushed. After an appointment like some of my parenting cohort endured, I know I would have had an impossible time stepping into a family bathroom and delighting with my husband in the diversity of body shapes. I would have carried the heaviness of "normal" and longed for it even more than I otherwise did.

Instead, I felt—at least for a few hours after the appointment—a little buoyant. Even wondrous. Who knew? We'd watch and see. We'd help her grow. I'm grateful to our cherubic resident. He was probably a product of progressive medical training, but I see him as a gift from some unknowable beyond.

If the first few days of motherhood entailed losing things, so did the first few weeks of knowingly parenting a kid with a rare syndrome. We surrendered the certainty that our child swallowed saliva. We offered up the assumption that her kidneys worked just fine. We handed over the expectation that our child would one day walk or talk. We relinquished all these things with the hope that someday they'd come back to us.

Despite occasional glimmers of equanimity, I don't think I ever felt more distraught than in the months following Fiona's diagnosis. After a day of teaching classes, I found myself pumping gas into my car and crying into my cell phone. "This is the hardest time," I said to my sister, who was listening in Philadelphia. "This is harder than the other times."

I didn't have to name those other times for her. She'd been my companion on the couches of child therapy and in grief. Three years older, she'd also been my trailblazer, traversing first into major life stages like college and marriage and motherhood, then reporting back gems of survival. *Don't ever sign up for an 8 a.m. class. If your baby cries, just put her on your boob.* But I was in uncharted territory now, and she was five hundred miles away, hearing me weep through a flip phone about a daughter who lived inside huge question marks.

Drivers around me filled their cars with fuel, decidedly not sobbing into their phones. The metallic fumes of gasoline wafted. "I can't fix this," I told her, and it seemed a ridiculous and unfair truth.

A month earlier, when I told her the pediatrician suspected a syndrome, her words were the singular wheel-hole around which all the chaos could spin, and I knew if I just focused on it, I'd stay clear-headed: *Whatever she has,* my sister had said, *nothing will change the fact that she's beautiful and we love her.* I needed nothing so much as that sentence.

Now, my sister could only listen. I cried through a long pause and then said, "I didn't sign up for this."

I meant I signed up for interrupted sleep and poop on my hands and decisions about preschools and guidance about snotty schoolgirls. I meant I signed up for the responsibility of stewarding a human being from smallest, most fragile suckling babe to eighteen-year-old independent adult. I meant I'd never intended to care for a child whose future was so uncertain, who offered so many terrifying chances: kidney failure, seizures, aspiration, death.

My sister replied, softly, gently, empathetically, "No. You didn't."

But she was wrong. Of course I signed up for it. Every parent does. When we venture to become parents, we sign up for the fragility of life. We sign up for the precarious vulnerability of being human. We just don't always know it. Or maybe we know it, but we try to prove otherwise—try to prove that being human doesn't have to mean ever hurting, ever struggling with your fractured bone or heart or chromosome. So we drink green smoothies and put Beethoven against our pregnant bellies and pray to the god of our meticulous, faithful pursuits.

We were on our fifth doctor in four months, and one thing had become clear: they were now our age. I found this funny, that somehow I'd gone to graduate school and taken a few teaching jobs and turned thirty-three, and the doctors no longer had gray hairs or wrinkles. They had Adidas and Starbucks lattes and opinions about indie rock. They had the verbal quirks of Gen Xers—a well-placed *like* for dramatic pause, a love of the word *totally*. The ENT was a tall, thin guy with spiked hair and happy, caffeinated spunk. He pulled out a black tube as thin as shoestring licorice. On the tip of that black shoestring was a red light. When he worked it into Fiona's nostril, her entire nose lit up, Rudolph-style. (Was Rudolph just a deer caught in a swallow study?) Naturally, she screamed. The light faded as the doctor's blue-latex hand eased the tube deeper up her nasal passage and eventually down her throat. At the end of the tube was a camera. Two televisions in the examining room now broadcasted my daughter's airway as a wet, pulsing red planet. She gagged and spit and cried.

The doctor then told me to try to nurse Fiona. Breastfeeding requires a certain degree of calm, so this was like asking a person to relax through a massage of needles. I held Fiona's thrashing seven pounds to my chest. Our bodies sweated together, and she slipped down my torso. I eventually got her mouth around my silicon-encased nipple—she still used the shields. She latched, and her taut limbs went loose. She sucked, and I felt the pins-and-needles tingling as my milk let down. The doctor and nurses turned to the televisions. I did not see what they saw, which was breast milk traveling safely down my daughter's esophagus and not into her airway.

"Looks good!" the young doctor said, still staring at a screen.

"All right!" a nurse said, her eyes also on a TV. It was like Ground Control just watched a rover touch down on the moon. I thought they'd erupt in applause. I think they wanted to.

Afterward, Justin and I sat in a booth of a daisy-decorated breakfast joint. I treated myself to eggs Benedict. Fiona, probably traumatized from the morning, had passed out in her car seat carrier beside me and was hissing deep breaths through her nostrils. I felt a thin line of giddiness course through me. I was repeating things to Justin across the booth like, "She can swallow her own spit! She can swallow breast milk! Formula! She can protect her airway!"

It was terrifying and wonderful. Maybe it was so wonderful because it contained something so terrifying.

For her first kidney function test, I went alone. I laid her on a paper-covered table and peeled back her teensy newborn diaper. A nurse held a clear bit of tubing.

"She's tinier than I expected," the nurse said, and went to a drawer. She sorted through medical supplies. "I don't think we have anything smaller."

Another nurse helped her find the very smallest catheter tube at Cincinnati Children's Hospital. When she tried to insert the tube into Fiona's urethra, my daughter screamed.

I got my face within inches of Fiona's. I tried to become all that she saw. I sang "Twinkle, Twinkle." Her toothless, screaming mouth bared red-hot gums. I moved on to the ABCs.

"I just . . . can't . . . get it . . . ," the nurse said.

When the hairdresser's blow-dryer is too hot, I don't tell her. When the dental hygienist pokes bloody patches into my gums, I don't relay my discomfort. *Be convenient. Don't let your pain become a problem for other people.* I never send back my plate at a restaurant. I don't know where exactly I learned this, but it's an expectation plenty of women internalize. *No, you go ahead.* Yet in the nephrology department of Cincinnati Children's, I watched Fiona's tomato-red face, splotched yellow and white where her brow furrowed. "Get someone else!" I told the nurse.

The nurse put down the plastic tubing and left the room. She returned with another nurse. The second nurse managed the catheter in one try.

Mothering Fiona was turning me into a different kind of woman.

Fiona had an ophthalmology exam to check her eyes for abnormalities (they were fine); a thirty-minute EEG to determine if her brain wave patterns were normal (not quite); a developmental assessment to see if she was delayed (she was, in all categories but social and emotional). She had a kidney ultrasound to determine if her kidneys were normal (not exactly) and not one but two kidney function exams, to tell whether her kidneys worked okay (they did). Justin and I also learned the results of our blood tests—we were not carriers of the syndrome. It had occurred "spontaneously," the doctor had said, a word I liked because it evoked something wild and fun, like booking a last-minute red-eye to Paris.

Because I now only taught half-time, I became the primary manager of Fiona's complex medical calendar. The squares on our "month-at-a-glance" filled with hospital appointments and therapy sessions. I called our health insurance on my off-days, fought incorrect bills, and set up appointments for early intervention. At least monthly I found myself wandering the halls of Cincinnati Children's Hospital, lugging Fiona in the car seat carrier that banged against my calf with every other step. When sunlight from the hospital's atrium hit my worried face, I fought the urge to weep. If I could design purgatory, it would look like this: walking through a hospital atrium on an immaculately sunny day, heading to another specialist, readying to soothe your infant through another test, after which you'd find out if your baby's body did what bodies needed to do to live. Purgatory is this atrium and tears.

Mondays and Wednesdays, I got a break: I sat in a circle with my students, their notebooks splayed open. Among them was a pale, thin blonde, a bearded hipster, a mousey brunette. I told them things like, *Find meaning through the senses.* I said, *Pay attention to your insides and to what, on the outside, triggered your reactions.* I told them what Jack Kerouac had said: *The de-tails are the life of it.*

As an undergraduate, I'd sat in the office of my favorite pro-fessor, a poet and playwright, who gestured to the ceiling and said the university had given her a roof to do what she loved: write and teach. I spent much of the next ten years building a résumé to acquire the same type of job—I got degrees and pub-lished and learned to teach and found I loved it. In Ohio, I felt lucky that I'd landed a position in a commutable distance to Jus-tin's church. The year I was pregnant with Fiona, I managed les-son planning and grading around my constant nausea. The only time my queasiness lifted was when I stood in front of a class-room, leading a discussion and bumping my burgeoning belly against the whiteboard with a dry-erase marker in hand. Teach-ing brought me out of myself, lit me up with purpose. My favor-ite course was on contemporary memoir, where I showed students the weird meta-narrative of Dave Eggers's *A Heartbreaking Work of Staggering Genius* and the fractured, lyrical prose of Nick Flynn's *Another Bullshit Night in Suck City.* I reveled in helping students see how writers framed their lives to say something true, and I wanted to help students figure out how to do the same.

Now I'd cut my workload and paycheck in half, squeezing most of my teaching life into two six-hour days on campus. I felt like a visitor from another country, one where my citizens thought more about swallow studies than literary studies, more about tummy time than writing time.

One day I gave my students a short assignment: *Walk around town. Don't drive—walk. Take notes. See what you see. Return home, and write two pages.* The pale, thin blonde raised a hand. She said this town was too dangerous for walking.

I recalibrated, asking if there was any place she felt safe. She mentioned a street with a café she frequented. Could she walk there, I asked, but pay more attention than usual? She shrugged as if to say, *Fine.*

In reality I had no idea whether the town I taught in was dangerous. On the two days that I drove to the school, I blew by gas stations, tiny houses with striped awnings over windows, and billboards advertising detox programs. I parked at the edge of the small campus, rushed to my office, planned, pumped milk, taught, pumped milk, then busted out: back to the baby and whomever was taking care of her. On Mondays, it was Justin. On Wednesdays, a babysitter. The bulk of my forty-minute ride home followed highways that zipped beside or above other Ohio towns I also didn't know. I knew better the hospital's atrium.

One night I came home to find Fiona's sitter on the couch, bouncing up and down while wearing my baby in a wrap. Fiona was making her high, weak cat cry. "She won't eat for me," the sitter said, distraught. I noticed two half-empty milk bottles on the coffee table.

We'd found this young woman in a miraculous stroke of luck. Four days a week she worked as a nanny to a pediatrician's kids, and she happened to have off the only day we needed her: Wednesdays. She had a few years of experience and usually spoke in a singsong. Today she was rattled.

"She's only had seven ounces today," she said. And then she dropped a bomb. "Maybe I'm not the right person for her."

"No, no," I said, recognizing the emergency. We were about

to lose our only support, our only sliver of a village to raise this child. The grandparents and aunts and uncles were all five hundred miles away. "It's not you. You're doing great." I said Fiona didn't drink much more than seven ounces for Justin either. I told the babysitter Fiona was very, very hard to feed.

The sitter was visibly eased. She said she'd see me next Wednesday. She never talked of quitting again.

The details are the life of it. When I told my students this, I meant the specifics will tell the story. The pitch of a mother's holler. The lilac in late spring. The names of people, places, things. Which was precisely why I couldn't yet bring myself to tell the sitter the name of Fiona's syndrome. Neither Justin nor I trusted that there were people in this world who wouldn't write our kid off the minute they heard her diagnosis. Google offered cruel portraits of "Wolf-Hirschhorn syndrome," with words like "severe mental retardation" and images of a dead fetus with a face like Fiona's. If I gave the sitter all the details, she could tell her own version of my daughter's story, and what if that story was one of tragedy, and what if she sang that tragedy as a lullaby to my baby every Wednesday?

A week after the walk-around-town assignment, the pale, thin blonde wrote a brilliant essay critiquing a subject I'd never once noticed: the town's bronze political statues. A soldier looking triumphant with a musket. A founding father with a finger in the air.

Me? I was a new mother. I wasn't writing a thing. I was living inside a labyrinthine essay as baffling and bright as a children's hospital, and I didn't know how to find my way out of it.

. . .

A decade earlier, in that scrappy basement apartment we'd lived in, Justin had once shown me a photo spread of six American Zen teachers, and I'd picked out Pema Chödrön without knowing her work. "I like her," I said. Since then I'd read a few of the Tibetan Buddhist nun's books, but I didn't buy her bestselling *When Things Fall Apart* until things felt like they actually had.

I brought the slim beige copy with me to Fiona's hospital appointments. I held the book in the back seat when Justin drove us, even though reading in a car turns me green. I carried the book around like an instruction manual for chaos. Chödrön's words were the anti–Louise Hay of my youth, the anti-Hypnobabies of my pregnancy. I read as she advised the opposite of daily affirmations.

Not: *I feel safe.* Not: *My baby will be born perfectly.*

Instead: *Things don't really get solved. They come together and they fall apart.*

Not: *I am confident. I am relaxed and peaceful. I am in control.*

Instead: *We don't know anything. Let there be room for not knowing.*

On the way to one big test—maybe the swallow study or the echocardiogram—I laid my hand over Fiona's little rib cage and talked to Justin in the driver's seat about the tender agony of the Buddhist nun's instructions. I was trying *to stay with a broken heart,* as she said, *with a rumbling stomach, with the feeling of hopelessness.* I was trying to feel the uncertainty of Fiona's life and not attempt to fix it, or smooth it over, or hush it up. How tender I felt, doing this. How raw and squishy and sore was that spot an inch below my sternum. Speeding down I-71 toward another test for the little seven-pound human, I longed to be consoled.

She's not gonna need a tracheotomy, I wanted to be told as I fingered her soft onesie.

Her kidneys are perfectly fine, I wanted the voice of God to say through the car radio.

She'll defy every odd, the pep-talking Uncle Sam in my American head would have said if I'd let him.

If I thought it would have helped, I would have also fantasized about a shopping spree and a trip to somewhere tropical. I wanted to jettison myself from this fear, this uncertainty, and I knew I could try through wishful thinking or avoidance or distraction or even blame. Blame God, blame myself, blame chromosomes, blame sperm or egg or Earth.

When things fall apart and we're on the verge of we know not what, the test for each of us is to stay on the brink and not concretize. I'd underlined *not concretize* twice.

"Concretizing" was writing a story that offered logic, whether soothing or searing:

She'll be fine.

It's somehow my fault.

Special babies happen to special people.

"Concretizing" was even what diagnosing doctors had done to so many other parents, predicting their kids would die by age two, or foretelling that their babies would never walk or talk. But concretizing was also what some relatives did after I used the

word *if*. As in, *if she walks. If she talks*. People rewrote my sentiment with a single word—*when. You mean, when she walks*. I understood their intentions: they believed in the power of positive
thinking. But plenty of kids with Wolf-Hirschhorn syndrome
didn't walk or talk, and it wasn't because their parents hadn't believed.

Not concretizing was, instead, like floating in outer space. It
meant I stayed with the warm tingle of a face before tears. *Not
concretizing* gave me nothing to hold on to. It was like being suspended amid the cosmos, beholding their vastness, getting a
glimpse of my smallness among the Everything. It was awesome
and terrifying. I found myself in awe of the painful vulnerability
of being human. In awe of the fragility of me, my daughter, my
husband—everyone. We were always on this brink, on this edge.
Always possibly headed for collision or creation. We just pretended otherwise.

Justin took exit 3, veered right onto Martin Luther King Drive,
turned right again, and then left. Up ahead we saw the sand-
colored buildings of the children's hospital. I held my breath, I
kept breathing. There were certain kinds of answers in those
buildings. Other answers would have to be found elsewhere.

One question doctors believed they'd answered: Why was
Fiona so difficult to nurse? It was her syndrome, they said.
Not a tongue-tie, like a few nurses had suggested. Babies with
Wolf-Hirschhorn syndrome have "low tone," which means their
muscles are limper than usual. Because their brains aren't telling
their muscles to contract, their mouths sometimes aren't taut

enough for a good latch on a bottle, let alone on the unwieldy cartography of a breast. The other problem is that many people with Wolf-Hirschhorn hate things in their mouths. *Orally defensive,* doctors called it. The phrase made me think of cartoonish boxing gloves accordioning from a person's mouth and knocking out any approaching finger or bottle.

"I think the syndrome explains her difficulty breastfeeding," the pediatrician said when we visited her again after the diagnosis. "Not a tongue-tie."

She saw my dubious expression.

"But we could make an appointment with an oral surgeon anyway. . . ." She paused. "If you want." Something in that pause and in her tone implied that I probably should not want, that wanting would be a waste. But her shrug and half-smile also said, *You could still try, I guess.*

A fork in the road lay before me. Justin and I could let the medical information about our kid's syndrome lead us. We could treat our daughter *by* her syndrome. We could say, *Well, people with Wolf-Hirschhorn syndrome typically don't or can't. . . .* We could call the breastfeeding quits, throw in the nursing towel, and let my milk "dry up" because *babies with Wolf-Hirschhorn syndrome almost never breastfeed.*

But groundlessness didn't just mean giving up security or misplaced hope; it also meant giving up despair.

I thought about what this pediatrician might have done if Fiona had no syndrome. I believed the doctor would have nodded when I pointed out Fiona's scalloped tongue tip. I believed she would have listened thoughtfully when I said that at least two nurses suspected Fiona's tongue was tied. If Fiona had all her fourth chromosome, I believed we would have been making an appointment with an oral surgeon immediately.

"Let's call the oral surgeon," I told the pediatrician, who nodded and made a note.

A week after the tongue-release procedure, I tried to nurse Fiona without the ubiquitous silicone shield. She latched. "Quick," I said to Justin, hunched over my baby's body to keep the seal intact. "Take a picture!" In the blurry results, I have the ecstatic, high-eyebrowed face of a can-can dancer. She never needed a shield again.

I t's hard to say who woke first. The waking was like swimming up from the bottom of a pool—rising from the depths to the surface. There was often nothing to hear, not at first. Consciousness brought me to the here and now: my side of the queen mattress, Justin's heat to my left, Fiona's cream-colored co-sleeper to my right, and no light yet breaking through the window. Why was I awake?

Then it came: the beginning of her cat cry. I knew before I knew: time to nurse.

Is she sleeping through the night now? elderly women loved to ask, I suppose because in some alternate universe of baby-raising, five-month-olds sleep soundly from dusk to dawn. Fiona woke every few hours. But now, so did I. I slept a few hours, I woke. She slept a few hours, she woke. We must have smelled each other's waking, sensed our collective swimming upward from our respective dream states. We woke together.

It was hard to say whose need I was meeting. If I didn't nurse her, I'd swell, turn rock hard. I might leak all over the bed. Her need for milk was my need to release it. My need to give was her need to receive.

We don't care for children because we love them, Alison Gopnik writes. *We love them because we care for them.* It had finally happened. Our needs held hands.

Love is a verb, as bell hooks points out. It's not static. Not a concrete object to dust on a mantel. It's a flowing between—an unpinnable exchange between a blessed someone and their beloved.

Here's an interesting thing: God too is a verb. At least that's what the God of the Bible declares. When Moses sees the burning bush, he asks to know God's name. *Who should I say is burning, God? What should I call you, Oh Lord Omniscient?* According to Exodus, the mysterious flame called God says, *I am who I am. . . .* And later, *Tell them I Am sent you.* In other words, God wants to be called a verb.

In my thirty-three years, I didn't think I'd figured out much about God, but one thing I did know: the Divine was probably found not in any static object but in the ancient ever-becoming of being itself. And loving my daughter was bringing me closer to the verb of God. We were living something divine, my daughter and me.

Chapter Five

⤳

The able-bodied babies were everywhere. They were giants. They were sturdy as small vehicles, their backs boxy and broad. They saw objects, grabbed at them, and yanked them from people's hands. They were wizards of muscle and mind. They held their own bottles! They wrapped their giant hands around the plastic cylinders and kept five, six, seven ounces at their mouths! Then they gulped that milk down in minutes. I watched, mind-blown. They sucked and sucked and finished and wanted more. They were fierce beasts of strength.

The able-bodied babies were at supermarkets and clothing stores and doctors' offices. In the waiting room of a pediatric ophthalmologist, a baby twice the size of Fiona sat in a stroller. Her dad attached a spinning rattle to the stroller's handle so that the toy dangled in front of her face. As soon as her father dropped the toy in her line of vision, she banged it in rhythm. *Bam bam bam.* She beat that toy like a punching bag. She ruled that rattling thing. She smacked it right off the bar.

I sat amazed: that the baby had the eye coordination, rhythm, and strength for such domination. A few minutes later, her dad looked up from his phone and saw the toy in her lap. "How'd you do that?" he asked, and he didn't know because he hadn't been watching, and why would he watch the dazzling, able-bodied actions of this baby, who did these things daily? And why *wouldn't* I watch, because in this child I saw not just infant athleticism and maybe even baby magic but the atlas of my own child's delays. I now knew what "severe developmental delay" looked like.

The therapists who visited our house explained the trajectory of typical baby development. They showed me milestone charts and pointed out all that Fiona wasn't doing. She wasn't moving objects across her midline like a four-month-old. She wasn't putting objects in her mouth or pushing up on her arms during tummy time like a five-month-old. She wasn't sitting unsupported or rolling over or grabbing a cube with a palmar grasp like a six-month-old. She wasn't copying the gestures of others, and she wasn't eating anything other than pureed carrots, and she wasn't making any bilabial speech sounds like *mmm* or *buh*, all of which she would do if she were "typically developing." She was eight months old. Belly down, Fiona could prop herself up on her elbows and look around, which meant she was gaining strength in her neck. She also sometimes held an object in her hand, although within a minute or two she loosely dropped it to her side. The therapists looked at their charts and said my daughter was functionally a three-month-old.

Every other week, an early interventionist named Tiffany came to our house. She observed Fiona, did a few exercises with her, made a list of recommendations on a triplicate form, and tore off a yellow copy for me to keep. Sometimes Tiffany came with an occupational or physical therapist, and they made their own recommendations. When they left, they bequeathed to me not just handouts on speech development and infant massage but a list of tasks. I once tallied everything I was supposed to do— fifteen therapeutic activities, including tummy time, arm stretches, leg stretches, hand massages, supported upright sitting in a modified infant chair, exposure to new food textures, rocking (for vestibular therapy), book reading (for literacy development), music listening (for cognitive development), and so on.

I was grateful for the therapy. In the sixteenth century, theologians Martin Luther and John Calvin suggested that people like my daughter were possessed by evil spirits. In the nineteenth century, social Darwinists would have considered Fiona "unfit" for the state programs she received. In 1972, American public schools neglected to educate one in five kids with disabilities. Thankfully we lived in 2012, which meant Fiona benefited from a 1986 federal law declaring that kids like her deserved therapeutic support.

I didn't realize at the time, though, that my Ohio county used a "teaching model" of early intervention. This meant that instead of working with a child directly for a few hours a week, a professional came biweekly to teach the *parent* to work with their child. It was a cost-saving measure, one in which parents were expected to learn the skills of occupational, physical, and speech therapies. This was why the OT, Karen, typically spent her visits observing Fiona from a chaste kneel and then giving me a dozen suggestions. When I finally asked Karen to engage directly with my child, she replied, "I'm not really supposed to touch her. In fact, I've been touching her too much already." She'd given Fiona a hand massage and stretched her arms above her head.

But I didn't know about the teaching model at the time. With a gripping sense of duty, I internalized the message that I needed to become three therapists inside one mother. Each minute that Fiona wasn't napping or nursing, I tried to do something with therapeutic purpose: I offered spoonfuls of textured purees; I did tummy time with her on my chest; I drove her to a feeding therapist, who started an egg timer and watched me offer her still more spoonfuls of textured purees until the ticker blared *stop*; I did tummy time with her on a quilt; I put plastic rings in her hands; I propped her beneath dangling animals; I did tummy time with her on a yoga ball; I placed her in "side-lying play" and scattered the floor with brightly colored rattles; I bounced her in a chair beneath still other dangling animals; I wore her around the house in a cotton wrap and narrated mundane chores like laundry because experts said her brain was a sponge and that's how she'd learn language—if she learned it; I read her Dr. Seuss. I didn't read to her for the fun of it, even though *Hop on Pop* is some raucous good poetry. I read out of a sense of duty that I couldn't fail her. "Walk, talk, we like to talk," Dr. Seuss said, and I pointed out the furry yellow creatures walking, talking, not knowing if my kid ever would.

I got bored out of my mind meeting all these therapeutic suggestions, so I once, once, drove to a bookstore. I carried Fiona in the detachable car seat and could not shake the guilt that she was lying flaccidly in molded plastic rather than working against gravity and strengthening her low tone. I spent the bulk of that anomalous bookstore trip in the children's section, stacking more Dr. Seuss.

Justin didn't internalize my pressures. He still spent hours communing with our black-eyed girl and listening with her to chill downbeats. But he did buy me a yardstick. Feeding Fiona still required a full day's labor, eight hours of bottle and spoon and breast. Were my efforts paying off? Was she making progress? I wanted tangible proof, so weekly I lined the top of the wood yardstick with her peach-fuzz head, then pulled gently on her leg, stretching her socked heel as far as it could go. Most weeks, her gains were invisible. She started her life at eighteen and a half inches. Eight months later, she was twenty-four inches, a half-foot shorter than most kids her age.

As a snaggle-toothed child, I could tell that my mom genuinely enjoyed the job of mothering. She was a stay-at-home-mom in my early years, and her hands usually smelled of bleach, the stove often simmered with some one-pot chicken dish, and her rouge-cheeked face smiled at requests to play. I remember her joining me in coloring or Play-Doh shaping or Lego building. She didn't long to be elsewhere. She didn't, unlike future me, have something she wanted to go write or teach. "You're the only mom I know," my stepfather told her more than once, "who doesn't want her kids to go back to school in the fall." She conceded with a nod: September made her sad.

So when I was having no fun as a new mom, I considered it a mark of a "bad mother." Good mothers reveled in the work, I thought, even if that work was hours upon hours of textured purees and tummy time.

But then my mom flew to Ohio for a weeklong visit. And although she doted on her third grandchild—changing Fiona's teensy

diapers, cradling her body to her chest in awe, weeping at tiny
fingers—she also found herself, days into the visit, dangling a toy
in Fiona's face and feeling uncharacteristic stress. The toy was
made of purple rubber tubing bent into a G. It was the aroma
and color of grape bubble gum. A therapist had given it to us.
Justin and I were supposed to encourage Fiona to gnaw on it,
but she refused, so the toy became a perpetual companion to
the keys on the coffee table. My mom, noticing my stress about
getting Fiona to meet this milestone or that, wanted to help.
So she resurrected the toy as a literacy tool. "Guh," she said.
"Guh, guh." She held the G-shaped thing to Fiona's face, trying
to get a closed-mouth baby to produce a consonant sound. "G
makes guh."

And that's when my mom realized: There is something inherently unfun about trying to get your beloved to be different than
she is. The therapeutic pressures stole the joy out of life with a
baby. So she dropped those pressures and focused on just loving
her granddaughter.

My mom had, like me, shed much of the mind-body fundamentalism after my stepfather's death. In her years as a widow,
she'd resumed her Bible reading and church attending, and she
never once told me I needed to "think positively" about Fiona's
diagnosis like some of my stepfather's family members did (as
though I could will my kid into different chromosomes). It was
not a wild pendulum swing for my mom: through all the decades,
even the ones filled with affirmations and Louise Hay, a painting
of Jesus had stayed affixed to her living room wall. If my mother
had struggled a ton over Fiona's diagnosis, she didn't tell me. But
she did tell me this story: One morning, during her devotional

time, with her Bible opened on the kitchen table, the prayer she offered was a tear-filled and desperate *why?*

As in, *Why did you give this child Wolf-Hirschhorn syndrome?*

The reply she heard was so striking and clear, so separate from herself, that it stopped her straight. The voice said: "You have no idea what I intend to do with this child."

And after that, my mother trusted the body my daughter had been given.

In the halls of my university, I stayed mostly silent about Fiona. I'd always been a personable, candid professor with my students, but motherhood had encroached into nearly every minute of my life, and work offered a rare reprieve where (at least when I wasn't pumping milk) I could be someone else, *to* someone else. Plus, if Fiona's syndrome came up, I didn't know how I'd hold myself together.

One afternoon I bumped into a former student from the previous year's memoir class. He was a charmingly honest Irish kid who spoke with an accent and always wore jeans and a denim jacket. After discussing yet another dark unfolding in a memoirist's life, he'd once called out, "Why are all these books so depressing?" When I laughed, my pregnant belly jiggled up and down. I'd chosen the books, I said, because they all related to the theme of family. I said I'd originally considered designing the course around disability.

"Oh!" he moaned in his Irish accent. "That would have been *mis*erable!"

Several months later, we were now face-to-face in a hallway. I was no longer big-bellied; he looked virtually the same—jeans and denim jacket. I blurted hello like he was an old pal. How was his semester?

"Eh." He shrugged. "I found out I have thyroid cancer." He said he'd been trying to manage the fall semester while also getting radiation.

"I'm so sorry," I said.

When he asked about me, I offered a benign answer and pivoted back to him. How was he holding up?

"You know." He took a step backward. "Cancer," he said, and shrugged, as though that should sum it up.

Later I realized that when the Irish student had groaned however many months earlier and said, *Ugh, disability*, he had probably been carrying cancer, just as I had been carrying a daughter with a fractured fourth chromosome. We were in that very moment carriers of things that disable the body, even while he believed *disability* to be a curmudgeonly, depressing topic that wasn't his—wasn't ours.

By the time Fiona reached eight months old, the mysterious Magic 8-Balls of her eyes finally offered up their answer: they turned Lake Tahoe blue. She mesmerized strangers with her intense, aquatic gaze.

At nine months, I spent my first full day and night apart from her. Justin's gig as an assistant priest was up in five months, and my own position was tenuous and underpaying. One of us needed to find stable work. So on the last day of February, I flew to Philadelphia, where for a day and a half I was at the mercy of a university search committee who weighed my ability to hold a position I'd always wanted: a tenure-track professorship. I spent ten hours answering questions, giving a reading and a talk, teaching a lesson, and attempting to prove in all modes and manners that I could do the job. I'd asked for one break during which I could pump milk; I never got it. The day started in Philly at seven in the morning. Seventeen hours later—at the stroke of midnight—I was crawling into my bed in Ohio, desperate for sleep.

But Fiona wasn't sleeping. She was grunting and tossing. The grunts were new sounds for her, weird and distraught. I tried to nurse her; she refused. Justin brought her into our bed and laid her on his chest. We spent hours trying to put her at ease.

At five a.m., I stared at myself in the bathroom mirror. I'd been awake for almost twenty-four hours. In the disorienting pre-dawn, I looked like a puffed and pale stranger, caught in a portal of a different life. Who was I? Who would I become? A professor? A "special needs" mother? A circus performer?

Just then, I heard my husband bark what I somehow believed I'd never hear, despite the odds: "She's having a seizure."

Fiona's eyes were fixed on the ceiling, unblinking. Her abdomen contracted, bringing her head and knees together, then pushing them apart. Her hands were fisted. Her mouth drooled a puddle out the left side. Her limbs jerked in a foreboding rhythm, like she'd become the metronome of every person's mortality. We checked the clock and started timing. One minute. Two minutes. Three. We called 911.

It was the first morning of March. In the pitch-black cold, I carried my bundled baby out the door and to an ambulance. Her eyes were now closed; her breathing was short like a sprinter spent from a race. *Postictal*, they call it—the altered state of consciousness after a seizure. The red lights of the ambulance were weirdly silent as they flashed onto our white house, across my stunned face.

Within the hour, Fiona stirred, woke up, screamed, and then fell into a deep and regular sleep that relieved me. By late morning, she'd returned to an ornerier version of herself.

The cause of her seizure? A fever. Her first.

Our family of three checked into the neurology wing of Cincinnati Children's Hospital, where doctors monitored Fiona overnight. Justin and I shared a pullout vinyl couch as our bed. The neurologist, another energetic, spiky-haired thirty-something, said it was good that Fiona's seizure had stopped at five minutes. He said seizures could cause permanent damage to the brain, but probably not until they went longer than five minutes. He conceded that no medical expert really knew at what point a seizure did damage. And in my sleep deprivation, his shrugging seemed simultaneously beautiful and brutal. The neurologist knew enough to know which things nobody knew.

A nurse showed us a video of people having different kinds of seizures. The patients jerked and stiffened, yes, but they also went limp and collapsed and then came to. They cawed and they crowed, they twitched and they laughed. With each seizure, I had the sense that I was seeing a person nakeder than naked. For their own privacy I wanted to look away. But I didn't. Today I knew who I had to be: the kind of mother who couldn't avert her eyes. The kind of mother who knew the difference between a tonic and a clonic seizure, a myoclonic seizure and a *petit mal.*

Then the nurse schooled us on what to do if Fiona ever had a seizure that didn't stop at five minutes. We would have to insert emergency medicine up her rectum. Justin and I both practiced by sliding a white, fat syringe between our index and middle fingers, pretending they were butt cheeks. *One, two, three,* we counted as the syringe fit between our fingers. *One, two, three,* we counted as we pretended to squeeze the medicine into our daughter's body. *One, two, three,* we counted as we pretended to hold an invisible butt together. This is how you did it: by counting to three, three times.

The cause of Fiona's fever? She'd cut her first tooth.

The night I'd found out I was pregnant, I called my sister, herself just weeks away from giving birth to her second child. "Is this good?" I asked. "Do you think we'll like being parents?"

I wanted my sister to say, *You will be forever changed in the best possible way!* I wanted an answer like, *Yes, of course! You made a wise and brilliant choice! You can't possibly go your whole life without at least trying to experience the crazy and satisfying and joy-inducing ride of parenting!*

She'd just spent the last eight months puking. She was too pregnant to lie. "I think if anyone knew how hard it would be, they'd never do it."

"Wait!" I said, feeling betrayed by the tardy feedback. "If it's so bad, why are you doing it again?"

"Because I already did it once. Might as well have two."

They say parenting is "hard." They say parenting is "the

hardest job you'll ever do." When they say this, they're of course talking about standard-issue kids—kids whose first teeth make them inconsolably irritable, for instance. Most babies' dentition is ushered in with fussiness and frequent night wakings. Fiona's first tooth came with a *grand mal.* A.k.a. "big bad." The wolf of seizures. If raising a child was hard, raising my girl seemed to be ten times harder.

Feverless and fine a few days later, Fiona's Tahoe eyes resumed their brightness. She stuck her tongue out of her mouth like Charlie Brown in contemplation.

The able-bodied babies were even at writing conferences. A twenty-some-pound giantess dangled from her mother's Björn while flipping a book. Her feet were brick-like and bare.

Two days after Fiona's seizure, Justin, Fiona, and I drove six hours north to a conference in Chicago so I could interview with two more universities. It took all of us to make this happen. We were a Celtic knot of need: she needed me to nurse, I needed Justin to watch her when I wasn't nursing. The night before my interviews, I nursed Fiona at midnight, four, six, and six thirty. Later that day, wearing a black pantsuit, I tried to nurse her again in a greasy booth of a place called Harold's Chicken Shack, but my milk supply had taken a serious hit from the pump-free Philly interview. I didn't know yet that it would never quite recover. In the booth, I kept my suit jacket open and my blouse lifted up. I held my baby between my chest and the edge of the greasy laminate table. She wailed and refused.

Then I went to a panel about how to be both a mother and a writer, where a bestselling author advised the audience to never, ever apply for a tenure-track professorship.

Minutes later, I rode an elevator to a penthouse suite a thousand floors above Chicago. I knocked on a door and faced an all-white-male search committee. We sat in a circle. A wet bar waited to the left. The head of the English department remained standing in his suit. A poet kept turning around to look wistfully out the window. "Oh! It's raining," he said.

"Your cover letter intrigued me," said the department head, still standing. "You mentioned my favorite, Montaigne. What do you love about him?" He gave me a smile that said, *Tell me that your reasons for loving him are my reasons.*

I said I loved how Montaigne challenged people's expectations of the essay. That he was the first to call what he wrote an essay, and yet his essays were nothing like what we were taught in grade school. They were uncertain, meandering, exploratory. I mentioned "Of Thumbs," how it proceeded as a list of weird and curious facts about the thumb and concluded inconclusively. I didn't mention that my fractured sleep had fractured my brain, that I couldn't think of a single essay Montaigne wrote *other* than "Of Thumbs." I plowed forward, explaining what I taught my students: that the real essay is not a genre of proof, of didactic certainty, but of exploration and unknowing and discovery.

The department chair nodded, but he was already looking down at my application materials.

"What are you working on now?" a famous fiction writer across from me asked.

I said I was writing a memoir about falling in love with a monk. I didn't mention that I hadn't touched in months the memoir about falling in love with a monk.

"The tenure track is five years," the famous fiction writer said. "And for tenure, you'd need a book. Do you think you can publish a book in five years?"

I nodded. I had an epileptic kid with an unknown future, but I could totally finish the book I wasn't writing.

They asked how I'd teach this class or that. I didn't tell them I now prepped course syllabi with a babe napping against my chest, with milk trailing onto my stained and ubiquitous nursing pillow. I nodded to their love of literary fathers. I took cues when I mentioned literary mothers and they ignored me. I widened my knees, tried to *man up*, as they say, owning myself and my words about my love of essayistic uncertainty in a way that belied, ironically, anything questioning or uncertain, anything vulnerable or maternal or feminine. I rejected any implication that my body had, less than a year ago, yielded to accommodate another human. I ignored that, beneath my bra, my breasts yearned for a good latch. My black pantsuit felt like armor over my motherhood. I disavowed myself of the truth this penthouse suite didn't know: vulnerability possesses an earth-altering power.

Three days earlier, the world had stopped spinning and my daughter's consciousness had been stolen by a manic metronome made from misfiring neurons. Now I nodded in the black blazer and said, "Oh, absolutely, I could move to Miami." I shook hands firmly.

Then I returned to my little family in a hotel room, where Justin relayed the news: Fiona had another fever. We knew what that meant—she could have another seizure. In a foreign city. With no access to her doctors.

Should I even be here at all? I wondered.

We drove home that Saturday, relieved that she hadn't seized, and the next day Justin's boss, Mother Jackie, stood at the lectern in her white robe and preached this to a few dozen people: "You know you need to die to the self when not getting what you want causes you distress."

It was Fiona's naptime—she lay sleeping in her car seat carrier. I thought of what I wanted. I wanted an able-bodied baby. I wanted all of Fiona's fourth chromosome. I wanted this with aching desperation. I imagined hunting each corner of the earth for the missing bit. I imagined finding it in a Dalí-esque sand dune among animal skulls. Or I imagined gathering up whatever I had that was valuable—my graduate degrees, my publications, my health—and handing it all over to some guy behind an arcade prize counter and saying, "This stuff for that?" Behind him would be jars filled with genetic material. In one I'd find Fiona's "pincer grab" at Cheerios, her ability to push her body up from prone position, her ability to say *bababa* and *mamama*. Her strength to grab something heavier than the thinnest plastic ring. If the man needed, I'd also hand over a bankrupting sum of money. I'd take the jar.

But this is where my fantasy stopped, because how could I envision what happened next? How could I unscrew the lid, hand the jar to my daughter, and ask her to absorb its contents? I wanted typical development to unfold naturally in the complex system of my girl's neurons and muscles and tendons. I wanted this without the aid of a hundred therapy appointments, without physical therapy and occupational therapy and hand massages and feeding therapy and vibrating oral stimulators and eons of tummy time. But that was not the child I had. And I loved my child. Mother Jackie had been right. I had to die to some version of myself, the desperate, clinging, distraught version who wanted what her child was not.

The service concluded, the organ played, a teenager in a robe walked a metal cross down the aisle, and Mother Jackie dismissed us with a blessing. We replied: *Thanks be to God, alleluia.* Fiona was waking up, so I loosened the straps on her car seat and lifted her into my arms. I fingered her lavender-socked foot.

"She just doesn't grow, does she," a retired woman, Greta, said. It wasn't a question.

I liked Greta. She was a pistol of an old lady with orange hair and tons of loudly expressed opinions. But I was exhausted from the Philly interview, the seizure, the hospital stay, the Chicago trip. I was worn down from waking three and four times a night, from the hunched-over position of nursing, the therapy appointments, the tests. So to Greta I couldn't smile or come up with something witty as Justin would have, something like, *We're trying to keep her as small as possible.* I spent almost every spare hour trying to get my kid to grow. The sentence stung, and I let it.

Justin and I still hadn't told many people about Fiona's fourth chromosome. We knew they'd visit Google. They'd see the photo of the dead newborn or the phrase "severe mental retardation." I couldn't bear the thought of people gossiping about my daughter's future when I was struggling to understand it myself. But

Greta's eyes were searching and piercing. And over the past week, I'd spent one night away from my baby, two nights in a hotel with her, one night in a hospital, and one night at home but utterly sleepless. So I said flatly, "She has a genetic condition that makes her small."

"Oh. I didn't know that."

I nodded. There was silence.

"You know," Greta said, "my mother had a genetic condition too. It made her small."

"Really?" I said.

"She was five feet, ninety-four pounds, and *that's* when she was pregnant!" Greta went on to say that her mother was strong and fierce and healthy.

"So there you go," she said. She looked at Fiona, who was rapt by her right hand. I understood what Greta was implying—her mother was small but also "normal." Fiona might be small but also "normal."

I'd been hearing stories like this lately. Last week a grandparent had told me that her grandson had been labeled "developmentally delayed." "You'd never know it now, though!" she said cheerily. "He runs and plays and everything." In exchanges like these, I was stumbling across a cultural pill, one that stuck in my throat and wouldn't go down. It said: Bodily difference is *charming* so long as it doesn't interfere with Normal. Or if it *does* interfere with Normal—if it is a *Disability*—it's charming so long as it becomes history, a tale to offer as inspiration rather than a real life to live. Disability is okay if it's overcome.

In conversations like the ones with Greta, I never heard what I really wanted to hear, which was, "Oh, genetic condition? You know, my nephew has a genetic condition, and he can't walk or talk, or feed himself, and you know what? He's awesome, a great man." If I'd heard that, I would have burst into tears of gratitude.

When I hedged on the evening of my positive pregnancy stick—*Did we make the right choice?*—my primary fear was that motherhood would detonate my writing life. This fear nagged me for nine months. Belly full of baby, I finally wrote that same professor who raved about a university as a roof for one's creativity. *Will I write?* "Of course you will," she replied. Her son and daughter were grown. "How else will you know what you think?" She warned, though, that she never baked a birthday cake from scratch, that she embraced grocery-store confections encased in plastic. I took this to mean: *You can't hold yourself to the high standards of typical American motherhood.*

My parenting life had already made one thing clear: it would require far more of me than typical American motherhood. Still, after my talk with Greta, I went home, fed Fiona and myself lunch, completed our therapeutic duties (tummy time, et cetera), put her down for her second nap, and, in the hour that she slept, typed frantically and single-spaced into a Word document. I wrote about Greta and the sting of her words—*She just doesn't grow, does she*. I wrote about the conference, the seizure, the two-night stay at Le Hotel de Children's Hospital. I wrote about how surreal it was to shop for tomatoes just days after riding with your baby in an ambulance. When Fiona woke, I saved the file "Fi Fragments." For months after, I returned to that file, opening it during the slices of time when Fiona napped, dumping into it any number of shards and snippets from this parenting life. I doubted it would ever impress any all-male search committee. But I was making a country for myself, a place where I could get down every raw and unsayable thing.

Another afternoon on campus, I walked into my classroom early and found a Women's Studies professor erasing the whiteboard. We hadn't seen each other all semester, and she greeted me enthusiastically. Her students were packing up their books.

"How's the baby?! How old is she now?"

I tightened, calculating how close we might get to Fiona's chromosomes. I said she was nine months.

"Oh, I love that age," she said, now putting her books into her bag. "They're already sitting up by that point, right? Is she crawling yet?"

A few of my students were shuffling into the room.

"No, actually. . . ." I stammered for words. My eyes filled. I was about to cry before two sets of students. I was too exhausted to stop myself. "She has a syndrome. So she won't develop like . . ."

My colleague walked toward me. "I'm sorry." She put her hand on my shoulder. "I shouldn't have asked something so personal right before your class. I'm so sorry."

It felt like an incredible kindness that she wasn't apologizing for my kid's syndrome.

"What can I do?" she said as I wiped my eyes. "Do you want me to teach your class? I can sub for you."

I shook my head.

"Are you sure? I'm so sorry. I can just take over for the first few minutes if you want."

"I'm fine," I said. And I was. In fact, it felt good to finally name, however briefly, this huge aspect of my life inside the walls of my work. She was the first colleague I'd told.

I went on to teach my class. When I returned to my office, an email from her sat in my inbox. It was a profuse and unnecessary apology, but something in it became a small treasure. She was sorry to have upset me, she said, but she was also sorry for something I'd never thought to receive an apology for, something I'd encountered again and again from medical professionals. She should not have assumed, she said, that all babies developed the same way. Of course they didn't, she said. Every human body was different.

This wise and big-hearted professor focused her research on women of color. She was an expert at analyzing the systemic ways that minority bodies are stigmatized and dehumanized. In her email, she had extended her perspective to people like Fiona. In her apology, I got a glimpse through a lens that contrasted the medical world's. This lens said: *Your kid's body isn't the problem. Viewing her as a problem is the problem. You have the right to expect better.*

A baby develops from the head down, Tiffany had told me. Babies can't learn to stand until they develop enough core strength to sit, and they can't develop enough core strength to sit until they develop enough neck strength to lift their heads. Tiffany began every session by testing Fiona's neck strength. She used her index fingers as handlebars and got supine Fiona to wrap her hands around them. Then she pulled her fingers toward her belly so Fiona bent at the waist and came into a seated position. After, she lowered Fiona back down. Baby sit-ups. I knew Fiona succeeded if she kept her head and torso in line, like her body was a board from her crown to her tailbone. Each time, Fiona's head lagged at least an inch.

"Come on, Fiona," Tiffany said one morning, like my girl was a slacker and her therapist was a tired track coach. "Have you been doing tummy time?" Tiffany asked, as though we hadn't been.

Did you do tummy time this week? How much tummy time are you doing? Tummy time became so frequent a recommendation from doctors, nurses, and therapists that I walked around with near-constant anxiety about it. While I peed or nursed or showered or ate, I also carried the ever-present guilt that I wasn't simultaneously coaching my kid through a few minutes on her stomach. I told Tiffany we were definitely doing tummy time. I aimed for six fifteen-minute sessions a day. I sometimes fretted to Justin when he *wasn't* doing tummy time with Fiona, when he was just dancing with her to reggae or letting her lie next to him while he read some Christian mystic aloud.

"How much tummy time should we do?" I asked Tiffany. I figured if she gave me a target, I could reach it each day and then relax.

Tiffany thought for a few seconds. "Really, you can never do enough tummy time."

It was the worst possible answer.

Tiffany asked me what I wanted to work on next. I suggested Fiona's fisted left hand. Maybe Tiffany could do some stretches or exercises for it.

"She used to open it, right?" Tiffany asked.

"She sometimes does," I said. "Other times it's like she's not aware of it."

Tiffany was quiet a moment. "I don't know, Fiona. You're a mystery." Much about Fiona surprised Tiffany. Her size. Her slow development. Even the uber-flexible nature of her tendons and the crinkly sound her ligaments made.

I asked Tiffany what she meant.

"Because once babies learn something," Tiffany said, "they don't usually unlearn it. Like, once they open their hands, they don't usually return them to fisted positions. When Fiona does that, it's like she's at zero again."

At zero. So many assumptions can get packed into two words.

"You should probably see someone about splinting her left fingers. To keep them open." Tiffany stuck her fingers up, palm facing me, and showed me how a splint would force Fiona's fingers straight.

Some things I knew, and I had no idea how I knew them. When I was pregnant, I knew, mid-sleep, that I was in labor even before the slightest birth pangs. I dreamed I had checked into a hospital to give birth. Only after a nurse greeted me did I dream I peed, and that's when I woke to warm fluid leaking down my legs. It was like those nightly wakings, when I met a hungry Fiona before she'd even cried. Having Fiona gifted me with a maternal intelligence that was beyond logic.

I knew my daughter wasn't "at zero."

I knew she sometimes fisted that left hand, and she sometimes opened it.

I knew she was much less aware of the left side of her body than she was the right.

I knew splinting a baby's hand was a horrible idea, that it would rob a baby of the freedom to use her hand, which would eliminate any opportunity for her brain to make connections with that hand.

I knew there was a certain way of looking at my daughter that made her a problem. *Bad seed. At zero.* I knew this particular way of viewing her valued milestone charts, scientifically mapped progress, data-corroborated growth and development. I knew it compulsively measured what humans could do and loved the results when they were average or better.

This was an evolutionary way of seeing humans, always plotting them left to right across a graph, zero to one hundred and onward. This worldview held up its charts, its maps of Normal, furrowed its brow, and offered splints and repetitions and carbon-copied to-do lists.

I sensed that in order to love my daughter well, I'd have to divorce myself from this way of seeing human beings.

But I didn't yet know how.

Facebook was the most dangerous place for my longing. When I watched babies on Facebook, I watched the infant equivalent of magicians making chairs disappear or eating three-foot flames. They yanked fistfuls of hair, sat on kitchen floors, pulled themselves up to standing. They brought food to their mouths! One friend posted a video of her baby crawling across the foyer, knee-hand, knee-hand, knee-hand, *slap-bump, slap-bump, slap-bump,* until the baby stopped, looked into the camera, and said, "Ba."

I watched this video in perplexed amazement. I watched it more than once, more than twice. I don't know how many times I watched it. The images carved longing into my gut like a spoon.

I read as the mothers of able-bodied babies discussed ways to further enhance their babies' high-functioning trajectory. What was the best first solid food? Avocado was a beloved choice: healthy essential fats. Which toys were necessary for stimulating the synapses of the malleable baby brain? Baby Einstein was a fraud, they said. Belgium-made wood toys were revered. What soft carriers ensured optimal position of Baby's hips and spine? The Björn was hated, the Ergo divine. When was it best to begin Baby's swim lessons? Before nine months, or Baby loses the breath-holding reflex. *Oh, I wish I had known that sooner,* a friend bemoaned in a thread.

The problems of the mothers of able-bodied babies were small and posited as large. I read as moms lamented that they now had to babyproof their houses. Their kids were into medicine cabinets. Their kids were into outlets. The moms were deep in the difficulties of their children's able-bodied-ness. They were rich with nostalgia for the earlier months. They mourned that their children no longer lay sweetly in their laps. Watching all of this was like watching a distant boat sail away, one I'd intended on boarding but now could not. I ached to have different problems than I had, which meant I ached for my daughter to have different problems than she had.

Or were they even problems? From her supine position, Fiona looked up at the manic, yearning world, calm-eyed, content.

Chapter Six

~

By ten months old, Fiona had developed such a fierce love of clapping that she appeared to be applauding all of life. *Yay, car ride. Yay, Mom's burp. Yay, random woman at church. Yay, middle-of-the-night waking.* It was one milestone she met on cue.

Despite this habitual urge to champion every nook and cranny, her pediatrician still labeled her *failure to thrive.* Our cherubic geneticist had insisted that Fiona was designed to be small, that no number of additional calories would help her leap onto the growth curve, but medical professionals still fretted over her weight—so I did too. Her pediatrician wanted biweekly weight checks. The egg-timing feeding therapist counted the calories I spooned into Fiona's mouth and urged toward the impossible goal of seven hundred a day. (Fiona usually capped at four hundred.) Tiffany and her team always wanted to know: *How much does she weigh now?* I started ignoring the pediatrician's penned *X* in the gutter of the growth chart.

Failure to thrive. It's a damning phrase for any baby. When a priest friend became a father, his baby too was labeled *failure to thrive.* Eventually, the baby started "gaining," as they say, but my friend looked back on the diagnosis with irritation. "It's like they're telling you that your baby refuses to participate in creation!"

I called my homeopath. She was the same woman who'd advised me while pregnant to avoid wheat and swallow mounds of vitamins, but she'd also saved me from countless bouts of bronchitis over the past decade. I'd always appreciated her quirky counter-perspective to the medical world. In one visit, she'd even mourned the decline of oak trees. She believed they were leaving this earthly realm, she told me, and moving on to other planes of existence. She said this sadly: *The oak trees are leaving us.*

I told her about Fiona's syndrome, mentioned *failure to thrive*, and asked if she had anything to help my kid grow.

"Wait." She stopped me. "How are *you* doing with all of this?"

I confessed it was hard.

"You know," she said, and I waited for her typical woo-woo inspiration. That my girl was a gift from the divine, maybe. Or that nothing about Fiona's life was failing, that she was precisely who she needed to be. Or maybe this cliché: *God never gives you what you can't handle*, which I did not believe. Plenty of people buckled under the weight of what they were given.

Instead she said, "You know, you can always put her in a home."

I sat speechless.

"And you'd still be her parent. I have patients who do that, you know. They visit their kids. They call me and get remedies for them. They take care of them. They're still their parents. You see?"

Her words hit pause on my breath.

"Oh no," I said. "It won't be like that." I didn't know if *that* meant I wouldn't resort to such measures, or Fiona wouldn't need them.

"Okay," she said. "But if you do need to do that, it's there for you. I just wanted you to know."

The standards for good mothering are impossibly high, and few people encourage women to invent unconventional paths. Few people give women permission to mother from afar and still call it good mothering. Was it a radical feminist notion to say, *This is another way to mother well?* Maybe. But I've since read accounts of male doctors urging mothers, right after labor, to put their newborns in institutions, to forget about them, to just go home and try for another. These stories are usually from past decades, but not always. The newborns had the almond eyes of Down syndrome, or the tight limbs of cerebral palsy, or some other feature that told the doctor: *birth defect, abnormal.* In these instances, health professionals think a mother's devotion is worth the world, sure, but they also think some lives aren't deserving of it.

In the winter of 2012, a three-year-old with Wolf-Hirschhorn made national headlines. CNN. CBS. *USA Today.* Amelia Rivera needed a kidney transplant. But the acclaimed Children's Hospital of Philadelphia, the children's hospital nearest my hometown, denied Amelia the life-saving surgery. In a blog post, Amelia's mother, Chrissy, described the moment a doctor revealed the hospital's decision. He showed her a form on which a phrase had been highlighted.

"This phrase. This word," Chrissy said to him. "This is why she can't have the transplant done."

The phrase was *mental retardation*.

The doctor said yes.

"I begin to shake," Chrissy writes on her blog. "My whole body trembles, and he begins to tell me how she will never be able to get on the waiting list because she is mentally retarded."

Without a new kidney, Amelia—or Mia, as her family called her—would die in six months, maybe a year. The story was covered by major news outlets. The hashtag #TeamAmelia spread on Twitter. More than fifty thousand people signed a Change.org petition, demanding that Mia be granted access to the life-saving surgery. In other words, over fifty thousand people had to argue with an esteemed medical institution that a child's life was worth saving. The fight was not over the availability of an organ. Amelia's mother was donating hers. The fight was over Amelia's right to receive the organ already gifted to her.

I followed the story closely. In it, I saw two hard truths. One: my daughter's syndrome could be life-threatening. Two: there were people in this world—powerful people—who didn't believe her life was worth saving.

After Chrissy's post went viral, a committee of doctors reconsidered the decision. They granted Mia the surgery. But not everyone agreed. In a *HuffPost* article titled "Denying a Transplant to a 'Retarded' Child?," journalist Lisa Belkin defended the doctor's original decision. She argued that because Amelia—whose parents described her as "happy"—was nonverbal and non-ambulatory, her condition was "heartbreaking." And because Amelia's inability to walk made her more likely to die of an infection, she was unworthy of a lifesaving intervention. "A waste of an organ," Belkin wrote.

In an ABC television interview after the hospital's initial denial, Amelia and her family are in their living room. Mia is rolling on a mat beneath dangling toys, the same kind Fiona lay under all the time. Mia was three years old. Her parents and two siblings surround her and smile. The reporter's voice-over says, "She can't walk or talk but *does* communicate, with her eyes and smile."

A beat later, her mother is being interviewed on the couch: "We just love her!" she says. "I mean, she's part of our family. She's just like *any other* child in *any other* family."

I watched this interview more than once. More than twice. I'm not sure how many times I watched Amelia Rivera rolling on the floor, making eye contact with her family members, while Mia's mother says, "We just love her!" I watched this life Lisa Belkin called "heartbreaking." And I watched this mother whose heart would surely break if doctors let her child die.

Months later, ABC returned for an update, showing Amelia sitting beside her parents on the couch. The surgery was a success. Mia's mom is stroking one of Mia's silky black pigtails. "She's just fun to be around," her mother says. "She definitely has that connection with people. It just kinda melts your heart."

Her words resonated. Fiona loved to link eyes with grocery-store shoppers and doctors' receptionists and strangers in elevators. She used her Tahoe-blue eyes to seek out theirs, intent on using no words to say "hello."

"It's almost unnerving," a friend once said, "her eye contact. It's like she wants to look *into* you. I've never seen a baby do that."

Beneath Mia's news update is one comment, written by a viewer. Because it's the only comment, it sits like a lone verdict on

Mia's good news. It reads, "This is wrong and terrible, that kidney could have gone to a child who was NOT severely mentally retarded."

In 2010 I got pregnant, and in 2011 I had a baby, and in 2012 I loved that baby, and all of this should sound as ordinary and mundane as any given Monday. But in my daughter's first year, I was learning: the simple act of loving her was countercultural.

t was Ash Wednesday, the start of Lent, the liturgical start of Jesus's forty days in the desert when he gives up pretty much everything—food and water and a bed and his friends. He's got nothing, so the story goes. Only his temptations and his longings and his fears, if Jesus had fears. And there's at least a sliver of proof that he did: Before he's crucified, he goes to a garden and grieves. The moment on the cross before his body gives out, he cries to God, *Why have you forsaken me?* As a lapsed Baptist, this was the Jesus I sometimes related to most: the one who sweats his impending death, who freaks out over all he's about to lose. The one who asks where the hell his divine Father is.

In my thirty-three years, I'd probably spent as many days doubting as believing. Still, I attended church. I didn't go out of any sense of guilt, or to appear the dutiful clergy's spouse, or even for community. I saw church not as a club to belong to but as a spiritual laboratory in which to conduct the great experiment. Was there an ultimate, divine reality? Spiritual masters said yes. I wanted to know for myself. I didn't believe—nor do I now—that Christianity was the sole path to know this ultimate reality. But it was one viable way, and the way my beloved Justin knew best. So I sat in the back and listened, and I loved the story of Jesus as it was taught to me in the Episcopal Church: God was so interested in humanity, so wanted to connect with humans, that God became human too. That God slept and peed and shat and touched and sometimes had low blood sugar and devoured fillets of fish. And, at least in one moment, God too feels forsaken.

On this Ash Wednesday evening, at the liturgical start of Jesus's forty days in the desert, Justin stood at the front of the church wearing a white robe and purple U-shaped chasuble. He asked parishioners to write down the things they wanted to "give up." What did they hope would die along with Jesus on the cross? What did they need to surrender? What was keeping them from knowing the great mystery, the ultimate reality, the infinite love we called God? It was dusk beyond the church windows. Fiona slept at my feet in her car seat carrier. From the pew in front of me, I got a golf pencil and a small slip of paper. I knew immediately what I wanted to punt miles away from my life. I wrote down, *Envying the mothers of able-bodied babies.*

A man who limped because of double-knee surgery, whose wife could not conceive a child, offered to take my slip of paper to the altar for me. I was the recipient of a thousand blessings and one thing I couldn't get over.

Die to the self, Mother Jackie had instructed.

Justin burned the papers. My envy of crawling and babbling and toddling became smoke. It disintegrated into the Ohio air along with someone's late-night Twitter habit and another's tendency to nag her husband.

But six weeks later, on Good Friday, on the very day Jesus was liturgically dying on his cross, a friend had a baby. She reported that the baby was a hearty, healthy eight pounds, twenty inches long. And I felt like I'd been broken open. And there was no covering up my sadness, even though I was in my office and about to teach a class on modern poetry. So I pulled my hands off the keyboard and felt a thin, reedy exhale, and cried.

Later I told Justin it didn't work. I still envied.

He said things work themselves out on their own timetables.

Here's what I wonder now: What did I long for more? A baby who could do this or that thing—suck a thumb or gum a cracker or pull to stand? Or a baby who was fully accepted by the world?

I suspect the two longings were near-equal, inseparable, conjoined. I wanted a baby who did all the things babies did, and I wanted a baby who was valued equal to typical children. If I'd lived in a world where babies like mine weren't called *bad seeds* or measured *at zero* or denied life-saving surgeries, I know my yearning for an able-bodied child wouldn't have nagged me quite so badly. If friends had simply said, "Oh, severe developmental delays? That's no problem. She'll be wonderful just as she is." If that nationally ranked children's hospital had said, "We will do everything we can to save this child." If my homeopath had heard Fiona's diagnosis and said, "What an interesting and beautiful package her soul has found itself inside!" If Tiffany ever once delighted over my daughter's being, delayed or not.

Easter came, Jesus rose, egg-shaped pastel candies drifted off the grocery aisles, and the weather warmed enough for me to take Fiona on walks. The walks were for me—so I could escape the house, leave behind the pressures of therapy, and keep my baby content all at once. Justin and I had inherited a brown pram from a British parishioner, and I pushed Fiona along sidewalks while she gazed at blooming trees.

"It's not therapeutic," I told a friend on the phone once, mid-walk, feeling guilty.

"Fresh air's always good," my friend said. "For everyone."

That season, I'd been flipping through *Birth: A Literary Companion*, an anthology of literature about childbearing. The cover featured a black-and-white photo of a pram, with one naked baby foot resting on the front edge. The toes splayed like the foot was waving at the reader. *Hello, world.* Whenever I saw it, I yearned for Fiona to be so aware of her feet, so strong in her abdomen, that she could lift her leg. Even while her arms had become more active, batting at toys or helicoptering around her playmat, her legs remained mostly limp.

But shortly after Easter, during one of our walks, I looked down and saw something miraculous: Fiona's newborn-size, yellow-socked right foot pressed against the front edge of the pram. There it was. *Hello, world. What's out there?*

I can sometimes be tough to please. When I read students' essays, their margins become a cloud of handwriting as I ask questions and make suggestions and point out unsupported claims. That spring, when I read my husband's job applications, I shouted from the living room, "You're not answering their question," and "What are you trying to say here?" There was always more to do, and more perfect ways to do them.

Now here was Fiona. If chromosomes had editors with red pens, Fiona's might have circled her fourth chromosome and shouted at the writer. But my daughter had taken down my internal editor—let's call him Warren. He'd buckled under the weight of her, fallen to his knees. Warren was now rendered awestruck by teensy raised feet. Fiona's projected outcomes for life were so uncertain that all my expectations were stripped bare. So when my daughter pressed her foot against the edge of that pram, which three months ago it seemed she'd never do, this was more than good enough. It was a triumph.

didn't get any of the jobs I interviewed for that spring. I wondered if I even could have said yes to a job if it had been offered.

Fiona had another seizure, after which she clapped. *Yay, seizure!* It was only a few minutes long, but we went to the hospital anyway. Days after, I fretted to Justin. Maybe because the backyard beyond the windows was black, and maybe because Fiona was asleep upstairs, and maybe because when a baby sleeps, a new mother is given the space to actually feel things—I panicked.

On the dining table was a brochure from the state about support services for people with developmental disabilities. The glossy, full-color photos featured smiling adults in fanny packs, engaging in activities like craft-making and walks in the park. I worried about whether their lives were fulfilling. I wondered if our daughter would wear a fanny pack. I told myself not to project so far into the future, since she was still the *size* of a fanny pack. But in that late hour, my panic grew. What would our lives look like? Would I have to quit working? What would she do with her days as an adult? Would she *be* an adult? Would she be happy? Would her life have meaning?

I discussed these questions with Justin, working myself up into a bigger and bigger upset, hedging around the unsayable. Then I finally blurted something with jittery honesty. "I mean, what will she do with her life? Will she bag groceries?"

I said this as though working as a grocery bagger were a disappointment. I would not have said this to any other person because I knew that such statements were snobby and classist and disparaging of grocery baggers. And not all of me believed that grocery bagging was a subpar existence. But it turned out that a part of me did. It turned out that a chunk of me was snobby and classist and disparaging of grocery baggers. I had to admit this out loud so that I could excise it from myself.

Here's the way this bastardly part of me thought: *There's a hierarchy of lives worth living. And a person who only has the cognitive function to bag groceries is lower than a person who can cognitively do more. And a person who does not have the cognitive functioning to bag groceries is lower still, because they "cannot even bag groceries."* I was proud of none of this thinking. But there it was inside me.

At this point, grocery bagging looked like a high expectation for Fiona, whose left hand still stayed mostly clenched. So what I really meant, which I had not said aloud, was this: *My child, my love, my heart worth more than a room full of nations, will probably live a life that a piece of me has ranked near the bottom.*

In graduate school, my advisor was the blind poet and disability advocate Steve Kuusisto, and I'd taught a writing curriculum co-created by Deaf and Disability Studies scholar Brenda Brueggemann. This meant that every quarter I read, along with my students, essays that unpacked implicit biases against people with disabilities. I listened as my advisor detailed the discrimination he faced daily. I no longer used words like "deaf" and "blind" as synonyms for ignorance. When *Million Dollar Baby* came out, I saw it through the lens of disability scholars who argued that because the main character, a boxing champ, wants to off herself once she's paralyzed, the movie reiterates the damning cliché that disability is a "fate worse than death." I scowled when the movie won the Academy Award for Best Picture.

But it turned out, I still carried a deeply buried prejudice, one I wasn't even aware of until after Fiona's diagnosis. Most of my life, I'd valued intelligence. And so I weighed as more valuable the body that could cognitively do more. I cried to Justin, and I didn't know if it was for my daughter's future or my own dismissive beliefs about that future. Probably both.

Justin didn't say, "I know. It's so sad."

He didn't say, "Think positively, believe in miracles."

He didn't tip the scales toward tragedy or triumph, both of which would have validated the hierarchy I'd caught in myself. He simply listened. When I was done talking, I looked at him like, *It's your turn.*

His reply was a short sentence of equal parts kindness and rebuke. He spoke it tenderly, with all the love he had: "She's not damaged goods, you know."

Boom.

"Of course she's not," I said, because she wasn't. Believing one's child was *damaged goods* was like believing one's heart was a hamburger. But inside, I also heard another response.

She's not? In reply, I heard two voices, both older than my own body.

One voice said, *Yes, of course she is. She's missing a chunk of a chromosome. It makes her small and epileptic and delayed. If you could fix every one of her cells, if you could find that small tip of her fourth chromosome, you would.*

But the other voice was as ancient as the first nanosecond of the universe. It said simply, *She's good, and she's whole, and she's holy.* It was so low and deep that it could hold me. It was the ground beneath me.

"But what will she do with her life?" I asked Justin. "What kind of life will she lead?"

Justin was unfazed by my questions. "She'll live *her* life," he said.

Then my partner of twelve years told me a story I'd never heard. In 1970, an eleven-month-old named Sarah Johnson fell out of a baby carrier. The accident caused significant trauma to her brain. For a while, she was deaf and blind, although she regained her sight and sense of hearing. But her development was halted. She lived to be thirty-four, and she never acquired speech. She could not walk or sit up. She needed round-the-clock care. Justin was friends with her mother, Pat.

"Pat changed diapers all of Sarah's life," Justin said.

I felt a bubble of pity rise into my throat. *How awful*, I wanted to say. But a pitying tone was entirely absent from my husband's voice. He was neutral, descriptive. The situation wasn't good or bad, just fact: *The mother changed diapers all of the child's life.* The bubble of pity in my throat popped.

Justin met Pat at St. Benedict's Monastery in Colorado, where he had been a Trappist monk, and where he still visited once a year. The monastery has a retreat center for people eager to learn Christian meditation from renowned teachers like Father Thomas Keating, who co-developed Centering Prayer. Pat worked at the retreat center—she gave spiritual direction to the monks and retreatants, and she also managed the kitchen. She brought her daughter Sarah along to work. While she cooked, Pat laid Sarah on the kitchen counter, and Sarah made eye contact with people who passed by. The retreatants came to St. Benedict's to learn about silence and presence from revered monks and meditation masters. But some said they learned the most from Sarah.

"Sarah had her own ministry going," Justin said. "She was an integral part of that place. She had her own way of teaching people."

"She didn't talk?" I asked.

"No," Justin said. "She just had a profound presence about her."

My husband said *profound presence* like it was no big deal, and in his perspective, it wasn't. He'd eaten side by side with monks and swamis and shamans. He knew that *profound presence* in a person could be as awe-inducing as the Colorado Rockies. He also knew some people had the presence of a buzzing and beeping cell phone. Sarah happened to be in the former category. Justin wasn't saying she had profound presence *because* of her disability. He wasn't turning her into the trope of the "disabled mystic." He was just stating a fact. "She figured out how to reach people in the body she had," my husband added.

Sarah's mother, Pat, eventually sent me a self-published collection of writings about her daughter, and I got a better picture of Sarah's "ministry," as Justin called it. Pat wrote that some retreatants would rush to Sarah's side after meditation sessions, eager to "just be in the present moment" with her. From her, they said, they learned connection beyond language. They learned openness and vulnerability. And they got to forget their bullshit.

"Her smile and laugh were . . . the most efficient forces of disarmament I have ever known," wrote her youngest brother.

How did I ever learn that people like my daughter were lessthan? Had the roots of my thinking been planted by the *defect* language, by the *bad seed* and *at zero* language? Had they begun in the hallways of that elementary school I attended? Not quite. The roots of my thinking were older than me. They were older than the neglected buildings that housed people with intellectual disabilities, older than the American laws requiring their sterilization. The roots dug deep into history's soil, reaching even past the story of Jesus's disciples, who found a blind man on the side of a road and asked their master, "Who sinned to make this man blind? The man or his parents?" Disability as punishment. Disability as sin. Disability as problem, as outcast, as other. These equations have been graffitied all over human history.

Sarah died in 2004, and eight years later, she was still schooling knuckleheads like me. What if my daughter had a significant place in this world precisely by living in the body she'd been given? What if the busying world—and its obsession with gross domestic products and increased profit margins and on-chart development of children—had it all wrong, and I'd erroneously swallowed the Kool-Aid? What if the things we valued in this world—accomplishments, exceptionalism, feats beyond grocery bagging—were halfpence? What if there was no editor of chromosomes, only artists of chromosomes, and my daughter's artist had looked carefully at her fourth, nipped off the top, then raised her DNA high and declared to the cosmos, *Here. Perfect. Genius.*

That the divine and the spirit of Fiona had conspired to form her unique body seemed suddenly clear. Likewise, it was clear they'd done so for reasons that would make zero sense to the Capitalist or to certain New Age thinkers or to Tiffany's developmental charts—for reasons that might never even become clear to me, but that made all the sense in the world to the vast and numinous Creator of sunsets and narwhals and snails.

"Her contribution had nothing to do with actions or accomplishments," I later read Father Thomas Keating say of Sarah. "It was just a celebration of life."

Maybe the point was not to be SuperHuman but ultra-human. *Ultra* as in *very*, as human as humanly possible. This meant being vulnerable, and sometimes aching, and sometimes struggling and weeping, and often fallible, but always open, and raw, and real. And present to the whole messy world.

But I note now that Sarah's teachings were only made possible because her mother insisted on bringing her to work, on including her in the day-to-day life of mostly able-bodied people. Sarah was not wheeled into a separate building. She was not "put in a home." She was in the kitchen with the cooks, on the couch with the retreatants. She was in the mix.

"She might not ever talk," I said to Justin.

"She might not," he said.

"She might not walk."

"She's sentient!" Justin said enthusiastically, belying his previously even-keeled tone. "She's capable of enlightenment!"

For my Zen-monk-turned-Episcopal-priest husband, this was
the mammoth trophy of life: Can you know the divine? Can you
see the nature of reality? Can you penetrate all the world's bullshit
and perceive things for how they truly are? Can you live in union
with the One True Source, truer to yourself than the "you" that
you call "you"? This was my husband's gold standard for determining "life-worth-living." Can you know God?

According to wisdom traditions, if you're sentient, the answer
is yes. For Fiona, that answer was yes. She could reach enlightenment. She could know God. Possibly much faster than her parents.

"You know what the Dalai Lama said, right?" he asked.

I shook my head, waiting.

"Some of the most enlightened masters weren't the sharpest
tools in the shed."

I laughed.

He added: "Intelligence isn't necessary for a fully realized life."

She was on her back in a floral pajama onesie, chipmunk
cheeks flushed pink. Her closed eyelids glistened with some
kind of mystical sleeping-baby dew. Her hands were lightly fisted
but relaxed. Her elbows were bent, her arms spread beside her so
they made a W.

W as in *who?*

W as in *Wolf-Hirschhorn?*

W as in *we*? She and Justin and me?

There was no single point at which my thinking about Fiona turned away from grief, from the sense of disability as deficit. This happened gradually. There was no single moment when I stopped envying the mothers of able-bodied babies, or when I fully accepted my kid as she was. This too happened gradually. When I look back at myself in that first year, I remember my anguish, and I feel the pain of that desperately yearning mother, her eyes regularly hot with tears about what she wanted and what she couldn't have. Somehow, I died to that self. And yet, the death wasn't a neat and tidy moment; it wasn't even a messy three hours on a cross. It took a year, and it took longer still. The process of dying to this one thing and becoming something else was more like climbing a spiral staircase—as the months went on, I circled back to the anguish, then drifted from it, revisited the longing, then released it, found myself again in the struggle, then was freed from it, all the while ascending to somewhere else.

When I adored my girl, I took steps away from the fear and the grief. When I gazed at Fiona—her effervescent skin and squooshy cheeks, her tuft of Kewpie hair, her bright blue eyes and teensy nostrils, her probing Charlie Brown tongue that poked from her mouth's side, her helicopter arms banging the shit out of dangling farm animals, her hyperventilating excitement at said farm animals—I thought, *My God. She's remarkable. She's the most remarkable thing in the house, on the Earth.*

In times like these I heard a sentence clear as a bell: *This doesn't have to be tragic.*

Chapter Seven

⁓

The knock on the door was right on time. I opened it and found a girl with blondish-brown hair in a mint-green T-shirt that read WAY 2 CUTE. She was about three and a half feet tall.

"They come small," her mother, Amanda, said behind her, with equal parts laughter and apology.

I stepped aside and let Amanda and her daughter, Lauren, inside. Behind them followed Dave, a stocky brown-haired guy with his hands in his pockets. He wore a friendly grin.

"I have no idea what size kids are supposed to be," I said. Only after having Fiona did I realize adults the nation over had internalized the World Health Organization's growth charts and responded with shock when your kid's body fell outside expectations.

"Well," Amanda said, looking down at her eight-year-old, "she's the size of a four-year-old."

A kid half the expected size! For the first time I was in the presence of people who might just get what raising Fiona was like.

A month or two before, I'd written a long email to a childhood friend, stressing about the challenges of raising Fiona. My friend—childless and busy—popped my tennis ball of trouble back to me with a short suggestion: Was there a support group I could contact? I got it: She couldn't relate, but maybe someone else could. So I did some googling, then wrote the 4p- Support Group ("4" for fourth chromosome, "p" as in *petit* for the short arm, and a negative sign to represent a deletion). The president, Amanda, replied to say that by coincidence her family lived an hour away. Amanda friended me on Facebook, then suggested twenty more parents for me to meet online. Soon my Facebook feed was filled not just with the triumphs of able-bodied babies but the lives of kids with my daughter's syndrome. Photos featured faces like Fiona's: tall foreheads, narrow chins, wide-set eyes. Some kids had tubes up their noses and trachs at their throats. The parents talked about nephrology appointments, the durations of seizures, subpar physical therapists, and hard-sought milestones like swallowing spoonfuls of pureed food. My family's life suddenly seemed a ton more normal in the context of this new scroll.

"Where is she?" Amanda asked, and scanned our beige-carpeted living room. "There she is!" Fiona lay on her playmat beside the bay window, batting at dangling stuffed farm animals. "Oh my God. If you let me hold her, I might not give her back."

I picked up Fiona and put her in Amanda's arms. Amanda cradled my nine-pound baby and gasped—not with shock but with awe. Absent was any worry people had when they encountered my tiny girl.

"Lauren, you were that size once," Dave said.

"That's the baby," Lauren said. "That's baby Fee-ona."

"We have a present for her, don't we?" Amanda said. "Lauren, get the present."

Lauren handed me a small, pink gift bag. I dug through the tissue paper and pulled out a plastic toy flip phone. At half a pound, it was way too heavy for Fiona's grasp, but for once I could receive such a gift without feeling like the givers wildly misread my kid's abilities. If Amanda believed Fiona would someday hold this thing, then maybe she would.

"Thank you," I said, wishing I'd bought a present for Lauren. I hadn't even thought of it. In truth, I wanted something from Lauren. How could I not? One in fifty thousand humans is born with Wolf-Hirschhorn syndrome, and Lauren was only the second person I'd encountered with the syndrome. I wanted Lauren to show me what might be possible for Fiona. I wanted her to show me that Fiona would be okay. And if Lauren could show me that Fiona would be okay, it would mean that *I* would be okay. It was an entirely unfair expectation for an eight-year-old, so I kept my desire in check. Lauren was not an ambassador for a syndrome, not a road map for Fiona's life, not my family's personal fortune-teller. And still. The stakes for this visit felt high.

Justin walked into the living room barefoot and introduced himself with a big smile. Then he lay down on the carpet, propping his head with his hand. He was wearing what he wore any Saturday—a pair of cargo pants, a random T-shirt so threadbare it was tissue-thin. This visit was clearly an afterthought for him, not a thing about which he wondered what he'd wear. (Me: favorite jeans and a dark blouse that wouldn't show sweat stains.)

Amanda sat on our couch and let Fiona lie on her lap so my

baby's twenty-five inches extended along Amanda's thighs. "Dave, look at her little tongue." Fiona did her thoughtful Charlie Brown, pressing her tongue out of her mouth and drawing it back in like she was tasting the air. "Lauren used to do that. What size clothes does she wear?"

"Newborn waist," I said. "Six-month onesies."

"Yup," Amanda said, nodding. "Lauren was like that. Growing long but not out." She looked at Lauren. "You want your lunch?"

Lauren nodded.

"My turn," Dave called.

Amanda handed him Fiona, then got a paper bag of fast food and brought it to the dining room table beside the living room.

"Hey there," Dave said, and held Fiona upright against his chest, above his belly. She curled easily into him like a newborn, a by-product of her low tone. Dave remained standing, but he didn't shift from side to side like a person nervous that the baby will cry. He stood rock solid, at ease with Fiona on his chest. It was like we'd instantly been gifted close relatives.

Lauren sat at the table, and Amanda set a takeout container in front of her, then tied a cloth around her neck. "She still needs a bib," Amanda said, again with that minor apology like her comment about Lauren's height. I wondered if maybe Amanda felt the pressure of this visit too, the possibility that Lauren could represent to us more than she was, more than she should be. *Your kid too might need a bib when she's eight.*

Lauren shoveled chili-covered spaghetti into her mouth—a Cincinnati-area specialty—and I went to the kitchen to get drinks for everyone. As I was pouring water into glasses, I thought, *Jeez, this is so normal. Other than the mentioning of bibs and body size, this isn't a meeting of Wolf-Hirschhorn syndrome. This is just two families hanging out.* So when I put the water pitcher back into the fridge and spotted our plastic container of field greens, I called out, "Does she want a salad too?" I could easily round out that kid's carb intake with some leafy greens.

But Amanda said, "Salad isn't good for her ileostomy bag."

When I returned to the living room, I noted the whoopee-cushion-like pouch dangling an inch past Lauren's mint-green T-shirt.

Would my kid someday need a bag to catch her poop?

We made small talk. How long had we all lived in Ohio? Where else had we lived? What did we do for work? Amanda said she couldn't work because of Lauren's health scares. She said she and Dave had made sacrifices to live on a single income. They rented a small house in a small Ohio town. *Would I have to quit working?*

Someone's cell phone beeped. Amanda looked at hers. "Time for your meds."

Lauren walked to her mother and lifted up her shirt, exposing her belly with the whoopee-cushion-like bag. Amanda drew liquid medicine through a syringe and inserted the syringe into Lauren's belly, or, more specifically, into a plastic thing on Lauren's belly that looked like an off-center belly button: a g-tube. Half of kids with Wolf-Hirschhorn syndrome had them.

"She eats well," Amanda said. "But when she was little, we needed the tube for hydration. So now we just use it for meds."

Amanda removed the syringe. "All set." Lauren went to a pile of Fiona's books near the fireplace and started flipping through *One Fish, Two Fish*.

"What health issues have you had?" Amanda asked, and sat back down on the couch.

"Not many," Justin said from the floor.

I mentioned the seizures, the heart murmur, the scoliosis. I listed the specialists we saw. The geneticist, the cardiologist, the neurologist, the nephrologist, the orthopedist, the early interventionist, the physical therapist, the occupational therapist. Every week our calendar held at least one appointment, often two.

Amanda said Lauren had pretty bad seizures, that she had them every day, but they were mostly controlled now by medication.

I nodded grimly, knowing that the worst of kids' seizures usually developed around Fiona's current age, sometimes later. *Your kid too might need meds for seizures.*

With Fiona in his arms, Dave head-nodded to their black SUV just outside the bay window. "That's why the tinted windows," he said. "Amanda got them paid for by the state." He looked at Justin and laughed. "Cops love to pull us over for it."

"It's illegal, right?" Justin asked.

"Yeah," Dave said.

"Tinted windows?" I asked.

"If you don't have the paperwork," Dave said. "We call it the limousine."

Dangling from the rearview mirror of their black SUV was the trademark blue placard with the stick-figure wheelchair man. *You too might have a handicap placard on your car.*

"I want her back," Amanda said, wiggling her fingers toward Fiona. Dave obliged.

"What's your name?" Lauren asked, standing over Justin.

He told her. "What's yours?"

She told him. Then she sat down on a nearby ottoman and put her legs on his stomach.

"Lauren!" her mother scolded. "Not everyone wants your legs on them!"

Lauren giggled and got off the ottoman. She started fiddling with a yellow plastic structure that looked like a castle straight out of Dr. Seuss: weird, asymmetrical, with spindly nonsensical things coming out of it. Unearthly creatures in primary colors were affixed to the side. Fiona didn't play with it yet. Lauren dropped a red ball into the castle. It rolled out the bottom as the unearthly creatures sang in no known language.

"Cognitively, she's at about a four-year-old level," Amanda said. This, she said, was "higher functioning" than most kids with the syndrome. "We expect she'll reach a five-, maybe six-year-old level."

Lauren dropped another ball into the Seussian structure, seemingly unaware of our conversation.

Fiona arched her back away from Amanda and squirmed. "You're done being held, aren't you?" Amanda set Fiona on her playmat by the window, beneath the dangling stuffed farm animals. Before backing away, she tapped my baby's belly gently. "No tubie, huh?"

I shook my head no.

"That's great," Amanda said.

I sat by Fiona on the floor. She helicoptered an arm, attempting to reach a black-and-white cow. Most babies Fiona's age were crawling, pulling to stand, cruising furniture. All the adults in the room knew this. But absent in our new friends was the usual silent concern. They just gazed at our daughter admiringly. And so I joined them, feeling my shoulders relax. Her right arm circled around and knocked a pink pig.

"Got him," I said.

"She's doing great," Amanda said.

I smiled, feeling her words deliver some peace into my bones.

Then Amanda sat beside me on the floor and told me about her first year as Lauren's mother. Like Fiona, Lauren was born very small. Like Fiona, Lauren didn't gain weight at the expected rate. Like Fiona, Lauren had been diagnosed "failure to thrive." But unlike Fiona, Lauren didn't have a diagnosis for over a year. The pediatrician believed Amanda wasn't feeding her baby enough. Amanda, though, saw other symptoms, like strange spasms she thought might be seizures. The doctor disagreed. She thought the whole thing was in Amanda's head. The doctor eventually diagnosed Lauren with Munchausen's syndrome by proxy. That is, the pediatrician believed Amanda was withholding nutrients from her child, keeping her small and delayed and inventing the seizures in order to gain sympathy from doctors.

I listened in shock. The challenges of caring for Fiona had been hard enough; I couldn't imagine handling them while an expert also accused me of having invented them.

"She was eighteen months old when we finally got a diagnosis," Amanda said. "From another doctor."

I shook my head.

"I faxed the diagnosis to the old pediatrician."

Amanda said she got involved in the support group when she realized she wasn't the only parent with this experience. Other parents in the community told stories of losing their children for a time or having to appear before a judge to prove they weren't harming their kid. Not only did this lay a ton of bricks onto the shoulders of a parent in an already difficult situation, it delayed the child's actual diagnosis. The mission of the support group was to spread awareness of the syndrome, which Amanda called "4p-," as in four pee minus, rather than Wolf-Hirschhorn.

"We were blessed with a higher-functioning kid," she said of Lauren. But then at age four, Lauren had a major health crisis. Digestive complications. Dave and Amanda almost lost her. That's how Amanda phrased it. "We almost lost her." She murmured the four words, glancing sideways to Lauren, who still seemed unaware of, or maybe uninterested in, our conversation.

Dave piped in from the side of the room. "We were at an event for four pee minus, and another mom once asked Amanda, what would she ask for? A kid with more abilities but also more health problems, like Lauren, or a child who was more limited but healthy?"

"Her daughter's in her thirties," Amanda said. "She's nonverbal. In a wheelchair. Never had any health scares."

"How could you choose?" I said from my spot on the floor, feeling a little sick from the question.

"We don't get to choose," Justin said.

Thank God, I thought.

Dave's face lit up. "You guys should come to the conference this year. It's in Indiana."

"We bring in speakers," Amanda said. "People to present on

neurology and feeding and different things. This year we're bringing in Dr. Carey again. He's the national expert on four pee minus."

"Wouldn't the national expert be Dr. Wolf?" I asked. "Or Dr. Hirschhorn?"

Amanda shuddered. "God, no. I was at a genetics conference once, and Dr. Hirschhorn was there, watching a slideshow of our kids. A boy in a wheelchair appeared on the screen, and he said, 'That child is severely damaged.'"

My face fell.

"That's why I don't call it 'Wolf-Hirschhorn syndrome,'" Amanda said. "I don't want Lauren associated with someone who thinks she's damaged. She has four pee minus."

"But the conference is awesome," Dave said, his face again a wide grin. "This year they're bringing in dance instructors. On the last day, the kids will all get to learn dance moves. They'll love it."

I tried to envision a bunch of bodies I couldn't envision, dancing a dance I also couldn't envision. But I loved Dave's enthusiasm.

"That's one thing people with four pee minus seem to have in common," Dave said. "They love music."

"Really?" I noted Fiona's affinity for reggae and dance and clapping. But how could this be? People with 4p- shared an *absence* of something. How could this create a *presence* of something? How could deletion create addition? It seemed both a mystery and a metaphor. A so-called deficit could surprise you. A so-called deficit could create an attribute.

Years later, I'd find an article that scientifically validated

Dave's observation: "Affinity for Music in Wolf-Hirschhorn Syn-drome: Two Case Reports." The article was co-written in 2014 by eight doctors two years after my conversation with Dave. It read, "An affinity for music has not previously been reported. . . ." I laughed. The doctors clearly weren't hanging out in the right living rooms.

"You," Lauren said from her cross-legged position on the ottoman. She pointed to Justin, then got up and tugged on his sleeve. "Sit there. Next to her." She pointed to me. "It's circle time."

"Yes, ma'am," Justin said, and moved beside me.

Amanda laughed and got up from the floor to sit in our rocking chair. I looked over at Fiona beside me, who was content with her gentle attacks on a woolly sheep. She couldn't grab it hard enough to get it to play music, so I leaned over and triggered the tinny lullaby with a squeeze.

"Sit up straight," Lauren said to me.

"Oh!" I said. "Okay."

She opened Dr. Seuss's ABC. She pretended to read: "In the earthly morning, in the dark earthly morning, on the deep dark planet earth. . . ."

She looked up at Justin. "I have to move you." She walked toward him and tugged on his arm. Justin let Lauren lead him a step in a different direction. "Sit there," she said, and pointed to the floor. He sat back down.

Amanda and Dave snickered behind us.

Lauren returned to her spot in front of the fireplace. She splayed the book apart again and showed Justin and me the pictures. "See?" she said like a librarian.

Justin raised his hand.

"Yes," she said

"I have to go bathroom," he said.

"No. You can't go. It's story time." She turned the page. "In the earthly morning, in the dark earthly morning, on the deep dark planet earth. . . ." She stopped again. "Wait. I have to move you again." She grabbed my husband's arm. He stood up. As she led him a foot in another direction, her parents could not stop chuckling. She returned to her spot in front of her mock classroom. When she showed us another page of pictures, Justin and I oohed and aahed.

"In the earthly morning," she repeated, "in the dark earthly morning, on the deep dark planet earth. . . ." It was the weirdest, coolest poetry I'd heard from a kid.

Justin raised his hand again.

"No," she said. "You already asked a question."

Then Lauren turned toward me. And Lauren, the first person I'd ever met with my daughter's syndrome, the person I secretly hoped could tell me *all will be okay*, looked at me point-blank and said, "It's your turn. It's your turn to ask me something."

At two a.m., Fiona's arm struck her mattress with a *bam-bam*, calling me from the deep leagues of sleep. My consciousness crawled sluggishly toward waking. It always felt like trying to swim to the surface of something thicker than water. It was almost painful, but once I was at the surface, I was a go: Sit up. Prop my pillow vertically against the headboard. Wrap the nursing pillow around my waist, click the plastic buckle, and lift the baby. I pressed my daughter's face to me. She latched and tugged, awaiting milk.

It was May, a few weeks from her first birthday. There was no morning light through the bedroom windows yet. Justin's breath hissed long inhales and exhales. It was just me and my girl and the stillness of the world, and a mind too tired to think.

In the earthly morning,
in the dark earthly morning,
on the deep dark planet earth. . . .

We were sitting above the abyss of the unknown. Two months from now, Justin's job as an assistant priest would end. We didn't know how we'd cover all our bills. We didn't know where we'd get health insurance. We didn't know where we'd move next.

"How stressful," a friend had said over the phone. Strangely, I didn't feel stressed. Now that I was connected to more parents like me, their uncertainties loomed larger: A four-year-old boy with Fiona's syndrome had died after suffering a seizure that had lasted hours. He'd just spoken his first words. A baby two months younger than Fiona had received five vaccines at once, then suffered a seizure that put her on life's edge. She was sedated, couldn't breathe on her own, and was given a 50/50 chance. She lived. And then I learned that another kid, several years older than Fiona, had spent the first few years of his life developing quickly. He'd learned to sit up at eleven months, crawled by the age of two, and was on his way to walking before the early age of three. Then he had a *grand mal*. He'd never returned to the trajectory he'd been on. His mom still hoped he'd walk one day.

Justin's job precariousness didn't keep me up, I suspect because we already lived over the abyss of uncertainty in a situation far more precarious than work.

Fiona and her fourth chromosome offered a profound truth: There were no predictions to make. No sculpted narratives, no expected plot lines to lean on. Having a medically complicated kid might initially put a parent closer to this truth, but we all eventually face it.

So maybe we could just trust the uncertainty. Trust the abyss. I began to believe, however shakily, that if my family fell straight into my greatest fears, the groundless darkness would somehow cradle us. Not that *everything would work out* according to my will, but that we'd find benevolence in those murky depths. I suppose this was a way of imagining God, a form of faith.

In the earthly morning,
in the dark earthly morning,
on the deep dark planet earth. . . .

Lauren's story reminded me of the first words of Genesis, before anything begins, when anything is possible. The world is but an abyss, covered by darkness. There is nothing.

And then, that nothing explodes into everything, into all of creation.

Chapter Eight

~

She turned one. Family and friends drove to Ohio. I put her in a white cotton dress, and her father drizzled holy water over her forehead in baptism, and Mother Jackie gave a sermon:

As we soak her in God's love and healing grace today, we invoke the Holy Spirit, praying, with God, that as Fiona grows she will be part of the Spirit's work . . . part of the transforming of this world and all our lives. . . .

We said *amen.*

Afterward, we crowded a dozen extra people into our rented Cape Cod and donned party hats and ate off of watermelon-shaped plates. We stuck a candle into a plastic container of baby carrots because it was our girl's favorite food. We sang "Happy Birthday." We blew the candle out for her. I wished she would be who she would be.

She was rolling over by then, front to back, back to front, usually to grab a set of plastic keys or a light-up toy. She got most of her calories through formula now, having rejected my boobs after the Chicago trip. Her hair had grown into a light brown mohawk that Kewpie-curled at the very top—a combo of cutesy and badass. Her eyes remained piercingly blue. Her mouth stayed mostly shut, and the sounds she made were usually M's. *Mmm, mmm, mmm.* When I tossed those plastic keys to the right of her supine body and she torqued to grab them, she rolled onto her back again and looked, not at the toy she'd just snatched, but at me—right in my eyes. It was people she desired—a face that loved her and the love from that face.

Vacationing while parenting is kind of like juggling while sleeping: an oxymoron. In June, we took her to the beach for a week with extended family, and I was caught off guard that the salt and sand didn't whisk away our regular parenting duties. Justin and I spent much of the time as we did at home: holding a bottle to Fiona's mouth while she lay on the floor, or cradling her in our arms while she drank formula, or propping her up in the narrowest high chair on the market and offering her spoonful after spoonful of mushed veggies. She ate every two to three hours; she napped at ten and three. But when we got to the sand, we held her by her armpits and dangled her feet at the ocean's edge. Waves foamed around her toes. We knelt to her level and beamed giddy, ocean-drunk faces and looked at our girl, gauging: *Does she like it? Does she like the best place on the planet?* She smirked and clapped. She made squeaky noises with her mouth closed. When the cold water hit her ankles, she let escape a few vowels.

One late afternoon Justin's cousin and I stood on the wood

deck of the rented beach house, staring across the Atlantic. The sun was sliding behind us. His lanky preteen daughter was running in the sand, past earshot.

"She's in the ninety-ninth percentile in math," Justin's cousin said of his daughter. "She's in the ninety-ninth percentile in reading. She's even in the ninety-ninth percentile in height. Anything we ever test her in, she performs in the ninety-ninth percentile." He carried a father's pride, yes, but he also spoke with a combination of curiosity and confusion, as if the tests were a strange problem—they couldn't challenge his daughter. He couldn't find a yardstick that matched her extraordinary skills.

The beach was thinning out. People were collapsing large umbrellas and shaking out blankets of sand. The waves rolled in regardless: crest, then collapse, then foam and retreat. I stayed silent. A year earlier, I would have said, "That's great." And it probably *was* great—to have a child so exceptional. But I'd been carrying around the virtues of achievement for as long as I could remember. I recalled envelopes with their perforated edges, the ones I was handed semiannually in grade school. When I tore them open, I saw the graph of my performance on some standardized test. I followed a horizontal black bar all the way across the form, to the number that labeled me: 99 percent. His daughter's situation was once mine. In sixth grade, I was the fastest girl to run the mile. In middle and high school, the courses I took were called "honors" and "advanced placement." The older I got, the faster the other runners ran, the harder the exams became. The last SAT questions perplexed me. Perfect scores were now a few hundred points away. I'd met my match. In high school, we students were ranked in order of our GPAs, and we learned our rankings on our report cards. The three kids vying for valedictorian sweated incremental differences, mathematically out of my reach. I graduated twelfth out of four hundred. Decades later, I'd tell a Canadian friend my number. "They ranked you?" he asked, appalled. "Of course they ranked us," I said. "How American!" he said. It had never struck me as strange that I knew precisely where I fell among my peers.

In his essay "Constructing Normalcy," Lennard J. Davis argues that the concept of "normal" was developed rather late in human history. The word "normal" as we might think of it—*constituting, conforming to, not deviating or differing from the usual*—appeared in European languages in 1840, he says. Prior to that, "norm" was a carpentry term, meaning "perpendicular." Davis links the appearance of "normal" with the emergence of statistics, which seems benign at first until he notes that Belgian statistician Adolphe Quetelet championed "normal" as a virtue. By studying human features like height and weight, Quetelet created and hailed the Average Man.

Enter the bell curve, otherwise known as "normal distribution," the bell-shaped graph that represents at the very top the most average and expected outcome, and at the edges—the lips of the bell—the most unexpected, the unusual, the outliers. Before Quetelet, the bell curve hadn't been applied to human beings. Suddenly, it was illustrating what among us was typical and what was abnormal. As Davis puts it, "The average man, the body of the man in the middle, becomes the exemplar of the middle way of life." Quetelet himself writes: "Deviations more or less great from the mean have constituted ugliness in body as well as vice in morals and a state of sickness with regard to the constitution." Normal was good; deviations were bad.

But in the late nineteenth century, Sir Francis Galton argued that some "standard deviations" on the bell curve were more desirable than others. Tallness, for instance, and high intelligence. The traditional bell curve—or "normal curve," as it was also called—didn't reflect these priorities. It showed both tallness and shortness as outliers, deviants—"ugliness," in Quetelet's words. So Galton revised the bell curve to rank desirable traits and ensure that they were read as superior to undesirable deviations. You don't need to connect too many dots to see how this thinking leads to some of the great horrors of the twentieth century. Before the Nazis used their gas chambers on Jews, they tested them out on the disabled. "We must remember," Davis writes, "that there is a real connection between figuring the statistical measure of humans and then hoping to improve humans so that deviations from the norm diminish." It was actually Galton who first coined the term "eugenics" in 1883. It was Galton's ideas that led, according to Davis, "directly to current 'intelligence quotient' (IQ) and scholastic achievement tests." In other words, Galton's ideology is an ancestor both to the Holocaust and to the fact that I know my graduating high school rank.

"The 'problem' is not the person with disabilities," Davis writes in his essay, which I will read two years after this beach trip and which will nearly cause me to sing *hallelujah*. "The problem is the way that normalcy is constructed to create the 'problem' of the disabled person."

Even a year into Fiona's life, I was still just learning this truth. If you viewed my daughter through lenses that valued, above all else, normal or above average, then my kid was a problem.

"In mainstream America," writes Deborah Deutsch Smith in *Introduction to Special Education*, "quantifying human performance is the most common method used to describe individuals. Unfortunately, this way of thinking about people puts half of everyone 'below average' and forces individuals to be considered in terms of how different they are from the average. For students with disabilities, this approach contributes to the tendency to think about them as deficient, as somehow less. . . ."

I don't remember what Justin's cousin and I talked about after the ninety-ninth-percentile remarks. I only remember my silence and the ocean's rhythm as I sat with a new knowledge: I could no longer join Justin's cousin in measuring people. I couldn't bring my former virtues of rankings and achievement into parenting. I had to quit that game. Looking out at the gray-blue ocean, from which Galton's cousin, Charles Darwin, had showed us our evolution had crawled, I felt nudged toward a different way of seeing. *Go on, now. Learn something new.*

"Eugenics" can be translated to mean "well born" or "good creation." But its essential opposite is the reason we recoil from it today: *poorly born, bad creation.* We remember eugenics as an ideology that sought to weed out the unwanted, and we know the qualities of the unwanted were determined by the people in power, who deemed themselves wanted: white, straight, able-bodied, presumably Christian. I hear again the pediatrician on my child's third day of life: *Bad seed, bad soil.* A modern-day eugenicist.

But here's something beautiful. "Eugenics" shares an etymological root with the word "genesis." They're both related to the Greek verb *gignomai*, meaning "to come into being, to become." There are fewer passages in the Bible more satisfying to me than its first verses. In the beginning, God makes everything—light and water, land and sunflower, lemon tree and whale and star-nosed mole. After God makes each thing, the book reads, "God saw that it was good." I used to remember it as "God *declared* each thing good," but the Bible doesn't even say that God *made* each thing good. It says God *saw* that these things were each good. The verb is *eidō*, to know, to perceive, to behold. No matter how you read the Bible, as history or fiction or poetry or myth, no matter whether you believe it's the inspired word of some higher power or just another human-made tome, the writers of the first page want to tell us something: when we perceive with the lenses of the divine, we see goodness.

I hadn't yet come across a certain *teisho* (or Buddhist lecture) by Soen Roshi, but years later I would read a transcript, and it would again bring me right back to this moment at the beach, with a father and his ninety-ninth-percentile daughter and the mammoth ocean.

"Everything is our teacher," Soen said. "This!" *Bang*—he slammed his hand on a table. "This is the real one point; very easy to understand. Too clear, too easy to get This! . . . Everything is wonderful! . . . Each one is best."

The modern mind might cry out, *Impossible.* "Best" commands a pyramid-like hierarchy, of which "best" is at the tippy-top. "Best" is superior, premier, the One. If "each one is best," there is no pyramid. There's not even a bell curve. There's only a plain.

But the Zen master's words jam a wrench into the gears of Galton's eugenics. His words flatten the bell curve, scramble statistics, scribble crayon over Quetelet's Average Man. Fiona had been ranked her entire first year, and she always came up short. Justin's cousin's daughter had been ranked her entire life, and she always emerged far ahead. Each was best. Each had an opportunity to play a role in this moment's unfolding. Each was *coming into being*—as *gignomai* is translated—just like the stars *came into being*, and the first human *came into being*, and I, a mother—an imperfect mother—was continuously *coming into being*.

'd always considered myself "a poet," a literary writer whose audience was meant to be in the low three figures. My goal prior to being Fiona's mother was to publish in obscure journals with print runs of a few hundred and acceptance rates in the fractions of 1 percent. This way, by creeping belly-down through the eye of the prestigious literary needle, I'd know my work was good. And maybe some search committee at some university would think I was good too.

But raising a child who ate yardsticks for breakfast was having the effect of eating my own yardsticks too.

Grace laughs in the face of conventional wisdom, I heard progressive Christian writer Rob Bell say years later. *It doesn't keep score. . . . Because being good enough was never the point. . . . God was never keeping score.*

Fiona was teaching me grace. I was waking up to some new way of seeing the world, and I wanted to share this with tired parents across the globe in the sloppiest and most efficient way possible. So I wrote blog posts, unprestigious, unawarded, and unacclaimed blog posts, and I received emails of thanks from parents, and it became the most satisfying writing I'd done to date.

One day, an email I never expected arrived not from a parent but from a daughter:

> Reading about parents like you who strive to support their children and to be themselves over being "normal seeming" is so very very very important to me that I can't even express it.

This woman wrote that she was excluded from family wedding photos because her wheelchair couldn't access the grassy landscape that the bride insisted upon. She was cut out from Christmas dinners because no one would make space at the family table for her wheelchair. On holidays, she ate alone.

> I'm lying here with tears rolling down my cheeks just trying to find the words. . . . Some of us with severe disabilities have parents who have somehow never been able to move beyond denial and it never ever ever ever stops hurting. Thank you. . . .

Suddenly, the small, private work of exhuming my ableism never felt so high stakes.

Amanda had written me with news: my family had been awarded a scholarship to attend the national conference for 4p-. Amanda knew our financial future was uncertain. The scholarship took care of our hotel and conference fees. All we had to do was get ourselves there. All we had to do was fill my old Sentra with a tank of gas and drive. It wasn't until I booked the hotel reservations that the timing dawned on me: the conference fell on my birthday.

That summer, I'd decided I put way too much mental energy into Wolf-Hirschhorn syndrome. On any given day, after a therapist left the house, or after I got a call from a doctor who said the kidney scan looked like this or the EEG looked like that, I scrolled through the Internet. I chatted online with moms of similar kids. I gathered research, compared notes. I read a book on the Anat Baniel Method, an alternative approach to pediatric therapy that prohibited any "fixing" mentality and prioritized "connection." I couldn't *not* think about Wolf-Hirschhorn syndrome, about my daughter and what she needed and how to be a good mother to her. So I decided I needed some balance. More jogging. Some novels. A gripping TV series. Spending my thirty-fourth birthday at the 4p- Conference ran contrary to my new goal. Plus, a group of folks gathering in the name of a rare medical condition sounded like a problematic way to party.

When Justin and I stepped into the elevator of the Indianapolis Sheraton, I choked on tears because I readied myself to answer the question I thought the bellhop would ask: "What brings you here?" But he didn't ask. He just wheeled the brass cart of baby accoutrement and said, "What floor?" Justin held Fiona against his chest. She strained against his arms and whined, telling us her tiny belly was due for another three ounces of milk.

. . .

Some folks held babies. Some held toddler-size kids like babies to their chests, rocking and rolling their hips in that universal parenting sashay of soothing. Some knelt to the level of a person in a wheelchair, and some just stood beside a person in a wheelchair. One person kept chasing after a kid who ran away from him. "Arnold!" a man shouted, trailing a child who emitted a shriek of glee as he blurred by. There were very slender kids steering silver walkers across the ballroom carpet's bold curlicues. And there were very slender kids taking stilted steps with plastic braces on their ankles. And there were grown adults in wheelchairs looking up at the chatter, and there was even a woman with a vibrant cloud of red hair scooting on her butt.

The conference room of the Indianapolis Sheraton was like any conference room in America: windowless beige walls with chestnut crown molding, giant crystal chandeliers overhead, and a vast stretch of bold geometric carpeting. But whenever large groups gather in the name of some common purpose—God or graduation or even elementary-school field day—I tear up. Triple that for a gathering in the name of my kid's rare syndrome.

"How old?" asked a tall, broad, middle-aged guy with an amiable expression. He nodded toward Fiona. She was drinking a bottle in Justin's arms. She wore a mix-match of turquoise florals and turquoise stripes, a fashion combo only a baby can pull off.

I answered. He didn't flinch. This was the gift of "normal." In this room, my kid was perfectly unsurprising. Then he launched into a monologue about life with his daughter. She was twenty-something, over there, in that wheelchair. Between the angled bodies, I didn't catch which wheelchair he meant. She was a delight, he said, such a joy. She was in many ways like a two-year-old, he said. He nodded to himself. Yeah, he said enthusiastically. That's what having a child with Wolf-Hirschhorn syndrome was like, you know? He looked at Justin, hoping for recognition, nodding. It was like living with a two-year-old, he said, the rest of your life.

I imagined there were good things about two-year-olds—openness and unpretentiousness and an affection for turtles—and hard things too, like diapers and poor music taste and the inability to self-bathe. Justin smiled at the dad, and the man smiled back, and I saw in his eyes a puppy-doggish droop of something like sadness or resignation or maybe just fatigue, even while his face was also a portrait of gratitude for his girl. Justin called him "partner" and said we'd see him around.

Early the next morning, Justin and Fiona lingered in the hotel bed while I showered and appeared at the opening session like it was my job. It was my thirty-fourth birthday, and I was tweaked with adrenaline. The "meet-n-greet" ballroom had been turned into a lecture hall, with rows of chairs facing a podium and a screen. The conference proceeded as conferences do—with experts giving talks, and people listening in chairs, and an audience member occasionally raising a hand to ask a question.

But the real learning happened in the gaps, when families got to talk. We met a girl in a wheelchair with lustrous red hair and a plump, Angelina Jolie–style upper lip. Her name was Maggie, and she reclined slightly in her chair wearing several strands of Mardi Gras beads—metallic purple and opaque pink and shimmering emerald. With slender fingers, Maggie fiddled with the beads, gazing up at people with a serious, gorgeous face. She was about the size of a five-year-old.

"She loves them," her mother said of the beads. She pulled a string of opaque fuchsia off Maggie's wheelchair handle and gave the necklace to Fiona. Fiona worked it through her hands, clenched it, and swung it around. When she finally dropped the necklace, Maggie's mother picked it up and draped it around my daughter's neck. "There," she said. Now Fiona could play with and drop the beads for hours, never losing them.

"That's awesome!" I said. Rarely did Fiona love a toy.

Maggie's mother smiled a *You're welcome.*

Maggie was thirteen. When she was born, doctors never expected her to leave the hospital. They told her parents that she'd never have the mental capacity to recognize her mother. Not only did Maggie know and connect with her mother, she had a crush on Justin Bieber and she'd at least once flirted with a cute male nurse. "Typical teenager," her mother said. She couldn't roll over on her own. Her parents took turns rolling her over at night so she didn't get bed sores. She'd been hospitalized several times in her thirteen years, and, as with Amanda's daughter, her parents had *almost lost her.* Maggie's interest in beads hardly waned throughout the conference—she fingered them for hours as she took in the world around her.

If, on my drive to the conference, I had been asked to describe the stories I feared hearing, the ones over which I'd picked the skin around my fingernails, Maggie's would have fit the bill: a child who didn't walk or talk, who was so medically fragile that she'd nearly died. And yet, *and yet*, I found myself lingering beside Maggie and her mother way longer than courtesy required. I loved being around them. So did Justin. Maggie's mother was honest and warm and compassionate. She was loving and tired and smiled often. She was utterly disarming, and she shared her experiences easily. There was a bareness to her, a beautiful vulnerability, and I don't know if she had those qualities before Maggie or if her life as Maggie's caregiver brought them out of her.

I met a woman named Rebecca, who had a rounded back and short black hair that clung to her head in tight curls. She was in her twenties. I watched Rebecca's dad spoon macaroni and ground meat into a small portable grinder and churn the handle. Then I watched him open the grinder, dip a spoon in, and feed Rebecca the food, spoonful by spoonful. She mashed it with the roof of her mouth. At one point, her father got very close to her face, and the two of them looked at each other, communing something ineffable, beaming straight-up love. He mumbled to her. Her broad grin remained. I stood on the edges of their intimacy, beholding the tenderness. Rebecca chewed, and her father wiped her face with a cloth.

This is another way to parent, I thought. *This is another way to love*—this caring for a child who would not grow beyond her need for you.

. . .

We went to the indoor pool. I watched Maggie delight on a flotation device while her parents spun her slowly around. The child who kept running from his father thrashed happily in a life vest. One very slender teenager with the high forehead of the syndrome set her towel down on a lounge chair and plunged right into the pool with nothing to help her swim but little flotation devices around her biceps. She made a small splash.

"She can *swim*," a mother whispered with awe from a lounge chair.

Justin and I brought thirteen-pound Fiona into the pool. She wore an inflatable ring around her neck, which sounds as terrifying as it looked but was a bona fide therapeutic device meant to keep her head above the surface while her limbs could explore the viscosity of water. I stood beside her, waist-deep, breath held, ready for her head to slip right through the ring. It never did.

"How old is she?" a woman asked poolside.

"Thirteen months," I said. For the past twenty-four hours, I could answer this question without first strapping an emotional shield over my chest, guarding myself quickly against whatever strange response the inquisitor would give.

"She's so chunky!" the woman said.

I puffed up, proud. "Thank you." Fiona jerked her legs in the water, unintentionally making herself spin in the neck ring.

"Does she have a tube?" the woman asked.

I shook my head. "Orally fed."

"Nice work, Momma."

Three typical boys splashed. They had wide, hardy bodies of heft and agility and speed. Their legs and arms were full of muscle. But I didn't envy them quite like I would have in the real world outside the Sheraton. In this Sheraton, about one in four people had a deletion on a fourth chromosome, which meant many of them had a face like Fiona's. And many had a body that resembled Fiona's, lean and willowy, with thighs you could encircle with a single hand. It was strange relief, being around so many bodies, so many faces, that resembled the one I loved.

met a woman in her fifties who pushed the stroller of a two-year-old. The child's eyes were cloudy, and the woman told me the girl was blind. I knelt down to say hello. "It's just the two of us," the woman said to me. She wasn't the birth mother. The child's parents had given her up at the hospital, right after birth. The hospital had called the woman and asked if she would foster the baby.

"How could I say no?" the woman asked me. "I'm so glad I learned about this conference last minute." They'd driven over ten hours.

And later, in a cramped, windowless room, I sat with a bunch of moms in an unmoderated chat session. We faced one another in an amorphous attempt at a circle, and moms of younger kids asked about feeding and seizures, while moms of older kids asked about day programs and puberty. When a middle-aged mother mentioned nocturnal emissions, the two-hundred-pound guy in a wheelchair behind her exploded in a punctuation mark of laughter. *Hah!* Up until this point, he'd said not a single word.

He'd made no indication that he'd understood anything in our thirty-minute conversation about this or that parenting concern, but he totally, totally got that someone was talking about erections.

When I sat back down in a row of chairs and listened to another presenter, I thought again of my stepfather. I'd been loved—dearly, truly—by a man who fixed people, who believed that many things about a person could be fixed, at least partially, by aligning their spines. My stepfather cradled heads in his stocky, sun-flecked hands and turned necks just so, until *pop*, he'd adjusted the cervical vertebrae. He believed an aligned spine enabled the body's energy to flow, increased the body's ability to heal and thrive. I lay facedown on his vinyl adjusting table and let him tweak my achy runner's knees, press on my hip joints, crunch my thoracic spine, and set my bones right. When I stood up from the table, I inhaled and felt giddy. Euphoric. Clear. I laughed. A rush of oxygen reached my head. This was one way he loved me. Giving wellness was like giving hugs. His hands aligning my spine were affections, affirmations.

In the evenings I'd sit beside him, his thick arm draped over the length of the love seat, my head resting on his bicep, and we'd watch TV, and this was another way to love: this wordless belonging of a daughter to a father figure. We'd watch *60 Minutes*, and he'd ash a cigarette into a metal tray because people are living/breathing contradictions.

The people with Fiona's syndrome were anomalous and raucous and serene; and rascally and skinny and replete; and agitated and entertained and curious; and quiet and laughing and crying; and loved and loving and human, and not a one, not a one would have been called a SuperBaby. Every one of my daughter's peers was a person I had not strived for when pregnant. Let me rewrite that: every one of my daughter's peers was a person I had actively striven not to have when pregnant. Among their company, something about my former pursuit of a SuperBaby seemed very, very wrong.

My family's mind/body fundamentalism was just another way to force the lepers outside the town walls. *Vulnerability cannot enter here. Mortality cannot enter here.* But when you push away disability, you also push away your humanity. When you push away any fissure of vulnerability, you also push away the tender truth about yourself. You are not, were never made to be, SuperHuman. You were made to be human. And this doesn't exactly break the heart, but it does split apart every clapboard and nail and piece of barbed wire you've hammered to it.

"I'm not crying because I'm afraid of dying," my stepfather had said to my mother on his deathbed. "I'm crying because I don't want to leave you three." By *you three*, he meant his wife but also the two daughters he bore no biological requirement to love. Pain came from loss. He loved anyway. If maximizing health was a way of protecting ourselves against pain, then he, the woo-woo doctor, couldn't even do that for himself.

Maybe he would have come with me here, to the Indianapolis Sheraton, where the conference might have jabbed at his fears masked as ideology, poked at them like a finger into the tenderest wound, and said, *Right here. Here's your fear of fragility. Here's your fear of vulnerability. Here's the sore place you shield futilely. And this, this soreness is what makes you human. This ache. This openness. This ability to break open. Break open.*

In *New Seeds of Contemplation*, Thomas Merton says that a tree glorifies God by being a tree. It's a profound thought for anyone who strives to be something *better*, something *else*. All a tree has to be is itself, says Merton, because that's all it was made to be. In being the tree, it consents to the creative love with which it was made. "The more a tree is like itself," Merton writes, "the more it is like [God.]" Trees are satisfied with this directive, Merton says, but not humans. "It is not enough for us to be individual men," he writes in 1961 (so I cross out "men" and pencil in "people"). "For us, holiness is more than humanity." Because humans are free to do much more than trees, Merton says, they are free to be themselves or not: "We are at liberty to be real, or unreal. . . . We may wear now one mask and now another, and never, if we so desire, appear with our own true face."

I've seen and worn a hundred thousand masks in my lifetime: the mask of authority to hide a fear of being wrong, the mask of aloofness to hide a fear of being rejected, the mask of cleverness to hide a fear of being dull. But deep inside me was a belief—no, it was bigger than belief—it was as unequivocally a part of my body as my own DNA, delivering an unwavering sense that I had to *be something else*. Something better. Healthier and holier and happier. Higher-achieving and faster and smarter and whatever. Always. And yet here I was, surrounded by people who seemed absolutely accomplished—triumphant, even—at being themselves. Rebecca wore no mask of embarrassment when her father wiped her chin. Maggie seemed uninterested in impressing anyone as she side-eyed other conference goers, beads in hand. The man who barked an uproarious punctuating laugh at the mention of an erection did not express one sliver of shame. No blush to the cheeks, no dip of the head or raise of the shoulders toward his ears. What I saw in many of my daughter's peers was a predisposition toward simply being, without mask, without lie. I was surrounded by people who wore, as Merton said, their true faces.

These folks with my kid's syndrome, they did not exist to teach me something, or anyone anything. But I was learning something anyway. I was getting a taste of Merton's truth: that holiness was no more than being human. That humanity, with all its fallibility and vulnerability, was precisely the point, was plenty holy.

One day is never enough to change your deeply fixed wiring. That's what tomorrows are for.

The next morning, I sat on a couch of a hotel suite and swiped the inside of Fiona's cheek ten times with a cotton swab. A smiling young woman—a genetic counselor—dipped the swab into a blue solution and sealed it for a lab, where technicians would examine the cells found inside. They'd look closely at that fourth chromosome, map the size and specificity of her deletion, and write a report. What genes did she have? Which ones was she missing? I didn't much care. I knew the results wouldn't tell us anything significant, not until the field of genetics advanced. I knew the cotton swab was more for the doctors and scientists who looked carefully at DNA and learned cool things about them and gave genes names as meaningless to me as the numbers they assigned to distant stars.

What mattered came after, when the smiling genetic counselor led my family through the doors that joined the suite's living room to a bedroom. A woman with short brown hair and glasses sat cross-legged in a skirt on a bed. She was Dr. Amy Calhoun, an assistant to one of the nation's leading experts on the syndrome, Dr. John Carey. Beside the bed were two empty wingback chairs. Justin and I settled into them, and Dr. Calhoun smiled kindly across from us. She asked if we had any questions.

It turned out I did. It turned out I wondered, oh just slightly, if I'd done something, oh just something, to make my daughter have a deletion on her fourth chromosome. I know: it's absurd. After all this time, I still wondered. But I was thirty-four and a day. My belief in a person's responsibility for wellness ran decades old. Any inkling I'd gotten otherwise seemed as fresh as a day-old babe.

I later learned that plenty of mothers ask this very question, even when we know the science. Even when we know a deletion is found usually in a sperm or an egg. And our eggs were nestled in our ovaries before we left our mothers' wombs. Maybe we subliminally carry the long history of maternal blame. In the twentieth century alone, experts have blamed mothers for Down syndrome, autism, schizophrenia, and homosexuality. So I told Dr. Calhoun I wanted a more thorough explanation of genetic deletions. I told her what I knew—that Fiona's chromosomal deletion occurred in either the sperm or the egg that conceived her—but how did that deletion occur in the first place? What was the source of this four pee minus? I wasn't just hoping for a scientific understanding of chromosomal deletions. I was secretly hoping to destroy, once and for all, any trace of my self-blame.

"Good question." Dr. Calhoun nodded with her hands on the knee of her crossed leg. "Chromosomes don't get passed down in their entirety," she said. "So, Justin doesn't have a whole fifth chromosome from his great-grandfather, for instance. He might have bits of chromosome five from this person, and bits of chromosome five from another person, and bits from another. Which is what makes his fifth chromosome completely unique—different from anyone else's."

In order for Justin's fifth chromosome to become this never-before-seen version, Dr. Calhoun explained, the chromosomes that made it underwent a tricky little dance called meiosis, something I probably learned in high school but didn't retain. The chromosomes copied themselves to become something called chromatids—exact replicas. They then joined with other chromatids to exchange genetic material. Dr. Calhoun let her index fingers become chromatids. She raised them up, pressed them together, and wrapped them around each other like intertwining snakes. "They tangle up," she said, "get stuck together, exchange genetic material. Then"—she untangled her fingers and tore them away from each other—"they rip apart."

My eyes widened.

"You can already see the issue, right?" she asked.

I nodded vigorously. To make a thing as precious as a chromosome, there was ripping involved.

When they rip apart, Dr. Calhoun explained, they collect new material, but they also leave other material behind. This is how genetic deletions—and even additions—happen. There's always a risk that some *necessary* genetic material will remain behind, or too much genetic material will attach.

Why is cellular reproduction so messy? Why don't chromosomes just transfer in their entirety, avoiding the whole "wraparound, stick together, rip apart" procedure? Dr. Calhoun explained that the process maximizes diversity. "We want a diverse gene pool," she said. "It makes us more resilient as a species, so we have a greater chance against things like the plague."

Biology wants randomness. It wants risk. There's an order to the chaos—or at least a reason. It increases survival. But I took Dr. Calhoun's message further than just survival, and further than just disease prevention. The sticky swapping and ripping of genetic material enables some of us to be immune to lethal viruses, sure, but also to be tall, short, wide, narrow, fast, slow, gay, straight, good with numbers, allergic to wheat, nonverbal, hypervigilant, social, flatulent, dyslexic, extra sweaty, musical, even-keeled, fiery, fat, skinny, prone to worry, or especially funny. Biology wants a wild mix.

Disability was not something to find blame for, because disability was not a problem. Through the neutral lens of science, my kid's chromosomal anomaly was a product of diversity, and who could be upset about that? Who could blame diversity, with its *Muppet Show* assortment of gregarious, bursting characters, each 100 percent unique?

Perhaps disability was an integral part of life's dance. Perhaps fragility was built into our very design. If the source of fragility was also the source of strength, then perhaps fragility *was* also strength.

"Actually," Dr. Calhoun said, "we probably *all* have deletions.

Little bits of genetic material that we don't even know about. Because there's so much redundancy in our DNA that it doesn't matter." Deletions, in other words, were normal, were par for the meiotic course. "But certain deletions are big enough that we notice them."

Downstairs were dozens of people with genetic deletions similar to Fiona's. But this conference had taught me nothing of who Fiona would become. It had only taught me that the trajectory of her becoming was far more wide open than I had imagined. And it had also taught me to respect her origins, not just for their holy or spiritual reasons, but for their scientific reasons too. *Trust the source of this deletion*, I heard. Trust the teensy paired ramen noodles found in every one of her cells. Trust that the combination of genes, nineteen thousand and nine hundred or so, were exactly what she needed in order to become exactly *who* she needed to be—and who the world needed too.

Part Two

Chapter Nine

⁓

The sensible thing to do when you're about to untether your family from your current state and head seven hundred miles toward a new life is, obviously, to get pregnant. Intentionally.

But sense had nothing to do with it. If inside each nucleus of my daughter's cells was an utterly unique and slightly abbreviated fourth chromosome, emerging from every nucleus of my cells were a pair of microscopic arms reaching outward, longing for a second baby. I was thirty-four. I did not approve of this longing. I had a teaching career to foster. Any writing life I once enjoyed was still being folded, origami-style, into Fiona's two forty-minute naps. To boot, Fiona was not yet sleeping through the night, and carrying her limp body knotted up my back in the same way that nursing a newborn would. I wondered how I'd transport two fully dependent humans to places like the grocery store or church. "You'll manage," a lovely elderly woman said, but I was dubious. Lastly, I am a terrible pregnant person. Even in photos where I make every intention to smile, I look at my image later and feel baffled by a strange fact: I'm clearly scowling. Near-constant nausea will do that to a person. But the longing did not care.

And so in September, a month after Justin solidified a new job as a priest at a Vermont parish, and as our home was being disbanded into cardboard boxes for our move to the Green Mountain State, we started "trying," as they say.

On our road trip from Ohio to Vermont, we stopped outside Pittsburgh. I was a solid week away from usefully peeing on a stick, and still I felt it: a fullness. A density below my navel that was by no means measurable in weight or mass. It was a familiar knock from inside, saying, *Hello, you're not alone.*

S trapped to my chest in a brown carrier, Fiona headed with me into the whipping autumn wind. The fresh air dialed down my nausea a notch, and I wrapped my wool coat around my girl, calculating the blocks to the drugstore. No more than four. I could make it, I told myself, without barfing.

Fiona was at peace in the carrier, her blue eyes open and curious as we passed the attractions of our new town: an old shoe store, a yellow bank, a river. We reached the drugstore, and I found what I was looking for: "seabands," Velcro bracelets meant to push on the acupuncture points that supposedly ease the need to upchuck. Immediately after the cashier rang me up, I ripped the box open and put the bands on. Halfway home, Fiona arched against the thick fabric of the carrier, straining to get out. Once through our apartment door, I removed my coat, took Fiona out of the carrier, set her on a quilt, and promptly went to the trash can to puke. That was our single outing of the day.

Thankfully, Vermont's early-intervention therapists come directly to your home. We moved to Vermont largely because Justin's job offer was a good one, and we figured we could nearly live on his income if we downsized. The job also put us in a five- to six-hour radius of family (the closest we'd been in almost a decade). My research on the state's services didn't turn up anything extensive, so we crossed our fingers that Fiona would receive the support she needed.

But when the county's speech therapist walked through our apartment door and saw Fiona clap and smile, her response immediately told me that my girl was in a different kind of therapeutic company than we'd known before. "Well, hello there!" the woman replied in a tone that was chipper without sounding condescending. The therapist sat down on our couch and told me that my daughter had already displayed excellent social skills within the first instant of her evaluation.

I'd been eager for a visit from a speech and language pathologist. Fiona was almost a year and a half and showed no inclination to "babble." The last time Fiona was assessed in communication, she scored a 5 out of 19. *Out of range,* Tiffany had written. I moved to Vermont believing my girl was woefully deficient in the area of communication. But the Vermont speech therapist asked me about my day with Fiona. When did my daughter typically eat? When did she nap? How did I know she was hungry? Tired? I realized that I could always tell when Fiona was hungry or tired, or even delighted or pissed, from the precise pitch and loudness of her *mmm*s.

"She's talking to you," the therapist said.

"Yeah," I said, a ray of optimism lifting my tone.

"She just doesn't have any words yet."

"No," I acknowledged.

"That's a concern," the therapist conceded lightly, and I agreed.

And yet, for the next hour, this stranger in my living room unveiled for me all the remarkable ways my daughter participated in communication. Fiona responded to her name. She paid attention to a book for a full minute. When I sang "Itsy-Bitsy Spider," Fiona rumpled her fingers together in an attempt to make the motion of the creeping, near-drowned arachnid. When the therapist handed Fiona a toy and then asked for it back, my girl's lax arm extended the toy toward the therapist. When the therapist asked Fiona to kiss a baby doll, Fiona tilted her head down and touched her mouth to the doll's forehead.

"Have you ever asked her to do that before?"

"No," I said.

The therapist was especially delighted by the baby-kissing move. And so was I. My girl was understanding full sentences and novel requests.

This therapist's view of my daughter was a far cry from the Ohio professionals' perspective. During one therapy session back in Ohio, Karen, the occupational therapist, knelt on our beige carpet and gazed disapprovingly at Fiona. By then, Fiona could roll from front to back and back to front but had a special love for lying supine. Karen shook her head. "It's like she's asleep, neurologically," Karen said. She was unsmiling. "We need to wake her up."

I didn't understand. Fiona had been lifting her legs in the air and grabbing onto the edges of her pant legs. She'd started "crossing her midline" by grabbing her foot with her opposite hand, which therapists said was neurologically crucial and a precursor to crawling. She was sucking on her fingers, a victory over her oral aversion. These weren't milestones parents and doctors of typical babies usually celebrated, but I'd learned that my daughter would break down every giant mile marker and turn it into a hundred incremental achievements, and these achievements were no less confetti-worthy. None of them, though, even touched on Fiona's greatest gift: a luminous aliveness in her eyes. A bright light behind those Lake Tahoe blues. She held in those eyes a sense of curiosity and connectivity and delight as she sought out my face, Justin's face, the faces of the ladies at church and the shoppers at grocery stores and anyone she met. She said *mm, mm,* and insisted people return her gaze and then basked in theirs, squealing. She was very much "awake."

But Karen spoke with conviction. *She needs to wake up, neurologically.* Then Karen grabbed twelve-pound Fiona by the shoulders, jostled her a few times, and said, "Wake up! Wake up!"

Fiona did not cry, or go uncomfortably silent, or do anything to indicate that she had been harmed. She wasn't exactly "shaken"— as in *Don't shake the baby!* She was probably jostled no more than if I'd driven over a bumpy road. So when I wrote the county's developmental services department, requesting another OT, it wasn't for any perceived physical abuse—although the department treated my complaint as such.

I wrote to register my disapproval for something more nuanced, even if, in my yearlong sleep deprivation, I didn't know how to articulate it. Karen failed to see what was good about my child. And yes, I partly mean she failed to look at Fiona as a complex expression of creation, although perhaps this is too spiritual a perspective to expect of a therapist. But I also mean Karen didn't perceive Fiona's developmental strengths, those things that even a lover of charts would have marked on a clipboard as "good." *Wake up!* she'd said, as though Fiona were a lazy teenager who'd slept past her alarm.

What I heard from the new speech and language pathologist, which I'd never heard in the twelve months that my daughter had received early intervention, was a detailed list of ways my girl was *bright*—and not just according to my own spiritual hunches. She was also bright according to measurable outcomes. The therapist noted that Fiona responded to requests. She saw how Fiona listened to conversations and paid attention to words. Fiona even exhibited something called "joint referencing," which was when she looked at me, smiled, and then looked at the therapist—her way of saying, *See that, Mom?* The Ohio therapists had never encouraged me to consider this stuff communication. And of course, Fiona had figured out her own way of communicating needs to me with her various *mmms*. It was kind of genius, given her mouth's limited range of consonants: she was working with what she had. She was innovating through pitch what her lips and tongue and teeth couldn't yet do. My daughter spent much of the session smiling and clapping at the therapist, and I wanted to join her. *Yay, speech therapist!*

"Despite our best intentions, we've created a system of special education based on deficits," writes Dr. Thomas Armstrong, executive director of the American Institute for Learning and Human Development. This "deficit perspective" is the direct offspring of the bell curve. Kids with physical and neurological differences are measured against the norm, and any deviation is labeled a problem. Plenty of educators have called for a paradigm shift, one that focuses not on deficits but on strengths and capacities. "We don't look at a calla lily," Armstrong writes, "and say that it has a 'petal deficit disorder'; we appreciate its beautiful shape."

Wading in first-trimester nausea, still unpacking boxes, I had stumbled across a new way professionals could perceive my child. Not with a "deficit lens." When the speech therapist heard in Fiona's *mmm*s a capacity to communicate, she was using what education scholars called a "capacity-building lens." "These educators . . . understand," write professors Emily A. Nusbaum, Julie Maier, and Jeanne M. Rodriguez, "that the 'things' that challenge [students] the most, 'things' that are often articulated as 'problems,' are actually evidence of student capability." Tiffany and co. only heard in those *mmm*s all the sounds Fiona *wasn't* making. Nusbaum, Maier, and Rodriguez explain that when therapists use a "deficit lens," they tend to limit a child's opportunities and view the child as a problem in need of "fixing." But a capacity-building lens will not only meet and celebrate kids where they are, it often will create higher outcomes for them. In other words, kids grow more when professionals see their strengths.

"Her skills in this area have some gaps," the speech therapist's final report read, "but she is a very social girl."

This strengths-based approach wasn't just limited to the speech therapist. The county's physical and occupational therapists each came to assess Fiona. Together with the speech therapist, they wrote up a comprehensive summary of Fiona's development in eight categories. Again and again, I read the words *she can.*

> She can roll back to stomach and stomach to back. She can support her weight when held under her arms. She can grasp her foot and bring her foot to her mouth. She can reach and grasp toys. She can just about hold two toys at once (emerging skill). She can express affection as well as anger.

When Fiona was hungry and the jar of pureed carrots wasn't coming fast enough, she fired her *mmm* sounds like nasally punctuation marks, sometimes flailing her arm. Nobody had told me a baby gets credit for being pissed off and making it known.

Again and again, I also read the phrase *she will*, not as a prediction of future achievement but as a description of what she already tended to do:

> She will assist when pulled to a sit and no head-lag was observed. She will work to obtain a toy out of reach. If something is placed in front of or offered to Fiona and she doesn't want it, she will turn her head to indicate refusal. She will vocalize when alone. She will become unhappy at the loss of a social contact or at the loss of a toy.

When, as a parent, you're in the company of someone who focuses on your child's strengths, there is a palpable emotional effect in your body. Your face lifts. Your chest feels lighter, more buoyant. You nod and say "okay" with pep and hope, because your child *can*. And your child *will*.

The therapists of course perceived all the ways Fiona was delayed, but they also set lofty goals. The occupational therapist, Anne, intended to teach Fiona how to chew. Chew! I knew very few people with WHS who chewed. The physical therapist, Rachel, noticed that Fiona didn't have a fall reflex. She didn't put her hands out to stop her face from crashing into something if, while I held her, she leaned one way or another. I always caught her from tipping over, but Rachel pointed out how much constant support I gave my daughter—which explained the unrelenting knots in my back.

"She'll need to be able to catch herself," Rachel said, "when she stands and starts to walk."

"You think she'll walk?" I asked, because I couldn't help myself.

"That *is* the goal," Rachel said.

Fiona was not yet crawling. She was not even sitting. But the new physical therapist took the long view. Then the Vermont team of therapists filled Fiona's calendar with more therapeutic hours in one week than she'd had in a month. Compared to Ohio, her services quintupled.

Vermont does autumn better than any pocket on the planet, but in the fall of 2012, too nauseous to take walks or drives, I was a combination of sick and stir-crazy. Fiona and I found ourselves alone together, stuck in a first-floor apartment in which every wall was white and every room was visible from the couch.

The therapists broke up our day, and because the church was a half-block away, Justin popped in and out, checking on my state. There were also loads of other gifts about our new life: not just the hours of therapy but Justin's health insurance, which was solid, along with Vermont Medicaid, which we got for Fiona within three days of moving and which covered nearly every other dollar of her medical expenses. But I was desperate for a window to a wider world. I wanted adult conversations, a public life, the ability to eat something spicier than Saltines. And despite Fiona's advanced use of the letter M, there were still chasms between us in communication.

Just a few weeks before, I'd watched a mother ask her two-year-old son a series of questions. Did he want water? The boy offered an exaggerated, bobbly nod. Did he want ice cream? The boy again nodded yes. Whatever the boy said yes to, the mother handed to him.

Envy yanked at my chest. How much simpler life would be, I thought, if Fiona could just answer a *yes-no* question. Although I sensed when she was hungry or bored, I didn't know most of her desires. She didn't yet point, a fact that the speech therapist noted in her evaluation, so if I knew Fiona was hungry and I put a row of choices on the table, she couldn't convey which she wanted. If I offered a spoonful of pureed carrots, she might smack the spoon, splattering orange mush. If I offered a mozzarella cheese stick, she might turn her head ninety degrees, pressing her food-covered mouth into the high chair. A permanent stain marked this dramatic dissent.

In *The Boy in the Moon*, journalist Ian Brown writes about his son, Walker, who has a genetic mutation so rare that there are only one hundred known cases. Cardiofaciocutaneous syndrome (or CFC) affects Walker in some of the ways that WHS affects people: Walker doesn't speak and gets his nutrition through a g-tube. Half memoir, half journalistic search for the meaning of his son's life, Brown's book takes him to Gilles Le Cardinal, a professor emeritus of communication and information studies and a man who spent time in a L'Arche community. These are communities created by the late Catholic philosopher Jean Vanier, where adults with intellectual disabilities live alongside neurotypical people. In the interview, Le Cardinal impresses upon Brown the importance of getting his son to answer a yes-no question, even if it's through a nonverbal sign or symbol. "With one word or sign," Le Cardinal tells Brown, "you and Walker can be synchronized—heart to heart, hand to hand."

I read this in the fall of 2012 during one of Fiona's naps, and my chest ached. It was true—my girl and I were not always synchronized, heart to heart.

Brown tells Le Cardinal that saying yes will be hard for his son.

Le Cardinal insists: "You must find it. . . . It could take as long as a year, but it's essential. . . . And it must be a strong sign that everyone can read, not just you or your wife. . . . It's liberty. It's the first step for him to be free."

Fiona stirred from her nap, and I set down the book, walked fifteen feet from the living room couch to her bedroom crib, picked her up, and got her a bottle, hoping it was the thing she wanted. If it was, she'd say *yes* with drooling sucks and satiated eyes. If she said *no* with grunts and a turn of her face, I'd go back to the kitchen, asking, "Do you want pureed carrots? Mozzarella cheese?" In reply, I'd hear silence.

My belly popped out, and the low mountains surrounding our town shed every last leaf, and the temperatures dropped well below freezing, and thank God almighty my nausea lifted at least half its weight.

There's one time an otherwise awesome and "strengths-based" physical therapist has to enumerate all the ways your kid has "deficits": when she communicates with insurance companies. Ours was questioning Fiona's physical therapy services. So one afternoon, Fiona's physical therapist, Rachel, sat down on our couch and reviewed some paperwork with me, which she had filled out in detail and which would hopefully convince the insurance company to continue to cover Fiona's services.

Rachel explained that Fiona's delays weren't simply delays but expressions of a global chromosomal condition. She explained that Fiona's delays didn't just cause slower development but, as Rachel said, "atypical compensation," such as a severe inward rotation of the hips, which could result in hip dysplasia. She explained—both to me and to the imaginary insurance execs in her mind—that Fiona's delays were "significant" (her word). To illustrate this, she put her hands in the air like they were about to connect in a clap, but then she spread them a foot apart. She concluded that Fiona, who was a year and a half, was displaying the gross motor characteristics of a four- or five-month-old baby.

I nodded. I appreciated Rachel's dutiful commitment to paper-work. I spent much of my newfound second-trimester energy on the crappy, unglamorous tasks of what some call "special needs parenting": filling out forms, calling insurance, scheduling over-due doctors' appointments, driving Fiona to a children's hospital two hours away, spending eight hours at that hospital to see this specialist and that. Rachel's suave argument was one task I didn't have to complete. And her explanation of Fiona's need for ser-vices was thorough and, I hoped, convincing. I thanked Rachel for her work.

But the rest of the day, I felt heavy. I didn't want to hear about all the ways my kid was "behind." I didn't want to think about what a typical day might look like if Fiona had her whole fourth chromosome. She'd be toddling around the apartment, eager to head out the door instead of lying supine, requiring support just to sit up. She'd be munching on crackers instead of needing me to spoon puree after puree into her mouth. Like most parents of kids with the syndrome, I still spent most of my time trying to feed my kid. Some days she consumed enough calories to sustain a toy poodle, but other days felt like a blur of hourly battles as I held every bottle for her, offered every spoonful, as she protested with frustrated whines.

That evening, Justin came through the door wearing his black cassock, a dress-shaped garment that made him look like Neo of *The Matrix*. Fiona clapped at her father's entry. He sat down on the couch with us. Fiona leaned away from me, toward her dad, and he scooped her up in his arms.

"Come here, you!" he growled.

She squealed. He kissed all over her face. She squinted in protection and touched her tiny hand to his beard. Her *mmms* were all delight.

I spewed at my husband all the shitty things about my day: The physical therapist's hands widening as she called Fiona's delays "significant." The hours I clocked trying to feed our orally defensive babe. The fact that my nausea still returned in waves and I was trapped in the apartment alone. The fact that Fiona still didn't have the hand strength to hold her own bottle.

At that moment, Fiona tilted toward me. Then she did something she'd never done before: she held out her hand and grabbed mine. She *grabbed* mine. She brought my hand toward her. She held my hand firmly, with the same strength she'd need to someday hold a bottle.

I stopped venting. I looked at my daughter—my daily wordless companion.

She cocked her head just so.

In those blue eyes of hers, I got the inkling of a message. And it was not the message one might expect. It was not, *It's okay, Mom. Everything will be fine.* It was not even, *You're a great mother.* The message was closer to this: *Woman, get over yourself. You're forgetting what's awesome. Like me. And this.*

Then she hurled her lean, wobbly body into the sofa cushion, where she buried her face into the gray upholstery and giggled.

I did the same, stuffing my face into the couch. I said, "Oof." She giggled some more. She repeated her move. We went on like this, back and forth, hurling our torsos into the couch cushions, giggling at the taste of upholstery in our mouths.

My girl did not yet have that all-important *yes.* But she did have a pretty effective, *Quit your bitching, Mom, and play.*

Chapter Ten

⁓

lay on a table while the technician pressed her wand around the greased hill of my middle, hunting for organs. When she found a certain piece of me, she named it with enthusiasm.

"There's your cervix!"

But I wasn't here for a glimpse of the entryway to my uterus. Nor was I even here to see the baby's organs, although I knew from Fiona's ultrasounds that they would interest the tech immensely. She'd carefully measure each. Anything "out of range" would elicit a phone call from a conscientious nurse. (Fiona's kidneys had always been "out of range," a small clue I'd shrugged at.) The tech kept clicking and naming objects in fuzzy black and white: a flapping, four-chambered heart. A black grape of a spleen. A brain, which looked like two hemispheres inside a globe.

But I needed the classic ultrasound image: that quaint profile, the one with the ski-slope nose and dainty pursed lips, the little fists held like white blooms around the baby's cheeks. I needed to see the face.

I'd taken to calling the tomato-size being inside me "Baby X."

It was not meant to be a distancing tool. It just came out one day: *Baby X*. Like a mathematical variable not yet solved.

The lights were off so I could watch the black-and-white movie inside my body. Here's what I imagined inside: a fraction. At age thirty-four, my risk of carrying a baby with a chromosomal anomaly was 1/238. My baby's risk of Trisomy 21, a.k.a. Down syndrome, was 1/500. Every chromosome could arrive in triples, become a trisomy, affect the body in a million ways. And every chromosome could have a deletion. There was Williams syndrome: 1/10,000. Edwards syndrome: 1/5,000. Noonan syndrome: 1/1,000. Cri du chat: 1/50,000—seemingly impossible but just as rare as Wolf-Hirschhorn.

I'd thought my risk of having another child with Wolf-Hirschhorn syndrome was the same as before, but a genetic counselor informed Justin and me that our chances were now 1/100. One percent. It was possible—although unlikely—that our reproductive cells harbored the deletion even while our blood cells did not. Every fraction was like a house, and that lone number "1" stood on the roof, shouting one word to the helicopters: *Possible*. I saw my second child in each skinny numerator. Because I knew the sticky, tangled dance of meiosis, I also knew the risks of reproduction, and I could not believe that the baby inside me had the usual makeup of genes. I could not even believe that the usual makeup of genes wouldn't deliver anomalies. As I said to my mother on the phone one day, "One hundred percent of my babies have genetic anomalies. I can't imagine anything different."

So I fretted, but I also fretted that I fretted. What did it say about me that I was freaked out about having another child like the one I loved? What kind of ableist asshat was I?

I didn't want to imagine a fraction in my uterus. I wanted to imagine a baby, syndrome or not. So I needed to see the face. I needed to call this child something other than Baby X.

"There," the tech said, finally landing on what I'd wanted.

The image was a square shot. I saw deep, ghostly eyeball cavities. The angular structure of cheekbones. A black opening for a mouth. It was a skull. A Halloween icon floating in my womb.

The tech sounded apologetic. "They look pretty skeletal at this stage," she said.

Ten months earlier, Justin had been sitting in our rocking chair, sewing his black cassock. This was back in Ohio, when I was a mother of one. I sat on the couch across from him, making a confession.

"The thing I'm most excited about, if we have a second child, is watching a typical baby develop. But this doesn't seem fair, because it makes my excitement contingent on the baby's abilities, and what if the baby isn't typical?" This was not some cool blue curiosity, asked in a tone that doesn't cling or care. This was a hot red question of desperation: *What if the baby isn't typical?*

Justin pulled the needle through the shoulder of his cassock and straightened the thread a half foot in the air. He was the seamstress of the family. His sewing was rough but effective. I loved this about him. He didn't know how to make clothes, but that didn't stop him from making them. He looked up from his cassock as if to say, *Go on.*

"I feel like I'm setting myself up for disaster. I long for a certain outcome I have no control over. But I so badly want a typical kid. I want to know what that's like, to see a baby sit up and babble and do all the things other babies do." I added, "Without hours of therapy."

He poked the needle back through the fabric.

"But again, this doesn't seem fair. To want something from a baby like this. I feel like I should be cultivating non-attachment. I should be free from the outcome."

This word "non-attachment" was code between Justin and me. I was referring to the Buddha's first two noble truths: First, there is suffering. Second, attachments are the cause of that suffering. In Christianity, the ultimate symbol of non-attachment is Jesus on the cross. He surrenders even to death. He lets go even of his own life. I couldn't let go of my desire: I still wanted, wanted, wanted an able-bodied baby. I didn't want that baby in Fiona anymore. But I wanted it in my next child. I knew what this meant in spiritual terms: I was setting myself up for a knife jab to the gut. How could I want from my future child anything more than what that child might be? How could I put that kind of pressure on my kin? How could I still call myself a mother and wish my baby were a certain way?

"I'm gonna need an amnio," I said decisively.

"I know," Justin said.

An amniocentesis—a needle plunged into the amniotic sac of a mother's womb and withdrawing a few drops of fluid—carried a risk of miscarriage, but it was also the only way to know for almost certain if your baby had a chromosomal anomaly. "I don't see how I can get through a second pregnancy without knowing."

Justin nodded. "I get it." Then he added a few more stitches in silence before he said, "Did you ever hear Trungpa's definition of non-attachment?"

Chögyam Trungpa Rinpoche was a Tibetan Buddhist master known for what some people called "crazy wisdom." He was also the teacher of my beloved Pema Chödrön. I shook my head. I'd assumed Trungpa's definition of non-attachment was some *blah-blah* impossibility I'd already heard in Buddhism, like *carry things lightly* or *live free from desires*.

But Justin's answer caught me off guard: "Hold nothing back."

I laughed out loud.

It was contrary to intuition. In order to keep yourself from suffering, wouldn't you in fact have to hold plenty back? Keep the longings of the heart at bay? Hold a certain percentage of chips closely so you didn't lose it all? *Hold nothing back* seemed emotionally reckless. But there was also something deliciously vulnerable about it. I imagined a poker player sliding every single chip across the table, then tossing into the pile their wallet and keys and wedding ring too. *I bet it all!*

Justin followed up the Trungpa quote with an idea from his favorite spiritual teacher, the Christian mystic Meister Eckhart. Detachment, said Eckhart, is embracing all things. "It's possible," my husband said, "to let go of all things in order to embrace all things."

I shook my head. "I don't understand."

The bay window behind him was black. Fiona was asleep upstairs. Justin's heavy dress of a cassock lay across his long legs. Eckhart's advice seemed as counterintuitive as Trungpa's, but their words were both cut from the same cloth. In order to be detached, you could both give over and embrace . . . everything.

"What does this mean?" I asked him. "For me?"

"Go full blast," said my husband without blinking. "Hope for what you want to hope for. Cry if you don't get it. Risk it all. Go full blast. Hold nothing back."

On the second day that I was pregnant with Fiona, I sat at a traffic light beside an outlet mall and prayed to the unknown being inside me. I said to the grain of light in my womb, *What's mine is yours. My body is now yours. Welcome.* But I hadn't done this my second time around. Months into my pregnancy, I hadn't bought anything for Baby X. Not a single soft cotton onesie. Contrary to Justin's advice, I was still holding plenty back.

In good news, I was thoroughly disengaged in striving for a SuperBaby, and this seemed a positive pendulum swing from my earlier pregnancy. I took some vitamins, sure, but I no longer swallowed a small mountain of them, or sweated my non-existent exercise regimen, or required myself to plan for a birth without the numbing river of pain relief. I mostly gave my body what it craved, including—*gasp*—Italian hoagies loaded with un-microwaved lunch meat. But because I no longer trusted that my efforts could sculpt a particular outcome, I also carried a mammoth fear that had been gloriously absent in my first pregnancy. My fear partly eclipsed the beam of love I'd hoped to emanate for this new, ambiguous human. It's hard to love a stranger, harder still to love that stranger through a rainstorm of *what-ifs*. *What if you too contain an anomaly? What if you are sick? What if you teeter on the edge of mortality? What if you break my heart?*

I wanted a fat and agile baby who never seized or needed an echocardiogram or threatened to go into kidney failure. I couldn't tell if this was an ableist desire or an understandably human one: to want a child who didn't threaten to break your heart into pieces.

On January 3, 2013, a few weeks before the ultrasound, two girls with Fiona's syndrome died. One was Fiona's age, eighteen months. She died from complications after a seizure. The other was a year or so older. I didn't know the cause of her death. She was the blind child in the stroller whom I'd met at the conference, the child who'd been abandoned by her parents at the hospital and then adopted by a senior citizen. I'd met the child in July, not knowing she had only six more months of life. A summer and a fall.

On January 2, just one day before the deaths of these two girls, Fiona was rushed in an ambulance to the hospital. She'd had another *grand mal*. Her fourth? Fifth or sixth? I was losing count. It was the third time I'd ridden in an ambulance, and by now I'd learned that the EMTs never did things the same way. Ride one: they asked me to hold Fiona while we lay down together on the gurney. Ride two: they strapped Fiona on the gurney separate from me, while I sat on a bench unbuckled and held onto a ceiling-tethered stirrup. Ride three was probably the least safe but my preferred: they let me sit up and hold her. She was postictal, that sleepy period after a seizure when her body went limp but her breath started regulating in rhythmic waves. They gave me a translucent breathing mask, ginormous and adult-size, and I held it above her wee mouth and nose. It shrouded half her face. The mask felt like a kindness to me as much as to her. It gave me something to do, some tangible way to call my daughter back, to reclaim her. *Here, child: oxygen.*

By the time Fiona was eighteen months old, I wore pretty easily the belief that she was not "wrong" in any way. She was as right as any human (which is, depending on your view of humans, debatable—but she was right to me). And yet nothing in the world looked so wrong as watching my girl seize. The grammar of it is erroneous. Fiona didn't *have* a seizure—the seizure had her. It took her, seized her. It was a thief. A *grand mal* could steal the ability to walk, to talk, to sit, to smile. And of course, some seizures didn't return a person at all.

During the minutes of Fiona's seizures, Justin and I hovered over her and waited and watched the clock and readied the rescue medicine—rectal Valium—which we were allowed to administer at the five-minute mark. We hoped with all our shallow breathing that the seizure might stop fast enough to give her back to us, just as she'd been before. We checked the clock and checked the clock. We watched her limbs jerk to that alien metronome, and we heard her grunt in time with her body's disturbing beat. *Uh, uh, uh.* For too long, we didn't hear inhalations. Once, her lips turn blue. Several times she unconsciously vomited out of her mouth's side, and then we heard the inhale, her chest now rattling with puke. Justin and I kept moving her around the mattress, away from the pools of vomit, trying to keep her airway clear.

Breathe, Fiona, we'd said, unsure if she heard us.

Fiona! I sometimes cried, as though she could be summoned back from wherever she'd gone.

And it did in fact look like she'd gone somewhere. *You'll know it's a seizure by the eyes,* a nurse once said. *Like the lights are on but nobody's home.* When Fiona seized, her eyes stayed hauntingly open. They were wide and vacant and unblinking. Very occasionally, she took in that crucial gasp of air.

Fiona's *grand mals* always happened at night, mid-sleep. And it was often Justin who caught them. When a fever unknowingly spiked in our daughter or broke through round-the-clock meds, it was often Justin who woke to that manic metronome of grunting. "She's having a seizure!" he'd call to me in the dark. I'd sit up, yank the lamp chain, scramble for my glasses, and he'd already be at her side. One time, I even slept with my body wrapped around her. She'd been feverish with a respiratory bug, so I tucked her below my armpit and tried to stay vigilant for convulsions. But when she seized, it was Justin who sat upright.

He'd been dreaming—of futuristic warriors and Jedis, he later told me. Suddenly a figure completely out of character, a powerful masculine force made of granite, got right in his face. It said, "Fiona is going to have a seizure. You must wake up." My husband, neither dazzled by nor skeptical of the supernatural, believed it was an angel.

Justin, the unshakably chill Justin, began experiencing symptoms of low-grade PTSD. He couldn't sleep deeply anymore. He slept in fits and starts. Heard something. Opened an eye. Worried it was a seizure. Asked, "What was that?" Tried to go back down. Tried to enter the forgetting world of sleep.

Many nights we found ourselves holding our breaths together, eyes open in the dark, listening for our daughter's breathing. Was it jilted? Was it even? When we heard the steady rush of air, or even the snort of her snore, we exhaled. We closed our eyes, tried to let ourselves fall back down. Although pregnancy ensured that I never slept longer than three hours straight, I could still let go of waking life more easily than my husband, perhaps because I had him and his seraphim to wake us. But who did Justin have? The granite guardian only came once. My husband felt the weight of his daughter's life on his shoulders.

Fiona's seizures almost always stopped, thank God, at five minutes. And by the next day, she was back to her usual self. But when I rode that ambulance on January 2, not knowing that two kids like mine would die the next day, I was riding with three people: myself, my daughter, and the baby inside me. And I think times like these—with Fiona postictal, sleepy and heavy and pale—led me so fiercely to want a child with every last bit of her chromosomes.

Why do we become parents? At our basest, we're called by biology. We feel in our genes the archaeology of our ancestors, hear them chant inside us: *keep going, keep going.* We feel this pressure humming in our bones—to continue, to carry on. Not everyone experiences this pressure as a desire to hold a mini-me. Some make art or computer programs or skyscrapers instead of babies. But even if a person manages to get through life without ever desiring a kid—an immunity to the biological clock that I fiercely admire—there's still inside our cells a drive to regenerate. Cells feed, and grow, and replicate their DNA. They divide. They make more of themselves. This is one way of defining Life.

When I was pregnant with Fiona, I'd once offhandedly asked a doctor if sperm that carry genetic anomalies are less effective at reaching the egg. I was wondering if sperm that carry disabilities would be disabled themselves. I remembered grainy video footage I'd seen of microscopic tadpoles, some jabbing pointlessly into uterine walls, others swimming in circles with double tails. The doctor shook his head. Sperm are indifferent to the contents they're carrying, he said. They're just two things—propulsion and luggage—and their engines are separate from their cargo as they sniff manically toward the egg, toward the thing that will on one hand end them, on the other hand let them perpetuate.

But the project of modern parenting isn't this simple or neutral. It's tangled with the desires of the ego, something I'm pretty sure no spermatozoon has had to contend with. Our cells want us to make, and seem indifferent to the outcome. It's our egos that want us to make better, better, better, believing we know what *better* even is.

Why was I having a second child? It was not—or not only—to satisfy the indifferent cellular yearning to make. It could no longer be to create a specimen of Humanity 2.0. I didn't just stop believing in the ability to make a SuperBaby—I questioned the morality of it. Our values were too twisted to know what would make for better versions of ourselves.

What is the point of parenting at all? Maybe it's not to raise children who succeed us, not to raise children who will eventually "become the future" as long as we "teach them well," à la Whitney Houston's "Greatest Love of All." It's to be leveled. To be brought to our knees with a love we have no choice over. To say *yes, yes, yes, I will love* whomever we find ourselves holding. There are ways of being brought to one's knees that don't involve parenting. But parenting is as good a path as any, requiring such self-sacrifice that we, once and for all, empty ourselves of our ridiculous egos, let them pool on the floors beneath us, and surrender to the sloppy, drooly, inconvenient, aching needs of another.

"He . . . emptied himself," Paul says of Jesus. This is, in other words, what God supposedly did when God lived inside the body of a human being.

Maybe this emptying, after all our centuries of striving, is the real blueprint for Humanity 2.0.

When we drove two hours over a snowy mountain to the hospital, we didn't just do it to learn that the mysterious being inside me was a girl (a girl)! We did it to get a needle in my belly. A message withdrawn by a syringe, an inspection of my baby's DNA, telling me whether to fear and, if so, what.

I'd signed a consent form. I'd learned that the needle was seven and a half centimeters long. I'd learned that the procedure could cause bleeding and cramping. I'd learned that the risk of miscarriage at this hospital was 1/300—yet another fraction. I'd received all this information from the genetics counselor in a cushy but windowless room with a tissue box and a fake orchid. So when I found myself in the examining room, perched on the paper-covered table, I nodded when the doctor poked her head in. A twenty-something nurse followed her, carrying a foot-wide circular tray that was divided into sections like a makeup kit. On that tray, I knew, was the needle.

I'd been resolute about this decision for months. *I'm getting an amnio.* And not because I'd terminate the pregnancy if doctors found something. (I was and had long been "pro-choice" for the world—pregnancy is such a complex knot of two lives that a woman should be able to consent to carrying that second life. But I was equally "pro-life" for myself.) I wanted the amnio because I desperately wanted to know.

So it shocked the hell out of me that, just as the needle entered the room, I hedged.

The doctor wore supportive clogs. I looked down at them as she approached the examining table.

"I'm worried about the risks," I told her.

"That's understandable. We have very good success rates here. But there's still a risk."

"We wouldn't do anything differently if we knew," I said.

The doctor seemed a hint surprised. "Well, that's something to consider. If you wouldn't do anything differently."

Of course we would do things differently. We'd research. I'd cry. We'd gather a team of doctors. We'd imagine a life with two disabled kids. I'd mourn. I'd feel guilty for mourning. Justin stood beside me, lightly swaying Fiona, who slept in the brown carrier on his chest. Her face angled upward, mouth agape. Her eyelids were a set of tiny watercolors, feathered by capillaries in pastel purples and pinks. All adult eyes were on me. How had months of resolution landed me here, in I-Don't-Know Land?

"Why don't we give you two some time to talk about it," the doctor said, and I nodded. She and the nurse left the room.

"It's your decision," Justin said.

"It's *our* decision."

"It's our decision," he said, "but you're the first among equals."

At eighteen weeks, my baby had ears. Websites told me they'd moved to their permanent position and now stuck out on the sides of her head. She could probably hear her parents.

"I want to know," I said.

"I know you do," he said.

"Don't *you* want to know?" I asked him. Our words would have been foreign to the baby—clipped whale moans. Mine worried, his resigned.

"It would be nice to know," he said. "But you seem like you *need* to know."

"But what if something happens?" I asked. Her own language was the drum circle of two heartbeats: hers fast, mine slow. Mine was beating faster than usual.

"It probably won't," he said.

The baby was the size of a mango. She was oblivious to mangoes. She was oblivious to rain and paper and refrigerators. She was oblivious to needles and chromosomes. Was she oblivious to my fear? Pop science told me no, that she could feel my feelings, that somehow she sensed my chemistry.

"But what if she has a syndrome?" I asked Justin. "Then I'd get to know the syndrome before I got to know her. At least with Fiona, I met her before I met her syndrome."

"That's true," he said.

Fiona's head languished sideways in the carrier. Looking at her, I felt those pangs that proved the cliché true: having a kid is like *having your heart go walking around outside your body*, said Elizabeth Stone. Because Fiona didn't walk, and might not walk, having her was more like *holding* my heart outside my body, and learning it was an extra fragile heart, one that might always require careful handling. My love for her was vast and full and all-consuming, and also hard. The hardest thing I'd ever known. I wanted the needle to tell me that, for this second child, love would be easier.

"But if something happened . . . ," I said, and I tried to think about that something: the cramping, the bleeding, the baby I wanted leaving me. All so I could get my assurance. The ground solidifying beneath my feet. The anti–Pema Chödrön. Twenty-two weeks of certainty and a sigh of relief.

There was a knock on the door. It opened, and the twenty-something nurse poked her head in, eyebrows raised hopefully. *All ready?*

I shook my head. *No, not yet ready.*

She bowed her head an inch and let the door close.

I sat with the weight of my pregnant belly on my lap. My baby was made of something like ten trillion cells, and each cell contained the chromosomes I sought, which meant I carried inside my body ten trillion messages that my eyes couldn't read and my hands couldn't reach and no mind could know, except by way of the needle.

"This is what we came here for," Justin said gently.

"I know," I said, and recalled his straight back in the driver's seat as he drove us over the snow-covered mountains.

When the doctor rapped her knuckles on the door and reentered, I nodded.

"Okay," I said.

"Yes?" she asked expectantly.

"We're ready," I said.

"Okay!" the doctor said with cheer, and nodded to the nurse behind her, who brought in the makeup tray and set it on the table. I lay back on the paper and inhaled, listening to the sound of the nurse unwrapping plastic.

But then the doctor said, "I know you already know this, but I'm required to tell you again. Afterward, you might feel some intense cramping—"

And that's when I sat up. "I can't do it," I said.

My certainty stunned me. It came with a ferocious decisiveness. It came from something inside me I didn't know I contained. And it came with a strange, hard-won ease: I had to protect this stranger-child. I didn't know her. I didn't know who she'd become. But my sole job was to keep things like seven-and-a-half-centimeter needles out of her room.

The doctor nodded, eyes closed, like she knew all along.

New England's rare winter sun streamed through the hospital's atrium. Beyond the doors, the snow on the ground glared white, the sky was bright blue, and the crisp, cold air hit my face. It filled my lungs. I opened the car door, squinting, giddy, laughing, and not just from high-pressure weather. I'd chosen love instead of fear. I'd chosen the baby over myself. I'd said yes to her over me.

This, by the way, is not to judge any woman who gets an amnio. There's enough mother-shame on this planet to fill oceans with sludge—we don't need more of it. Months later, when I tell this story to a forty-year-old friend with a toddler, she'll confess in a guilt-bound voice that she'd gotten an amnio with her son— just to know, just to ease her mind. And she'll say she thinks she's a lesser mom because of it, and I'll attempt to send her all the support a telephone receiver will transmit. *Hell no, friend. You are a kick-ass mom, a triumph*—because she is. But I'll also say: *You probably weren't calling your child Baby X.* To which she'll admit, she was not. Declining that needle was, for me, a powerful step in surrendering to the task ahead—which was to love this unknown child through my big fat fear. I didn't know my baby, my skeletal-headed, mango-size baby, but I'd sacrificed my yearning for her safety.

Days later, the euphoria dissipated. At three in the morning, awake from the bizarre hormonal injustice of pregnancy-induced insomnia, I tried to imagine the face of my future baby. The black blobs in my mind morphed into blurred ghosts. I sat upright in the dark for two hours, worrying, consigned to this truth: there was no way to make love easier.

In the winter of 2013, Fiona learned to sit. Her version was unconventional. Rather than bend her knees and bring her feet together like those uniform infants on the cover of *The Baby Book*, she locked her knees so her legs stayed straight, rotated her thighs inward so her toes pointed toward one another, and leaned forward. Her right hand splayed out on the floor in front of her as an anchor. I snapped a photo and cheered. Her wet coral lips spread wide in a grin. Lashes fanned from her eyes. As the minutes passed, she bent slowly at the waist so that her face crept closer and closer to her knees, like she was a limber athlete in a state of post-workout stretching. Eventually she tipped over. At twenty months old, she could sit independently for several minutes.

This was not all she'd recently achieved. Maybe due to her rigorous new therapy schedule, our girl could now eat a variety of strange textures, like cottage cheese and scrambled eggs and steel-cut oats—although she still needed us to spoon-feed every bite. She could grab things with her feet. She could use an "inferior pincer grasp" on bits of cereal. She could even sign "all done" after she finished eating, although her version of "all done" bore an uncanny resemblance to her version of "Itsy-Bitsy Spider."

Most usefully, she could choose what she wanted to eat in a lineup. If I put a few foods on the table—cottage cheese, pureed peas, pureed sweet potatoes, a cheese stick—she'd direct her fist toward something, her version of pointing, and say, "Mmm." This took some of the guesswork out of our long solo days together.

She'd also learned to feed herself things like pickles and orange slices. This might sound simple, but it was a feat for Fiona to grab hold of an object, bring it to her face, and let it enter her orally defensive mouth. She'd gnaw on it with a few front teeth—the only teeth she had so far—and this gave her a degree of independence, not to mention released some of the knots in my back.

That winter, bound up in the white-walled apartment that served as a barrier to Vermont's single-digit temps, I let literature become my window into a wider world. At any given moment, the tabs of five articles by disability scholars were open on my computer, and disability-related memoirs came through the mail. During Fiona's naps, I immersed myself in the stories of "minority bodies," as writer Elizabeth Barnes puts it, bodies that differed from that omnipresent *Norm*, a phrase that now conjured for me a man with average height and average weight and brown hair and a slight gut. He loved himself so much he put a definite article before his name. *The Norm.*

But it probably made sense to no one that, just as I was cresting into my third trimester, I added a particular book to my disability reading list: Emily Rapp's *The Still Point of the Turning World.* When her son is nine months old, Rapp learns that he has Tay-Sachs disease. Regardless of anything she does, her boy, Ronan, will lose all the developmental skills he has acquired in his short life—including seeing and eating—and die by the age of three. As such, *Still Point* isn't the starred book-club selection for pregnant women. But I needed this story. I needed to get as close as possible to the absolute worst that I feared.

One afternoon, I sat propped on a paper-covered table, half reading Rapp, half hoping that whenever my midwife walked into the examining room, she'd be too busy to ask the question she'd asked every other time. *What's your book about?*

By the grace of God, the midwife plopped herself in the office chair opposite me, opened her laptop, and said, "This will be short." She tapped at the keyboard. "I've got a baby in distress downstairs." Her eyes stayed glued to the screen.

"Any cramping?" she asked. "Any swelling?"

I answered in the usual way.

"I didn't get the amnio," I said, like she was a priest and I was making a confession.

"That's fine," she said, her eyes still on the screen. To my surprise, midwife appointments weren't the touchy-feely sessions I'd expected when I'd first chosen midwifery for prenatal care. My midwife ticked boxes, checking urine and weight, made sure neither I nor my baby were in obvious danger. But we didn't ever talk about the wild spiritual or even emotional dimensions of gestating a human person inside one's human person.

Toward the end of the brief appointment, though, I leaned back and let the midwife press her Doppler to my belly. Together we heard the heartbeat. A rapid horse. A runner. And my rushed midwife said something unnecessary, something as decadent as dark chocolate: "She's gonna be awesome," she said.

I was able for a short minute to believe her.

"I'm still terrified," I said.

"Why? Don't be!"

"It's just hard to imagine that there's no syndrome."

"Oh. Right." She thought for a few seconds. "Why don't we order you another ultrasound." She seemed buoyed by her idea, and she went to her laptop with gusto. "For therapeutic reasons."

"Really?" I said, like she'd just offered to pay for next week's groceries.

"Yeah. That's totally justified, medically speaking." She started typing. "You have a history. We'll order you a second ultrasound. It'll put your mind at ease."

Nobody is immune to disease or sickness or any other catastrophic event, read the book in my hand as I left the office; and yet, in my other hand was an order for images that I hoped would tell me otherwise.

T wo weeks later, I met with the midwife again. She explained the results of the test. The technician had found something concerning. My baby had an abnormally large abdomen.

"What does that mean?" I asked.

"Well, it might mean nothing. But it could mean something."

"Like what?" I asked.

It took several versions of this question to get my midwife to admit the worst-case scenarios. Eventually, she explained that my baby could have a gastrointestinal issue or microcephaly. The latter diagnosis appeared in Fiona's medical charts, listed beside *hypotonia* and *scoliosis*. I knew *microcephaly* was a marker for bigger concerns.

"Well, now I'm terrified," I said.

"Yeah," the midwife conceded. "It's terrifying."

Chapter Eleven

At twenty-two months old, just two months shy of her second birthday, Fiona had found it: her *yes*.

It was adamant and clear and universal: a nod. She didn't hinge at the neck with a subtle gesture. The root of her nod was her waist. She bowed her sixteen pounds back and forth in her high chair, knocking against the plastic. It was a full-bodied yes involving what seemed like half her muscular system. It was definitive and deliberate and adorable.

It also cut our mealtimes by a third. Combined with the powers of her itsy-bitsy spider version of "all done," a typical lunch now went something like this:

"Do you want water?" I ask. She does the full-bodied nod. I give her some water. This sounds simple, *I give her some water*, but she can't yet close her lips around the mouth of a sippy cup, let alone suck from it, so to *give her water*, I take a straw, drop it in a glass, close the top hole with my index finger, and put it in her mouth. Then I lift my finger so the water pools into her mouth. The hope is that one day she will close her lips around the straw and suck it herself. I keep doing the straw thing until she rumples her fingers together. "All done."

"Mmm," she says. It's half command, half request. She wants something.

"You want eggs?"

No response. Thanks to the power of yes, no response is now its own response.

"You want yogurt?"

Instant full-bodied nod, like she was waiting for this offer. I feed her spoonful after spoonful of her preferred flavor: plain, whole-fat. It collects in a white goatee around her chin. I wipe her face. "You want out?"

Full-bodied nod. I lift her out of her chair. Lunch is done. What once took sixty minutes now takes twenty.

"Do you want music?" I would sometimes ask, a ridiculous inquiry because Fiona always rejoiced at tunes. But now she could consent. Her full-bodied nod was furious in reply. I hit play on her favorite—Florence and the Machine's "The Dog Days Are Over"—and her face lit up at the ethereal opening notes. When the bass drums entered, banging out the rhythm in aggressive joy, she body-nodded to the beat.

"Do you wanna dance?" I'd sometimes ask, another silly question. She nodded, and I pressed her string-bean frame to my globular middle and bounced her to the thrumming bass drum. I was sporting a belly so big that friends told me *their* backs hurt just from looking at me. Her eyes shone with delight, her coral-lipped grin widened, and she let out her faint, almost accidental giggles—airy, high-noted bubbles. We were *synchronized*, as Le

Cardinal had said, *heart to heart, hand to hand*, string-bean body to gargantuan pregnant one.

But the most interesting thing about *yes* was its ability to clarify her desires to herself. In the middle of changing her diaper one day, I broke out into a tickle session. I walked my hands up her legs and toward her neck. She panted and wriggled, squealed and grimaced. I couldn't tell: Was she liking this or not? She sometimes responded to tickling with fussy whines, and I knew to stop. But on this day, she was borderline. Happy or mad? She hadn't decided.

"Do you want more?" I asked. "More tickles?"

She could have whined. She could have delivered that response of no response. Instead, she nodded. I resumed the hand-walks, and now my girl was all giggles. Why? Maybe because she'd had a say. Le Cardinal told Brown that helping his son find a *yes* was "the key for him to meet his intelligence." Maybe in the act of choosing, Fiona had met "her intelligence." Or rather, maybe she'd met her*self*, heard her desire and then made it known. This was liberty: to discern, and then to declare.

My water broke on St. Petronilla's Day. I had no idea that it was St. Petronilla's Day. I had no idea there was a St. Petronilla. I knew there was a St. Peter, and that the feminine form of Peter was *Petra*, meaning rock, but I didn't know Petronilla was another version of this name, and that she was rumored to be either the spiritual or actual daughter of St. Peter, Jesus's stubborn and loyal disciple. I just knew it was super inconvenient for my water to break on this particular Friday. Justin had a wedding rehearsal to lead that afternoon, a deacon's rehearsal and ordination that evening, and a wedding to officiate the next day. The baby was early—the baby we had already planned on calling *Petra.*

We hadn't given her this name so much as she'd claimed it for herself. A name came into my mind, and it wouldn't let go. *Petra.*

"Yes," Justin said. "That's it."

And that was it.

Why was it *it?* I'd asked on countless occasions. Of all the beautiful names I'd adored in my life, letting *Evelyn* and *Annabelle* roll around in my mouth like marbles, I'd never once given a thought to the somewhat obscure *Petra.*

"It's just it," Justin said.

The name attached itself to the baby inside me, or the baby inside me clung to the name, elbowing aside *Baby X* once and for all, and Justin and I could only oblige. It was another version of the lesson parenting continued to deliver: We're not in control of the people we're given to parent. We can only open our arms, say *welcome.*

So on a Friday, with my husband gone for the day, amniotic fluid leaked into a diaper-style towel I wrapped between my legs, and contractions cinched my middle like a thick belt. I moved from room to room, hiking up my towel with one hand and carting Fiona with the other, shoving things into a hospital bag. Fiona helped by sitting beside opened drawers, grabbing random articles of clothing, and throwing them on the floor with glee.

By three o'clock, a friend's car pulled into our driveway, and I gave Fiona a look. This look froze, for just a few seconds, the time-space continuum of my thirty-four years. Fiona's face was utterly unexpectant. Innocent and opened. I heard myself think, *I'm sorry.* She'd been touching my belly for months, reaching her tiny hand and letting it rest on the basketball of my stomach and looking up at me curiously, like *What's going on, Mom?* Justin and I had never left her overnight with anyone before. The next time she'd see me, her world would be rewritten. I would no longer be hers alone. I realize every parent of two must manage this potential tug-of-war, knowing a newborn will pull them from a child who only ever experienced their undivided attention. But in many ways, Fiona still required the care of a baby. And in other ways, she required even more care than a baby. Could I handle her needs as well as the ones of a newborn? I didn't know. My friend swooped Fiona up, gave me a minute to cover her face in kisses, and took her out of the house.

Two hours before I first became a mother to Fiona, I wanted to climb the walls of Justin's hatchback. He sped up the interstate toward the Ohio hospital. I writhed in the back seat. I wanted out of the car, out of my body, off the planet. I wanted to the moon. The moon seemed a very good place to be during the throes of transition.

Transition. It's a laughably gentle word for the reality it's meant to name—technically the period of labor when a woman's cervix dilates from seven to ten centimeters. But *transition* implies that a woman simply steps from one room to the next, like gliding in fuzzy slippers from the foyer to the tearoom, from the kitchen to the parlor. It's a dainty word befitting of day gloves and crumpets. *Oh, don't mind me, I'm just transitioning.*

Transition is seismic. It rattles the body, ruptures it with quakes fit for a seismometer. It feels—or at least felt to me—like an apocalypse. With Fiona, the contractions didn't just take my breath away. They turned me animal. I was roaring in that back seat, clawing at the car door, desperate to leave my body.

Once at the hospital, nurses pushed me on a gurney toward the maternity ward. I was in between contractions, and the walls sped by with carnival-ride thrill, so I found myself shouting, "Wheeee!" That's when I realized I was no longer on the earth. I wasn't among regular people and their earthly concerns about hangnails and coffee breaks and whether that tomato they'd eaten for lunch was too old. No, I'd been catapulted into the stratosphere. I'd wanted to go to the moon, and now I was there. Minutes later I was birthing in a tub, and a lone, brief video of me looks strangely peaceful. I'm leaning against Justin, my eyes closed. I'm quiet for a minute and then moaning the next. But inside, there was a purposeful annihilation, a razing of cities.

For years after, Justin would marvel to people about the singular focus labor requires. My husband saw in me the concentration he'd needed in order to get through a Zen *sesshin*—the intensive training period when monks meditate most hours of the day. While sitting half-lotus on a cushion, he couldn't simultaneously plan his breakfast, or fantasize about sex, or consider his job prospects. He was in too much pain. If he did let his mind wander, he'd want to flee. Get a coffee. Head out of the Japanese monastery and down the Kyoto hill to a noodle shop. He had to give himself over completely to the meditation, even lose himself in it. Labor, Justin saw, was the same. The physical demands absorbed a woman's mind and body completely. Justin evangelized about this to family members, to friends, even to parishioners from the pulpit, praising the spiritual requirements of labor. It took being a monk for a person to edge toward becoming a mother.

But now, at six o'clock on that Friday of St. Petronilla's Day, when my husband walked through the front door in his black cassock and asked how I was doing, I was weepy. "I know how painful this is gonna get. And I don't want to do it."

An hour later, I was standing at the hospital admissions desk, moaning at a whalelike caliber, attracting the stares of people in the ER. I was asked to complete a form, and I signed it with an X. There it was: my name was gone. I'd "transitioned," gone to the other side, been catapulted to a planet where people are too engrossed to have a self.

Hold nothing back, Trungpa had said, and maybe this is what he'd meant: to be so immersed in something that you lose yourself. Your pleasantries and your opinions and your plans. Your beliefs and your pride and your name. Like Christ on a cross, you empty yourself. You moan like a whale and sign your name with an X.

When it was time to push, I got on my hands and knees. "I can't do it," I said to my husband, something I suspect every laboring woman ever says.

"You're doing it," my husband said.

And then the annihilation was over, the cities had been razed, and the baby was outside of me, into the hands of the midwife and onto the bloodied hospital sheets. I was facing the mattress, still on my hands and knees, gasping from the pain.

And here is the important part, the weird part, the part I returned to again and again for months: I'd forgotten to worry. Forgotten to ask the questions. Forgotten to think about her face, or her chromosomes, forgotten to check her body for markers. I'd forgotten—*entirely*—about my concerns. I guess you could say I'd forgotten my*self*.

Instead, I thought, *Someone hold her. Someone love her*, because I was bruised and bleeding and gasping, and I couldn't do it myself. Love is perhaps what's left of us when we are no longer all the things we'd primped and planned.

So I told Justin: "Pick her up and hold her." And he did.

The next day, the on-call pediatrician told me what I already knew. My baby Petra did not have Wolf-Hirschhorn syndrome. She did not have any obvious syndrome. After he examined her, he actually said, "Lightning didn't strike twice here."

I understood what he meant. The rare thing hadn't happened again. My baby was well. "Perfectly healthy," he said. But I also registered the reality: a doctor just compared having Fiona to getting struck by lightning.

Petra's cheeks were already bulging, and her body was seven pounds something. The difference between my children's births was striking. With Petra, the room afterward was quiet and calm. The windows were dark from the night, and nobody rushed to blast bright light onto her body and inspect her. Nobody rushed to cut her cord. Nobody whisked her away from my view before I could even touch her. Nobody examined her with worried question marks in their brows, and nobody asked me if I did any drugs while pregnant. Nobody accused me of containing "bad soil" and nobody accused Petra of stemming from a "bad seed."

Instead, the midwife was congratulatory. The pediatrician called her *beautiful*. The nurses let us sleep uninterrupted—no frantic wakings every two hours—and they bid us farewell the next day.

So this is what it's like, I thought, *to have a baby the medical world sees as "right."* It is infinitely better to welcome a life into a world that also welcomes, unequivocally, that life.

When I got home, I looked up at the million stars dangling over the Green Mountains. I laughed at their inconceivability and rejoiced. *Thank you, thank you.*

Days after Petra's birth, I consulted Google. What interesting things had happened on the day of her birth? That's when I learned that she'd been born on the feast day of Saint Petronilla, otherwise known as Petranella, otherwise nicknamed Petra. That's when I'd learned that Petronilla is among the oldest saints. And that's when I'd learned about St. Petronilla's area of expertise. She's the saint invoked against the very thing that triggered Fiona's seizures: fevers.

I am prone to both wonder and skepticism. But about this serendipity, I felt more wondrous than skeptical. My daughter had, in utero, claimed for herself an unusual name and then been born on the saint's day of that name. And that saint is the one invoked against the thing that triggered her sister's greatest threat. I don't mean to say I thought that Petra was born for Fiona. But I've said it before—a family is a Celtic knot of love and need, the swirls of the selves looping infinitely around one another, binding together. There are over ten thousand saints canonized by the Catholic Church, and there are 365 days in a year, and what are the odds that a parent would choose a name for a child who would then go ahead and get herself born on the feast day of their namesake? I can't answer that math problem. I'm guessing the odds are even rarer than getting struck by lightning.

Fiona hardly paid attention to her new family member, and only then to claw at Petra's bald head and rake at it with zero concern for eyeballs. We'd said what every parent of a two-year-old must say when their child touches the new baby: *Gentle. Gennntle.* I was delighted by this singular expression of "Normal."

Normal is not just a range on the bell curve. It's also a community, a collective. To be Normal is to partake in a certain kind of belonging with others. This was one thing that made parenting Fiona unexpectedly hard—the isolation of *difference*. We could not often relate to other parents and their children. They could not often relate to us. About their two-year-olds, they bemoaned the task of baby proofing—plugging up outlets and putting locks on bleach cabinets. About our two-year-old, we hoped she'd maintain interest in eating orally so she'd never need a tube in her gut. Them: *She will not stop calling me—Momma, Momma, Momma!* Us: *I hope someday she can say Momma, Momma, Momma.* Their complaints were our longings. Even our moments of parenting comedy were in different realms. Them: *My kid found the tam-*

pons, removed every one from the box, and dropped them in our shoes! Us: *My kid totally seemed drunk after the technician sedated her for her last echocardiogram!* We longed to someday see our child possess the fine and gross motor skills for tampon hilarity.

The loneliness of so-called "special needs parents" is a statistical fact, and I think it's partly due to this invisible but palpable line that separates us from other families. Petra broke that line. She united me to others. Everything about her was what people expected, and as pathetic as it might seem, I cannot underestimate the relief of this, socially. Heading out into the world, I didn't have to don my armor against what I knew would be awkward stares and questions. I didn't have to hear the declarations of "How tiny!," which always preceded the nonchalant "How old?," which usually preceded either the uncomfortable silence or the nosy inquisitions of "Was she premature?" and even "Is she *okay*?" Women especially loved to ask of Fiona, in an incredulous tone, "How much does she *weigh*?," as though her body was an abomination in its smallness. I knew if I flipped the question around they would hear the offense: "And how about you, ma'am? How much do *you* weigh?"

Justin never sweated these encounters. One day, when he wore Fiona in a carrier during a walk, two college-age women fawned over her, then asked her age, then asked *why so tiny*. Justin explained her syndrome, and one woman replied, "But she'll live a normal life, right?" To which my husband laughed and, with characteristic warmth, said, "No!" That encounter would have sent me into a glum mood for at least an hour. Justin was unfazed.

With Petra, I didn't have to prepare myself for anything other than cheer. Her body made sense to strangers. It fit inside their expectations. "Oh, she looks new!" a woman would practically sing in an elevator or at the grocery store or in church, and I'd smile, because the story in the woman's head conformed to the reality. "Yes," I'd say.

"How old?" the woman would ask, and I'd smile again, because nothing about this encounter was going to get weird.

"Three weeks," I'd say.

And this was the best part: The woman wouldn't gasp or twist her face or go silent and look worriedly back to my kid. She would nod and smile in response, like the whole world made sense as a result of this dewy newborn.

Six weeks after giving birth to Petra, I let both girls lie faceup on the rug. One was eight pounds, the other sixteen. One was a newborn, the other was two. Fiona was long and lanky like a string bean. Petra, half her sister's length, curled into the shape of a coffee bean and rolled right.

Petra jerked her arms and legs. She brought her hands together and blinked at the lights and shadows of the living room. Fiona tapped her right fingers into the palm of her left hand, which the early interventionist told me was "stimming"—when a person repeats a sensory experience again and again, often for calming purposes. Fiona looked up at me with a grin. Scattered around her head were plastic stars. She could sit herself up and play with them if she wanted to, but she didn't want to. At two years old, she still preferred to be on her back.

Already you could tell that the baby was destined for a different trajectory. At just a few weeks old, Petra had legs springy with muscle, ready for reflex. Her body filled a floral onesie that had been loose around Fiona for months. Elastic-band pants that had always left an inch-wide gap at Fiona's waist now pulled tight across the baby's rump. If I laid Petra on her belly instead of her back, she could already lift her head off the floor an inch, something that had taken her sister four solid months.

Already—this was the word for the baby. *Already* rolling to her side, *already* eight pounds big, and I could tell in her dewy chub and taut, elastic muscles that she was *all ready* for a life of quick development. For sitting and crawling and walking, all without hours of therapy. The maps of baby milestones were embedded in her very DNA.

Fiona's body had always told a different story. Two years earlier, I'd been afraid to hear this story. Now, I heard it as no less beautiful than her sister's.

When I looked down at my girls, I noticed that my right foot was near Fiona and my left was near Petra, and this mirrored how I felt: It was like I straddled two countries. I had one foot in the land of "normal," one in the land of "rare." I was grateful to my girls for letting me hold dual citizenship. I could let both kids be themselves.

I got down on the floor with them. Back flat, I let the weight of myself sink toward the ground and heard my lower vertebrae and hip bones pop with relief. *Let go of the day,* a yoga teacher used to say when she instructed her students to lie supine. *Now let go of the week,* she'd say. *The month. The year.* A year always seemed an unfathomably large thing to release—each day its own pound. But today, with my kids on either side of me, I was happy to release three whole years. For thirty-some months, my body had attended to the demands of conceiving and gestating and birthing and nursing and supporting small humans. It was tired. It was gushy. It had little "core support," and it ached something fierce. So, *Let go of the last three years*, I heard myself think, *when you carried inside your body the bodies of two different girls*. Up drifted the smoky images of night feedings and nipple shields, an oxygen mask and an ambulance ride, a heart sculpture in a cardiology wing, a swaddled baby and a father bouncing her to reggae. My shoulder blades dropped a millimeter. My biceps and triceps and quads and calves released micro-distances from the bones. I let the earth, the wild and unreliable and beautiful earth, hold me.

And then I thought, *Why not release the future too?*—that uncertain destination, where the bodies of two girls would continue to tell their own stories.

Chapter Twelve

sat cross-legged on the living room rug with hunger-shakes. A screaming baby lay to my left, and a lean two-year-old lay to my right. It was lunchtime. The baby needed my boob. I needed a sandwich. The two-year-old was getting what she supposedly needed—a bottle—but she wouldn't drink it. I didn't know why. Fiona chucked it a good two feet. For a kid with arms you could encircle with a finger and thumb, she sure could throw.

Petra's screaming exacerbated my hungry, jittery nerves. New plan: I let her suck a finger on my left hand and used my right to grab Fiona's bottle and reposition it into her mouth. Fiona now drank as long as I held the bottle to her mouth. But hunched over, my back hollered. I'd already made it carry two humans for eighteen nonconsecutive months—now I was splitting it in two. *Screw this*, I thought.

Fiona's pacifier lay on the coffee table. I grabbed it and popped it into Petra's mouth. This calmed the baby for two sucks until she spit it out accidentally and wailed again, now with the ferocity of a steam train.

Fiona cried in response. Not her usual whiny "I'm not getting what I want" cry, but a red-faced frown with real tears. They dripped. I rarely saw this. I stood her up. "Come here," I said, and tried to press her against my chest. She'd spent most of the morning in therapy, and I'd spent most of it holding and nursing Petra. Maybe she needed to be held. But she wouldn't snuggle up. She just kept crying, looking down at her baby sister, who prevailed with the ferocious wails.

"Are you upset that she's upset?" I asked.

The other day, Fiona had reached out and held her baby sister's hand. After weeks of only raking the top of Petra's head, Fiona had made this gentle gesture of affection. Maybe my girl was experiencing empathy. Maybe she now loved her sister enough that, when her sister hurt, she hurt.

"Aww," I said as Fiona leaned away from my arms and bent at the waist. She had her eyes on Petra. She stretched her hand out. I let it reach her sister.

Fiona snatched the pacifier from beside her sister's face, made several attempts to put it in her own mouth, finally succeeded, and stopped crying.

It was a different milestone in sibling relations—the first rivalrous one. Perhaps no less vital than the first empathic response. I had to laugh at my mushy projections, as though Fiona were anything other than a two-year-old.

Fiona's sandy hair had grown into a ruffled mess befitting a bass player in a boy band. When wearing her mustard-and-brown-striped footy pajamas, she looked positively indie rocker.

She couldn't yet crawl, so she combined her most successful

gross motor skills to date: rolling and sitting up. One August evening, with Petra nursing in my lap, I watched Fiona arch her back on the living room carpet, spot a small orange ball several feet behind her head, sit up with the painstaking care of an exerciser doing the last of a hundred crunches, rotate sixty degrees, lie back down slowly so her head didn't bang, roll again, sit back up, and rotate so that, by lying down again and rolling one more time, the ball would be within arm's reach. She grabbed the ball.

"Got it," I said, but within a split second, she chucked it across the room. She played like this for several rounds. She rolled and sat up and rotated and rolled, making progress in zigzags. "Motor planning," the physical therapist called it. *Metaphor*, I called it. Her progress was never a straight line. My girl was a genius at finding abilities within her constraints.

She also continued to show off her unconventional communication skills. She combined the two sounds her mouth could muster—*uh* and *mmm*—and used the result to rename the most necessary element for the human body: water. She called it *um*, and she said it while waving her hand near her chin in a very rough approximation of sign language. When I gave her a sippy cup of water, she said it again, this time definitively. *Um.* I thought of her ingenuity: she was 70 percent water and couldn't manage the *W*, let alone the *T* or the *R*, so this most necessary element became what her mouth could say.

She sniffed whenever someone said the word "smell." She exhaled forcefully when someone said "glasses"—because she'd seen me clean mine countless times. She made a muffled woof when dogs I didn't notice appeared in picture books or passed by our window. This was especially impressive because she woofed without opening her mouth. In fact, all her sounds, save the *um*, were made in the back of her throat, lips closed. She even had a back-of-the-throat version of the word *poop*.

But I wondered about all the things she knew and couldn't say. All the things inside her that had no way of getting out.

Much of the events of motherhood—of parenting, of life—don't satisfy the chain-link effects of traditional drama. I can't think of any role in which this is more true than parenting a newborn, a job that requires round-the-clock tedium. There is the bottle and the other bottle and the other bottle after that. Or there is the midnight nursing and the two a.m. nursing and the four a.m. and six a.m. and seven thirty. There is soothing for the morning nap and soothing for the afternoon nap and then soothing for the hundreds of naps after those. The actions matter, of course, to the baby. But they don't contribute to some shapely portrait of your life's plot. Parenting a newborn might be the anti-plot.

For a year after Petra's birth, I continued to "stay home," which means my sole job was caring for two small children who were entirely dependent on me. This wasn't by choice. I wanted to teach again. I wanted to engage intellectually, to help students reflect on how smartphones or movies or buildings shaped their minds. I wanted to have a reason to wear something other than sweatpants. But I couldn't find work in our area. And if I had gotten work, I don't know that we could have found a daycare that would have met Fiona's needs. So Justin and I ended up in the traditional family arrangement I'd never expected: he earned the money, and I did most of the child-rearing, along with the emotional and physical work the role requires.

I once explained to my husband what it was like to prep the three of us—Petra, Fiona, and me—for a single Sunday church service. (He left the apartment at the same time that we woke up.) I explained the minute-by-minute orchestration, the juggling act of satisfying the baby's nursing demands, Fiona's hunger and feeding difficulties, both kids' diaper changes, the baby's cries of gas, Fiona's whines for attention, and my own caloric and hygienic requirements. I spent every single minute of three hours efficiently and entirely committed to very low-level demands on Maslow's Hierarchy of Needs. And if I didn't get the timing exactly right, we were locked in the apartment together another hour, caught in another cycle of feedings. It took everything I had, every minute, every muscle, to get all three of us fed, cleaned, and out the door. "And once I'm at church," I said to Justin, imagining Petra fussing on the carpet of the sanctuary's play area as I unstrap Fiona from the stroller, "Petra is ready to nurse again."

My husband shook his head in awe. "You gotta write that down!" he told me of my Sunday morning log. I shrugged. Why? To whom would it matter? "You might want to go back and remember it someday," he said. If, in my newborn fog, I did listen to my husband, I didn't, in my newborn fog, commit to memory where I put that log.

I haven't written about every echocardiogram, every EEG, every scoliosis X-ray, every seizure, every discussion about giving or not giving seizure meds, every way we had to measure and monitor and weigh our child for potential crisis. So many of them, narratively, would read like red herrings, sending a reader toward some possible disaster that never came. And yes, that is a blessing. With Fiona, we lived with a fairly high risk of wrenches flung into our lives, and this became its own kind of normal, a baseline, a horizon from which other stories emerged. It was tragic—and normal—to learn every few months that one of Fiona's WHS peers passed away. It was normal to drive a few hours every other month to see some pediatric specialist who always said, but might not next time say, "This is nothing right now. It could one day be something. It could even become life-threatening. We wait and see."

But in the fall of 2013, Fiona quit eating. Not altogether; yet food logs revealed to Justin and me that she was consuming about three hundred calories a day, less than half of what nutritionists said her body required. When I offered her spoonfuls of pureed sweet potatoes or a high chair tray's worth of rice puffs, my daughter clamped her mouth down like a fortress. She sung the song of her whiny *mmms*. No way that rice puff or orange glob was entering her body. My girl was on a modified hunger strike. Miniature Gandhi, and I didn't know the reason. Because she was teething? Because she now had a sister and wanted to exert some control? Because her oral aversions had finally caught up with her?

Her physical therapist, Rachel, always a voice of reason, expressed concerns that Fiona wasn't getting enough calories for day-to-day living, let alone therapy. How could she progress developmentally if she wasn't eating enough? I nodded, piling this concern onto myself.

"Eat!" I told her at meals, holding a plastic spoon inches from her shut lips. *Mmm*, she whined, and pulled her head as far from the spoon as she could. "Eat," I commanded, "or else we're gonna have to drill a hole in your gut."

That was the question: to get or not to get a g-tube. Roughly half of people with Wolf-Hirschhorn syndrome have one, and Justin and I wondered if now was finally Fiona's time. We consulted with doctors, nutritionists, feeding specialists. We agonized over this question for months. The look of Fiona's body amplified everyone's fears. She grew longways but never wider. Chicken legs, chicken arms. Her elbows and knees were wider than the flesh above them. She was two and still couldn't fill out the waistbands of her sister's six-month-old pants. I stored those pants as potential shorts for a future in which Fiona ate. Would getting her a g-tube increase her strength so she could better develop? Would getting one *decrease* her tolerance for oral feeding and make her reliant on the tube? Mothers online weighed in. *Get the tube! It changed our life.* Or, *Don't get the tube! It ruined everything.*

In the end, no doctor signed off on a g-tube. They thought we should press ahead with oral feeding. So Justin and I labored over every spoonful, tallied each cheese bite, sweated over the meager calories and the willowy body of our kid. "Eat!" Justin said, spoon held. "Or we're gonna have to drill a hole in your gut."

And then, after an eternity of six months, Fiona's appetite returned with a vengeance. She ate three scrambled eggs with ketchup for breakfast. She downed whole cups of cottage cheese for lunch. She devoured five cheese sticks in one day. To this day,

I have no idea why my girl stopped eating. "Teeth," I have told myself, because her teething was erratic and super-delayed compared to typical kids. But the red herring of her hunger strike revealed a deeper problem: our child had almost no way of communicating what was going on inside.

'd stumbled across Dana Nieder's "An Open Letter to the Parent of a Child with Speech Delays" when Fiona was not yet two. By that point, we had a small collection of oral motor tools, among them the G-shaped, grape-flavored chewy tube and a white-and-blue, bumpy-ended chewy tube. I'd also seen Fiona's speech therapist rub a large cucumber-shaped vibrating thing all over Fiona's mouth in an attempt to activate her muscles, and I did not have the heart to ask the therapist what this object was, because I did not want to hear the likely answer: it was a vibrator.

Many kids with WHS do not learn to speak. It was entirely possible that Fiona would not either. And yet we knew our girl had things to say.

In her letter, Dana Nieder offers a portrait of her daughter, Maya, who was five years old at the time. Nieder writes,

> With her voice, she can say "Mommy" and
> "Daddy." With her talker, she can tell me that
> today is Friday and she's going to the therapy gym
> in the afternoon and she wants to ride on the big
> swing and the tire swing and do an art project. With

her voice she can say "bus." With her talker, she can
tell me who she sat next to at school and what they
talked about and what she wants to have for dinner
and whether she's feeling tired or happy or cranky.

With her talker, she tells jokes and is sassy and is
proud, so proud, to tell us things and to connect with
us. If she only had her speaking voice, I would barely
know her.

What if my daughter spent her life in a body that could never fully express herself? What if I raised a child nobody—including me—could fully know?

If Fiona's mouth never mastered the complexities of consonants and vowels, there was another way. Nieder argued that if I woke up one day from an accident and couldn't speak because my voice needed healing, someone would hand me a paper and pen. They'd give me another form of communication. My child needed the same. She needed what the speech therapy world called AAC: augmentative and alternative communication.

Possibly the earliest electronic communication device was made in 1960: a typewriter operated by mouth. The designer, Reg Maling, volunteered at a hospital for paralyzed patients and saw that they communicated with a bell. In response, he invented the POSM, a typewriter with a sip-and-puff controller that extended like a gooseneck. A decade later, developers of electronic communication devices were thinking about portability. In a photo of one device from 1973, a suited man with a skinny tie is holding a clunky but small keyboard, which is connected by a wire to a rectangular display pinned beside his lapel. The pin reads "Hello." The system was called the Talking Brooch.

At about the same time, educators were designing communication boards for people who couldn't speak due to oral motor challenges or intellectual disabilities. The boards were covered in images or words or a combination of both, and nonverbal students gestured to them in order to "talk." Some educators worried that these boards would permanently halt a kid's oral speech. In some instances, speech pathologists were even fired for providing students with communication boards. But research showed the opposite: the boards often enhanced rather than harmed a child's oral speech development.

In the mid-nineties, communication boards and computer innovations coalesced to form speech-generating devices, durable portable computers that spoke words with the touch of a button. In 2010, Apple turned this ten-thousand-dollar piece of medical equipment into a tablet you could grab at your local mall. But another philosophical bump emerged, one that persists today: some educators believed kids needed to "prove themselves" on lower-tech communication systems, like laminated picture cards, before getting the opportunity to try out high-tech (read: costlier) systems. AAC advocates and experts reject this as a "burden of proof" dehumanizing to nonverbal people. They operate on a simple, beautiful principle: Communication is a human right. Everyone deserves a way to make themselves known.

.   .   .

'd asked Fiona's early interventionist, Blair, to help me determine a viable system for Fiona. She agreed but rejected an iPad
off the bat. They just turned into toys, she said, and recommended laminated cards with pictures instead. She warned that
it was a difficult skill for a kid to associate a picture card with a
real object or action, and only after Fiona showed proficiency
with the cards could we move on to something more expensive
like an iPad. In her blog, Dana Nieder calls therapists like Blair
"gatekeepers." They unconsciously stand between a kid and the
right to communicate. I had to figure out a way around Blair,
who, when she finally did bring cards three months after she
promised, decided they probably wouldn't work because Fiona
liked to "stim" on them.

Blair had taken the lead on AAC because she spent more
weekly hours with Fiona than the speech therapist did, and also
because she'd received recent training on AAC. But one afternoon I mentioned AAC to the speech therapist, Sue, who was
playing games with Fiona on the living room rug. Sue told me the
state had AAC resources up in Burlington. They were a part of
something called the I-Team.

Months later, the I-Team descended upon my living room. It
consisted of two middle-aged women named Maureen and Tammy,
who sat on our couch and watched Blair engage with Fiona in
therapy. It was December of 2013. Fiona was two and a half years
old, propped up in a small wooden chair with a detachable tray.
Blair asked Fiona to respond to different play cues. Fiona kissed
a doll. She made the doll dance. She put balls in a bucket. She

wanted things and got frustrated. She whined through her closed lips. She was given picture cards, and she sniffed them and tapped them against her left hand. Intermittently, she flirted with the new visitors. She rotated her head ninety degrees and blinked at the women on her couch and cocked her head to the side just so, as a way of asking: *What are you doing here? Do you think I'm adorable yet?*

Justin and I laughed from the sidelines.

After observing the therapy for about thirty minutes, Maureen asked me, "Does Fiona ever put two words together?"

"She doesn't really have any words," I said.

"I mean any form of words. Does she combine two signs? Or a sign and a point? Or a point and a sound that means a word?"

"Yes!" I said, thinking back to a few weeks earlier. After my laptop stopped playing a perky *cat-says-meow* type of kid song, Fiona banged two fists together—the ASL sign for *more*. "More what?" I'd asked. I'd expected her to look toward the laptop, or grunt or whine. Instead, she'd waved her right hand wildly in the air. For months, her speech therapist had been signing *music*—motioning her right hand over her opposite forearm like she was conducting an orchestra. Fiona's wild waving across her chest was an approximation. Two words. *More music.* I was ecstatic. "She made a sentence!" I said to my husband later that day, even though it wasn't grammatically a sentence. But it *felt* like a sentence! Two words put together was like two building blocks clicked into place. It was a way to build a house, a place to live. Language could work like that, could offer shelter. This I knew.

I told Maureen that, since that afternoon, Fiona had signed *more music* a dozen times.

Maureen nodded with very wide eyes, like she was gazing upon a miracle she entirely expected. "That's a *two-word utterance*," she said with all the reverence of a devout Catholic spotting the pope.

Maureen explained that this "two-word utterance" put Fiona in a different cognitive category than a child who only ever utters one word at a time. Typical children make their first one-word utterances at twelve to eighteen months. They combine two words at eighteen to twenty-four months. Two years old. At two and a half, my girl had never been assessed so closely to kids her age. Whenever a therapist measured her according to sound production, they noted the absence of *buh-buh* and *ga-ga* and said she was further behind than a six-month-old. But Maureen shook her head at all of that. My girl made two-word utterances.

This is partly why I bristle to this day when doctors ask me the question, "How old is she, developmentally?" I offer them her present age, and they tilt their head an inch and clarify what they mean. "But how old is she, according to developmental tests?" I say that she's been alive X number of years, and I let them suss out their normative obsessions.

The two-word utterance was significant, Maureen said, not only because it indicated Fiona's cognitive capabilities; it also indicated her vocabulary size. Kids use one-word utterances when they have twenty to thirty words at their disposal. They combine two words when they know fifty or more. Fiona knew a lot of words. Far more than we realized.

Justin couldn't stay for the whole session. In his black cassock, he stood at the door, waved to everyone, and split. Fiona looked at me, then looked at the shut door, pointed her fist to it, and said *Mmm*.

"Where did he go?" I asked for her. "He went to work."

"This gap between her expressive and receptive communication," Maureen said, "is only going to continue to widen. She's going to understand far more than she'll be able to communicate."

I sat on the floor of my living room, sobered by the thought. If we did nothing, my daughter would continue to understand more and more of the world around her, and yet have very little ability to make that world understand her. This seemed to me, the writer, like living in a locked glass box: you could see out, but you couldn't reach others.

Blair described their work with the cards and Fiona's "stimming" response to them. She mentioned Fiona's very limited fine motor skills, her inability to hit targets on an iPad with any accuracy.

Maureen cut through all of this. "Her fine motor skills don't need to stop her from having access to language. There are ways around that."

Tammy, her I-Team co-conspirator, chimed in. "There are special gloves. Key guards. A stylus. Or her partner can use the iPad for her until she has the fine motor abilities."

Maureen nodded. "Linguistically, she can handle anything."

I was holding a notebook and pen. I wrote down that sentence. I wrote it down because it shocked me. I wrote it down because it was unlike any sentence I'd heard about my child. *She can handle anything.* I even repeated it aloud to Maureen, like a question without the upturned intonation.

"Yes." Maureen turned toward Blair. "Are you starting her on an alphabet app?"

Blair was quiet a beat and said, "Um."

I looked at Maureen and shook my head.

"Why not? Get this kid writing!"

This kid writing. This kid who couldn't isolate a finger yet. *This kid writing.* Maureen was a beacon. A lighthouse in my living room, beaming optimism like it was nothing more than obvious truth.

"It's not a matter of *if* she can use a communication device," Maureen said conclusively, "but *what* and *when*. She has both the high-receptive communication and the motor control to use a device."

Communication is a fundamental human right. Maureen embodied this powerful ethos. She rattled off some options for us to consider. Apps that could be downloaded to an iPad. Companies that made designated speech-generating devices. We were nearing the end of our scheduled hour together, and the I-Team had other kids to visit. Maureen suggested that we meet again in a few months and, until then, Fiona should test out some systems.

I mentioned the app that Maya, Dana Nieder's daughter, used.

Maureen nodded. "She reminds me of Maya, actually." Maureen too read Nieder's blog. She looked down at Fiona, who by now had rolled herself beneath an ottoman and was doing leg presses with it. She lifted it three inches and then let it fall with a thud.

"The time to act is now." Maureen looked around at all the

adults in the room. "Because what do you have that's more important than language?"

I nodded profusely.

"What's more important than language?" she asked again. There was a pregnant pause. "Maybe health," Maureen acknowledged. "But after that?"

The I-Team stood up from the couch and collected their bags.

"Good-bye," Maureen said.

"Good-bye, Fiona!" Tammy said with cheer.

They both smiled and waved to my daughter, who paused her leg presses to gaze at them with her clear, knowing eyes. Somewhere from the back of my daughter's throat emerged the musicality of the phrase, the exact notes of the words, even as her mouth formed none of the consonants or vowels. *Good-bye.*

Chapter Thirteen

~⌐

once listened to the designer of the Apple mouse, Dave Evans, describe something called a *gravity problem*. "I'm getting older," he told NPR reporter Shankar Vedantam. "So I'm doing that thing of putting on a little extra weight. And it's starting to bother me, so if I said . . . I've got this terrible problem. It's gravity. . . ." We would laugh. Nobody can take seriously the person who blames gravity for their extra pounds.

"Design is oriented to action," Evans explained in the interview. "Which means if you can't do something about it, if it's not actionable, it's not a problem. It's a circumstance. And a lot of people have a problem that isn't a problem. It's just a circumstance." This is what Evans calls a *gravity problem*.

I listened to this interview a few years after my encounter with the I-Team. Never would I have guessed that the designer of the Apple mouse could offer so elegant a way into perceiving disability. Gravity is neutral. It's factual. It's the circumstance with which we live—the thing that keeps us bound to the earth and hurling around the sun. Likewise, Fiona's body was factual, a circumstance. Her fourth chromosome was as much a problem as gravity, which meant not at all.

What I loved about the approach of AAC was that, in the realm of communication, it freed my daughter's mouth from being a problem. In therapy, we didn't have to repeat again and again the sounds we wished she would make. Speech therapy didn't have to look like trying to "fix" a circumstance, because oral speech didn't have to be Fiona's only avenue of communication. Speech therapy could instead be an opportunity to design our way around the real problem, which was that my daughter needed a new way to talk.

From December to March, Justin and I and all of Fiona's therapists embarked on an intense deliberation over what communication system might best fit our daughter. We scheduled a meeting with a representative from a company that makes "designated communication devices." We learned that they cost ten grand but that Vermont Medicaid would pay for one. We researched communication apps for iPads and tried out several. I emailed back and forth with Dana Nieder. Meanwhile, to buy time, Blair and her assistant brought more laminated picture cards to our house, along with a binder, and we arranged the cards by category. There were pages of cards for people, for food, for songs, for activities, for TV shows. Fiona was now partial to *Yo Gabba Gabba*, a show with loads of music and a retro vibe, including a male host who wore a skintight orange jumpsuit and a foot-high orange beehive. She requested the show by touching a picture of his face and looking at me longingly.

One afternoon, Sue the speech therapist sat cross-legged on the living room floor and showed Fiona an iPad. On the iPad were several photographs of toys. A Mr. Potato Head. A ball. A set of stackable, star-shaped rings. Sue touched one of the images. A feminine, electronic voice said, *I want the Mr. Potato Head.* She brought the classic brown head and his bucket of parts from her ginormous tote bag. "Do you want to play with the Mr. Potato Head, Fiona?"

Long pause.

"I don't know what you want unless you tell me," Sue said in that animated, enunciating, chipper way only early childhood educators can master.

Fiona shook her head.

"O-kay!" Sue pulled out the varicolored, star-shaped rings stacked on a plastic stand. "Do you want to play with the star toy?" she asked.

Fiona nodded.

"O-kay!" Sue touched the photograph of the toy on the iPad. *I want the star toy*, the electronic voice said.

By the end of the session, Sue was encouraging Fiona to touch the images on the iPad herself. They were large enough that Fiona could cover them with her splayed hand without bumping into other pictures. *I want the shape sorter. I want the ball.*

I'd done enough research to know that this wasn't what Maureen called a "robust communication system." While it was accessible to Fiona's fine motor skills, it didn't offer a range of language functions. I'd learned that we used language for at least twenty different purposes. We described the sky, told someone they were wrong, declared things ours, changed subjects, exclaimed that this cookie was amazing. The problem with Blair's well-meaning and ever-growing binder was that it contained only nouns. Food and people and TV shows. These were high-preference objects—things Fiona loved—but nouns alone couldn't convey the range of a person's communication needs. In fact, nouns tended to lock a communicator into requesting. A child touches a photograph of an apple, and the adult with her says, "You want the apple?" But what if the child wanted to say, "That apple is smaller than the one I ate yesterday," or "Apples are hard like balls, but if you throw them on the floor, they will bruise." Likewise, an iPad app that only said, "I want the star toy," wasn't "robust" enough, as Maureen put it, to support a child's burgeoning creativity. Fiona might someday want to say, "I hate this star toy," or "This star toy reminds me of a spaceship," or "Can I have not just one but a hundred star toys and give them to every child on the block?"

According to Maureen, Fiona was already using a range of language functions, just not in words—she used vocalizations and facial expressions and gestures and signs. When she stared at the door where her dad had been, then turned to me, then turned back toward the door and made a sound, this was her way of asking a question. ("Where'd he go?") When she watched the orange-beehived host on her favorite TV show and then smiled at me, this was her way of commenting. (Perhaps, "That beehive is bananas!") When she reached for an object, looked to a therapist, and made a sound, she was requesting. ("Can I have that?") When I held a spoon of food in front of her and she thrust her cheek into her high chair and grunted, she was rejecting. ("Hell no, Mom!") I was learning that the design of a communication system had powerful implications. It could severely limit a child's potential or open it up.

Fiona needed a system that allowed her to combine words— all different kinds of words. Nouns and verbs, adjectives and pronouns. The problem was this: the more words a device had, the less accessible those words would be. An iPad screen had only so much physical real estate. If you put six words on a screen, they might be super accessible to Fiona's small but imprecise hands. But then, well, you'd only have six words. Some apps were designed to house folders upon folders of vocabulary, but that's a lot for a three-year-old to navigate. Fewer folders meant one of two things: fewer words or smaller targets. The app that Dana Nieder's child, Maya, used had 119 targets on the main screen. The designers of the app, Speak for Yourself, said these were the most frequently used and most powerful words in the English language. They include words like "no" and "stop" and "help" and "me."

Things I absolutely wanted Fiona to be able to say:

Stop that.

Help me.

But the targets on this app were teensy. At about one-by-one-and-a-half-centimeters wide, they were no larger than the print of an adult's index finger. For Fiona, this would be a problem. Still, if we matched the size of a communication system's vocabulary to her fine motor skills, my girl wouldn't be able to communicate all that we already knew she had inside her, let alone all that she'd have to say tomorrow or next year.

"How many words" became a frequent subject of debate among members of Fiona's support circle, and it came up again at our second meeting with the I-Team. Tammy and Maureen again sat on our living room couch, and the other adults—Blair, her assistant, Fiona's occupational therapist, and I—sat in surrounding chairs. We bounced numbers around. Everyone now agreed that Fiona needed some kind of technological device that produced speech. But what should be the vocabulary capacity of the device? How many words could she handle? How many could we fit on a screen and reasonably expect Fiona to touch with accuracy? Ten? Twenty? Thirty?

How many words would we give my daughter?

Maureen, blessed Maureen, interjected with a sentence as sharp as a tack. "You give her *all* the words," she said.

The room went silent. *All the words?*

"She under*stands* them," Maureen said to the silence. "So give them to her."

This was what Maureen had meant two months back when she'd said, "Linguistically, she can handle anything." Fine motor wise, Fiona couldn't yet handle thousands of words. Her fingers had a lot of development ahead of them before they could touch a centimeter-wide button. But this, according to Maureen, shouldn't stop us from giving Fiona access to all the words she can *linguistically* handle. She is hearing thousands of words. Give them all to her.

It sounded so abundant and hopeful. Here, child, *slipper*. Here, *lemur* and *butter* and *daffodil* and *rampage*. Here, *avalanche* and *ornery* and *alleluia*. Here, my beloved: all the words ever. I felt my chest expand, blooming a billion flowers. This was the way—this bold and big and brave way—this was the way I wanted to love my daughter.

And what about the fine motor limitations? someone asked.

"You model," Maureen said. She explained that we didn't start talking to babies once they showed the capacity for verbal speech. We started early. We started at birth. "It's the same with AAC," Maureen said. "You model the system. You use it when you talk to her. And you don't need to put any pressure on her to use the system in reply."

Maureen explained that a baby needs to hear oral speech for about a year before she utters her first word. AAC experts apply the same timeline to kids learning alternative communication systems. Expecting Fiona to use a system almost immediately would be a bit like expecting a wee babe, on the very day that his mother squeezed him from her body, to repeat *mama*. Whatever system we decided on, Maureen said we should model it for a full year before we expected any results.

"You're teaching her a new language," she said. "Right now, you don't have a shared language."

I nodded at this painful truth. Language created space. This I always knew. It made space for emotions, for needs and wants and refusals. I spoke English. Fiona spoke grunts and faces and fisted points. I could speak her language if I needed. She couldn't speak mine. I saw then that an AAC system could give nonverbal people and their family members not just a shared language but a place to meet. A common ground. A shared country, all on the terrain of something like an iPad screen.

We bought an iPad with money from Vermont's Flexible Family Funding. I set to modeling. I used both my mouth and the iPad, which we called "the talker," to speak to Fiona.

"What do you want to eat?" I'd ask, and hit *Want* and *Eat*, both of which were part of the front screen's vocabulary. This front screen, always open and available, offered 119 "core words," the most common words in the English language. Eighty percent of our daily speech draws from these core words. Each of those words could then open up an additional screen of another 119 words, considered "fringe vocabulary." The app spoke whatever words a user touched in enthusiastic electronica. *Want! Eat!*

I showed Fiona the real-life options, and she gestured toward what she wanted: a cheese stick. I opened up the screen of foods and touched her choice. The electronic voice said, "Cheese stick." Then I got her request.

This was called, in the AAC world, "aided language input": showing a person how to use the system. And there was, according to experts, no maximum amount of "aided language input" that you could do for a student. Use the device as often as possible, experts recommended. So I had my hands all over that iPad and, when he was home, Justin poked at it too. We modeled *stop*. We modeled *no*. We modeled *hi Fiona* and *find cup* and *big hair* and *love you*.

Fiona smacked at the screen with a splayed hand, lighting up several rectangular icons at once, drawing from the talker's electronic mouth a train of strange poetry: *Thing call then so from well up up up up.*

The average number of words an adult English language speaker uses is about twenty thousand. With a fourteen-thousand-word capacity and a built-in keyboard to help her spell anything she wanted, the system we'd chosen for Fiona's iPad made the assumption, vast and spacious as the American plains, that our not-yet-three-year-old girl could handle anything, that she might someday need or want, for instance, to name presidents and spell "Mississippi" and identify the Pythagorean theorem. This assumption felt grand and joyous and loving. But it still hinged on her ability to do one small, tedious, seemingly insignificant thing: isolate a digit on her hand.

When I took out her talker, Fiona panted with giddiness. She loved looking at it. But when she touched it, she splayed her hand like a person high-fiving, and I sometimes felt like a fool. When her tiny hand clumsily struck six words at once, and the device released its strange and garbled electronic poetry like a robot at an avant-garde reading, I again felt like a fool.

At out sleep

that right with

not not there color.

When Fiona's occupational therapist first saw the app and said, unmistakably loud, "Whoa!" I did indeed feel foolish. The therapist pulled her head back an inch, as if her eyes sought reprieve from the accosting 119-word screen. And when the physical therapist saw the device, she said, "Even *I'm* overwhelmed."

These highly experienced professionals we'd known and trusted for nearly two years, the same ones who'd set lofty, ambitious goals for my girl and then ensured that she met them, were now expressing *doubt*. They never said, *I don't think she can do this.* They swallowed their doubt and set to incorporating the device into therapy, straining to locate words that would be relevant to their sessions. But I couldn't stop myself from wondering if perhaps I was truly a fool.

The word "fool" comes from the Latin *follis*, meaning "bag." *Follis* eventually came to mean a person whose head was as empty as a bag. Full of air. Etymology points in a hundred directions, two of which are backward and forward. *Fool* is etymologically related to the Old French, *fol*, which meant a madman, an insane person, or an idiot. And there it is: bagged inside that last word, *idiot*, is a partial history of ableism in language.

At the turn of the nineteenth century, people with intellectual disabilities were called "feeble-minded." In 1910, American psychologist and eugenicist Henry H. Goddard decided that this term was too broad and imprecise. He translated an intelligence quotient test from French and used it to create three distinct categories, each with its own label: "The feeble-minded," he wrote, "may be divided into (1) those who are totally arrested before the age of 3, so that they show the attainment of a 2-year-old child or less. These are the idiots. (2) Those so retarded that they become permanently arrested between the ages of 3 and 7. These are imbeciles. (3) Those so retarded that they become arrested between the ages of 7 and 12. These were formerly called feeble-minded, the same term that is applied to the whole group. We are now proposing to call them morons. . . ."

Idiot, imbecile, moron. Today they mean the same: *Dumb, dumb, dumb.* In fact, according to an etymology dictionary, it took Goddard's coined term "moron" only twelve years to become an insult. And in turning these words into insults, we've underscored our cultural disregard for people with intellectual disabilities, although maybe we've also made an accidental point: it's inherently insulting to categorize a person by their so-called developmental age. But that was Goddard's professional focus. He shared an interest with eugenicist Francis Galton across the pond: both men sought to raise the intelligence of their respective countries. Both men sought to prevent intellectual disabilities from entering the population. "The idiot," Goddard said, "is not our greatest problem. He is indeed loathsome. . . . Nevertheless, he lives his life and is done. He does not continue the race with a line of children like himself. . . . It is the moron type that makes for us our great problem."

For centuries before Goddard's hierarchy, *idiot* was the blanket term for the intellectually disabled. A sixteenth-century English lawyer defined it this way: an idiot "is so witless that he cannot number to Twenty, nor can tell what Age he is of, nor knoweth who is his Father or Mother." When I walked through the front door, Fiona pointed her fist at me and said, "Om!"— Mom. Likewise, if I asked her, "Where's Dad?" she pointed her fist in his direction. But she could not say our names. If an English lawyer from the sixteenth century had asked her, "Who is thy father and thy mother?" I doubt her answers would have satisfied him.

Around the same time that I was researching AAC, I became fascinated by the etymology of these words. I learned that *retarded* was once considered progressive, an improvement from *feeble-minded*. I learned that Goddard coined the term *moron* by borrowing *moros*, Greek for fool. And with *fool*, we've ended up where we began: with *follis* and a bag of air.

So when I heard the therapists suggest skepticism at the complex iPad screen, and when I felt just beneath my skin that self-conscious feeling of embarrassment, I knew the word to capture my feeling—*foolish*—was ableist. My head was not full of air. My daughter's head was not full of air. I couldn't call myself a *fool* for trying to give my daughter the opportunity to define herself beyond that very word and its many rejected cousins.

With Maureen's help, Fiona's therapists and Justin and I tried out key-guards to make the app's icons more accessible. We tried a stylus. We took one of her socks and cut a teensy hole through it so that her index finger could poke through, so the device would respond to just one finger. But none of the accommodations quite worked in helping the complex app become more accessible for Fiona. (In the case of the key-guard, which was a raised clear grid that differentiated the rectangular icons on the screen, Fiona's enthusiasm for the talker deflated like a birthday balloon. She wouldn't touch it.) We had to stay the course, which was to model the words ourselves and wait for her fine motor skills to catch up.

We also responded enthusiastically to the talker whenever Fiona made it speak. We aimed to treat it like her voice. "Call," she'd say, and Justin and I would perk up. Given her fine motor skills, the word was most likely accidental, but that wasn't the point. To teach her the talker's power, we had to give it power. So we'd stop ourselves mid-conversation and ask, "You want to call someone?" Justin would grab his cell phone. I'd tap "family," and the page of family members would open, displaying tiny icons of grandma and grandpa and aunts and uncles. Fiona smiled, rapt, and considered her options. This was her favorite page.

Fiona's hand was not a problem. Fiona's hand was gravity. It was a condition under which we worked. The "problem" became whether I—and the other adults in Fiona's world—could incorporate the talker into our daily lives. And that was a problem I could solve. I could model the hell out of that communication device.

Because Fiona had aged out of early intervention, the summer that I was modeling the talker I was also prepping my non-verbal, non-walking, very tiny kid for preschool. It was a good preschool, where Fiona's occupational therapist and speech therapist already worked, and where kids with various disabilities learned side by side with typically developing peers. Fiona, who had spent most of her first three years at home with her mother, was getting sick of me anyway. By whining at me a lot and lighting up when people visited, she made clear that she was desperate for more action.

I was too. That summer, I had a phone interview with the chair of an English department at a college an hour and ten minutes away. After two years out of the workforce, and after logging at least seven thousand hours feeding small people, I worried I wouldn't sound relevant or valuable to an academic professional. But the chair invited me to teach two classes of composition. I would earn enough money to cover Petra's childcare *and* give myself a teaching life two days a week. (Fiona's publicly run preschool was fully covered by the state.) I'd have a reason to wear something other than hoodies, a reason to inhabit an identity other than *Mommy*, and I'd get to return to my beloved place in the classroom. I rejoiced. That summer, I was not only modeling the talker; I was making a syllabus, a freshman-level study in personal writing. It contained a unit on disability memoirs and the construction of Normal.

And I also made a video: it featured Fiona in a plush, light blue chair small enough for her. She's wearing a royal blue tank top that draws out her brilliant eyes, and she looks expectantly into the video camera. She's pink-complected and just a little cheeky. Her boy-band hair is now growing out into a wavy bowl cut. A few strands near her forehead are damp—we must be in the middle of a Vermont heat wave.

"Okay, Fee," my voice says from behind the camera. She looks to her right, raises her eyebrows as if discovering a profound thought, and grins. She knows what's about to come. "Can you sign . . . spider?" I ask.

A rare open-mouthed smile wrinkles the bridge of her nose. She brings her little hands together and rumples them like they're crawling on each other.

"Spider!" I say. "Very nice!"

She taps her right fist to her mouth. She's offering another word in her signing catalog.

"Eat?" I say. "Yes."

She drops her hand and looks down, waiting.

"Can you sign . . ." And again, as soon as I speak, her face is alight with smirking expectation. What word will I offer next? "Silly?"

She shakes her head around.

"Silly, silly, silly," I say.

She sticks out her tongue and grins, creating dimples at her cheeks. She is utterly silent, and yet she's speaking a thousand things.

"Can you sign shake?" I ask.

A baby from the background says, "Shay." It's Petra, already approximating speech at a year old.

Fiona stretches her arms out and shakes them.

"Shake, shake, shake," I say.

Preschool meant that my daughter was about to enter the public fray alone. Without an ability to fully communicate, hours of her day would remain a mystery to Justin and me. She'd be in the company of teachers who didn't yet know her, who couldn't yet read the subtle differences between her attempts at "wash hands" and "all done" and "spider." And I worried that because she was a somewhat limp, teensy, mostly quiet girl who we'd transport to school in a wheelchair, new teachers might take one look at her and make assumptions. So I made the video. It was a glossary of terms according to Fiona. It was a bridge, a way for her to carry her language into a new context and have it mean something. But it was also my way of saying to the teachers, *Look, this child knows stuff. She's smart, okay?*

For another minute on the video, I ask Fiona to sign her versions of *clean up, bounce, all done, windy, wash hands, change clothes,* and *hat.* Justin snickers from beyond the camera. I hand her a foam book. "Can you do open?" I ask. Blair taught her to tap on a closed object twice to indicate when she wanted it opened. But Fiona starts flipping the pages instead. She's done with this performance.

"Can you say bye-bye?"

She raises her right hand and flops it open like she's about to wave, but then she shakes her head no.

"You don't want to say bye-bye?"

She looks down at the book and smirks—a coy, closed-mouth thing that's suppressing her glee. I keep the camera on her. She wields power, and she loves it. She touches her head, trying to show me another sign. *Hair*, maybe? *Hat* again? But I miss the cue and instead shift the camera ninety degrees across the living room. The lens catches Justin lying on the floor and then rests on the big face of a drooly, runny-nosed baby. With wide brown eyes, Petra looks at the camera like it's a new form of intelligent life.

"Petra wants to say good-bye," I say.

Out of nowhere, a babyesque voice shouts, "Ahh! Ahh!" But Petra's mouth is shut. And Justin is grinning close-mouthed in the background. Who's making that sound? It can only be one person: the otherwise silent Fiona is blaring her vocal alarm.

"You don't want Petra . . . ," I say, and pause for a snicker, "to be on the video?"

Justin's laugh rises over the audio as I span the camera back to the sweaty kid in the royal blue tank top, the one who's under twenty pounds and demanding that the world orbit her. She's pointing her fist at me. "Ahm!" she says definitively. *Mom.*

"It's on you, it's on you," I say with reassurance.

"Ahm!" she says again, and she points her fist to herself.

Today I laugh at the end. I'd wanted the video to prove to Fiona's future preschool teachers that she was smart. But my girl's improv demands for the camera offered up her own message, just as useful as mine: *This child is feisty. And determined.*

A few weeks before preschool, I was prepping dinner in the kitchen. Fiona sat in her high chair at the dining table. A mozzarella cheese stick, broken up into bits, rested on the plastic tray, untouched.

"Mmm," she whined. "Mmm!" It was an *I'm bored* whine, a nonverbal but unmistakable version of *Mother, I reject the plans you have for me, your plans of cheese-eating while you cook your dinner. I refuse.*

"Eat your cheese," I said. When I looked through the kitchen's cut-out window into the dining room, she pointed her fist at a tablet on the table. "Ahm!" she said. She was doubling down, playing hardball. She wouldn't eat the cheese unless.

During Fiona's food strike, we'd started letting her watch videos while she ate. It was a bite-by-bite incentive. *Keep eating this jar of pureed carrots, kid, and I'll keep letting you watch this chipper kids' show.* It was precisely the kind of parenting strategy a person swears they'll never do before they actually have kids. But during the six months that professionals were seriously considering a g-tube for Fiona, Justin and I resorted—reluctantly at first, and then heartily—to TV shows at the table. These were music-heavy distractions for the genetically predisposed music lover in the family. Beyond *Yo Gabba Gabba*, she also favored a series of YouTube videos called *Super Simple Songs*, which paired cartoons with kid-approved tunes like "Five Little Monkeys" and "Mary Had a Little Lamb." It worked. Fiona would forget her oral aversion long enough to swallow a spoonful of something mushy. And when she stopped opening her mouth for the spoon, we stopped the show, freezing those five wide-eyed monkeys mid-bounce on the bed. Pressing pause on the video had the impressive result of unhinging our child's jaw. The food went in.

When Fiona broke her months-long modified fast, videos at the dining table became the trophy over which a nonverbal three-year-old and her parents sparred. I'd been putting my foot down lately. No shows while eating.

So on this day I rounded the partition between the kitchen and the dining room and came to the table. I looked down at Fiona's talker. I tapped my finger on it. "Eat," said the talker. I tapped my finger again. "Cheese," it said. I tapped the whole phrase, which the app now stored at the top of the screen. "Eat cheese," the high-pitched electronic voice insisted, like Fiona's mother had solicited backup from a chirpy but stern robot. Then I returned to whatever was simmering on the stove.

I started chopping carrots. I thought the last word was mine.

One of the features of Fiona's app was that it never took more than two hits to reach a word. This meant that to say any of the 14,000 possible words, you never had to touch your finger to the screen more than twice. But intentionally hitting two icons was still not possible for Fiona—she hadn't hit even one with accuracy. So for most of the 119 core words on the front screen, we'd turned off the secondary screen function, at least for now. We only enabled the secondary screens for a few necessary and high-preference categories: food, people, and TV shows. When she touched *Eat*, for instance, the device didn't say *eat* immediately but instead opened up a page of words related to food. Likewise with *Our*: that icon opened a page of people. And when she touched *Look*, it opened a page of videos and TV shows. *Sesame Street. Yo Gabba Gabba. Super Simple Songs.*

And that last phrase was precisely what I heard from the dining room table while I chopped the carrots. *Super Simple Songs.* Unmistakable and clear. My girl had reclaimed the talker from Mommy's backup robot to her rallying cry. Her voice.

Maureen had said, "Give it a year. Don't expect her to intentionally use the device that whole first year." Fiona had needed just a few months.

I set down my knife. I rounded the partition and looked at my kid, shocked. She looked back with those blue eyes, expectant.

"You want *Super Simple Songs*?" I asked.

Her full-bodied nod shook the high chair.

I opened the tablet. I searched through the Internet. By God, reader, I gave that girl her TV show.

Chapter Fourteen

⁓

The new neurologist was thin and gray-haired and ancient. He had small glasses and long fingers and a reedy voice as chill as an iced fillet of fish. "Her recent EEG," he said, "was beautifully normal. But an EEG only offers us a snapshot of a person on a specific day. And does a single picture give us a complete understanding of a person?" He waited two seconds before answering his own question. Justin and I sat in chairs, looking up at him. "No, it does not." He recommended anticonvulsive medication.

We were here because I was trying to cut corners. Making the two-hour trek over a mountain to the former neurologist felt damn-near impossible with Petra in tow. This new doctor was just an hour away. But neither of Fiona's two previous neurologists had ever recommended seizure meds. They'd both explained that the damage caused by anticonvulsants was greater than the harm done by her specific seizure activity.

"But the question remains," this new neurologist said, "which medication?" With his hip leaning against the paper-covered examining table, he mused about the pharmaceutical options. We could try such-and-such drug, he said, and then listed the side effects, which were alarming at first and then drifted into the category of unthinkable. He suggested a second drug with similar side effects. He listed a third, with side effects that were weird and terrible but not nearly as bad as the other two: headaches, dizziness, tremors, nausea, vomiting, insomnia. This drug was his recommendation. Fiona was sitting runny-nosed in her stroller. A doctor who had barely examined her was already interested in chemically altering her brain.

I shook my head no. Justin agreed.

This new neurologist said fine, but then he launched into a tale about a cardiologist he once knew, a "brilliant" cardiologist who had a daughter with epilepsy. She was, as the neurologist put it, "profoundly disabled." She was in a wheelchair, he said. She had a feeding tube, he said. There are ways of reporting these facts neutrally. The neurologist offered these details with flat despair and then paused, seemingly awaiting our pity.

He continued: It was very hard on the family, on the father, the neurologist said. Very hard. One day the father, who the neurologist reminded us was a brilliant cardiologist, took the daughter alone to her doctor. He asked, *How long will you let her live like this? When is enough enough?*

The neurologist explained what happened next as though it were a perfectly reasonable thing to happen, as though it would not elicit international protests. The brilliant cardiologist asked his daughter's doctor, *Is there anything you can do to end her life?*

The neurologist told us that the father was reported to the hospital's ethical panel. I was relieved. But the neurologist's deadpan delivery did not echo my relief. I couldn't tell where he stood.

Then he relayed the fallout. When the cardiologist's wife found out what happened, she filed for divorce. She petitioned for sole custody of her daughter, and she won. And after all this—the custody battle, the divorce—the brilliant cardiologist's career tanked. His life was ruined. It was about this last point that the neurologist expressed the deepest disappointment. A man's career had been destroyed.

"All because the father had asked the question," he said. "Now, was it a valid question?" He waited the requisite two seconds. "Yes, it was a valid question. Did the father have the right to ask the question? Yes, he did."

I sat stunned.

Here's something a parent of a typical child probably never has to suffer through: a conversation with a doctor in which the doctor wonders aloud whether a child like theirs can be ethically killed.

What exactly was the neurologist's point? He got to that: "You have a right to question my medical recommendation. Just like the father had the right to ask the question about his daughter's life."

Whenever I hear parents retell alarming encounters with doctors, I wait for the part of the story when the parent lashes back. Turns their tongue into a whip that cuts open the truth and puts the doctor in their place. But so often the parent says, *I had no comeback. I was too shocked to speak.* And that's what happened with Justin and me. We rode out the few remaining minutes of the visit, then gathered our things. Justin grabbed the handles of Fiona's stroller and pushed. We blew out of that windowless examining room. I called the old neurologist and got Fiona back on his patient list.

. . .

t's not off-limits in American society to deliberate on whether the disabled should die. Read online comments beneath a disability-related article. Or observe how newspaper reporters write sympathetically toward parents who kill their disabled children but would never think to extend such sympathy toward parents of typical kids. Or visit the faculty list at Princeton University, where Peter Singer holds tenure as the Ira W. DeCamp Professor of Bioethics.

Singer argues in his book *Practical Ethics* that parents of disabled newborns should be allowed to kill their babies. Why? Their parents might not want them. Or they'll bring less happiness to their parents than other babies. Or they'll be less happy themselves. His argument is laid out in reasoned, unemotional prose that, sentence by sentence, builds a steely architecture to house something horrifying.

On Singer's first day at Princeton in 1999, the disability rights group Not Dead Yet protested his appointment by blocking the university's main building. They chanted and held placards that read NO ONE SHOULD HAVE TO PROVE THEIR PERSONHOOD. But Singer remains at Princeton to this day, and the third edition of his book was printed in 2011.

It's not just Singer who makes the assumption that happiness determines a "life worth living." The year Fiona turned three and headed to preschool, evolutionary biologist Richard Dawkins tweeted that it was immoral for a pregnant woman to knowingly carry a child with Down syndrome to term because such a choice would decrease happiness and increase suffering. "Abort it and try again," he wrote to a mom.

You'll sometimes hear parents say of their child, "He has Down syndrome, and he's nonverbal. . . . But he's happy!" Or a mother will say, "She has cerebral palsy, and she doesn't walk, but she's brought us so much joy!" I get why parents add this caveat. It carries currency in a culture that otherwise devalues their kid. One way of countering people like Dawkins and Singer is to say, "My kid is happy." Or even, "I am happy."

But this can be exhausting. This turns happiness into a rhetorical strategy. This makes the faces of disabled people and their caregivers a walking argument that should never have to exist in the first place.

By the time Fiona turned three, I was very tired, and I adored her, and she was making progress with a walker, and she sometimes used her talker with intentional success, and her talker often spewed random trains of nonsense as she whacked at it. She made us laugh with a wild enthusiasm for hats, and she couldn't walk independently, and she ate by mouth, and she loved yogurt, and she couldn't feed herself the yogurt, so Justin and I fed her every bite, every single bite, of the yogurt. She was nonverbal, and she slept terribly, waking multiple times a night, and we were tired, and we adored her, and we made *her* laugh by cluck-clucking in the backs of our throats, which she could mimic because it did not require her to open her mouth. And I can't tell you if I was happier or sadder than the average parent—although she absolutely seemed happier than the average kid. But none of that, none of that should matter in proving the value of her life.

Sometimes we are joyful because we have known grief. Sometimes we know grief because we have dwelled—for full long days or microcosmic minutes—in the sun-soaked luminescence of joy.

What Dawkins and Singer don't understand is that often the two go hand in hand.

When I brought Fiona to preschool, she usually lingered in the school's foyer and looked around, reluctant to move forward. She'd only been attending a few weeks. Was she overwhelmed? Scared? Her classmates were regular-size three- and four-year-olds, which meant they were ginormous. They were a species of giant clobbering around the school with their hardy legs and thick bodies, singing and speaking and shouting in polysyllabic words, sitting in mammoth preschool chairs that would swallow my daughter. Once seated, they shoved spoonfuls of cereal into their faces and chewed.

Fiona did not chew. Fiona had her own chair. Fiona was still the width of a three-month-old, the height of a one-year-old. Although her Vermont preschool was legally required to maintain a population of kids that were half "typically developing" and half in need of special support, Fiona was by far the most visibly disabled child. At the start of her day, she stood in the bustling foyer, spindly as a willow tree, leaning against her mother for support.

One morning, I unfolded her metallic blue walker and lined it up so I could help her push it in a straight line toward the speech therapist's room. She placed a hand on it for support. But she was still just standing in the foyer, looking this way and that.

"Come on," I said, conjuring up a story that she was probably too scared to go into her class.

Then a boy's perky voice called out, "Hi, Fiona!" I didn't recognize him.

Fiona puckered her mouth and sniffed her nose—her version of an air kiss.

"Hi, Fiona," two girls said in sync as they waved, walking past her. Neither of them was in her class. How did they know her?

Fiona again acknowledged her greeters by puckering her mouth and sniffing her nose. *Air kiss to you, air kiss to you.*

"Come on, Fee," I nudged. We were late. She'd already lost five minutes of speech therapy. "Get in your walker."

To position herself inside the U-shaped walker, she only needed to cruise two steps left and turn. But she took the long way, cruising right, all the way around the walker's metal frame. Meanwhile, she eyed the room and fielded the greetings of her large classmates. It turned out, she wasn't overwhelmed. She was a mini-celebrity, reaping the benefits of an adoring public square.

Unlike most of our New England town's storefronts, the library had an accessible ramp. It also boasted a story hour for toddlers, and one afternoon I was eager to get out of the apartment. I pushed our beast of a double-stroller down Main Street. Once inside, we saw the cheerful librarian reading a book to an amoebic cluster of kids and their parents. I unfolded the blue metallic walker with a click. It was the most satisfying click. It also made people's heads turn. They looked. I smiled. I tried to smile because the pressure was now on: I was the mother with disability accoutrement. Is this too much to say? I was the mother they were glad they were not. So I smiled. *See,* I tried to say. *Walkers can be happy things.*

I sat on the floor with Petra and Fiona in my lap and the talker balanced on my right thigh. The librarian sang a song with rhyming and clapping and hand gestures. I modeled the words on the talker. "Happy" and "Know. It." The electronic voice cut through the kiddish chorus. There were a few stares. I smiled. *See? Talkers can be happy things too.*

But my back was now sore from balancing two kids and an iPad on my body. Craft time commenced, and I was relieved to get up. Petra joined the children toddling over to a table of markers and crayons and paper. I helped Fiona arrange herself in her walker. I hunched over and helped her push and steer it. I was eager to get her to the crayons. She could color, and I could try to make some friends in this town that, after a year, still felt new.

My heart sank: the activity involved scissors. Fiona would both want to use the scissors and be unable to use the scissors. As other parents sat on the sidelines and chatted, I stepped into the role of occupational therapist. Hunched over, back aching, I strained to get Fiona's wiggly, clammy, tiny fingers through the scissor loops. Sweat beaded under my arms. Fiona said, "Ah, ah!" and flung her hand around. I didn't know how to be an occupational therapist. I felt like a bad mom for lacking an advanced degree in scissor use.

I pushed my children's collective forty-eight pounds and the stroller's twenty pounds back to the apartment. I unbuckled them and helped them inside and collapsed on the couch. Two hours had passed, and I felt like I'd put in an eight-hour shift.

For over a year, this was how it had gone: Rachel the physical therapist placed Fiona's fingers on the handlebar of a plastic toy that had wheels. Then Rachel wrapped a hand around Fiona's narrow rib cage, encircling it halfway. This hand kept Fiona upright. With the other hand, Rachel moved one of Fiona's legs. Fiona's Converse sneaker hovered over the floor and came back down a few inches ahead. When Fiona would inevitably take her hands off the handlebar, Rachel would place Fiona's hands back on it. "Nooo," she'd say gently but firmly. "This is *your* job. To hold on."

For a year, it took four hands to get my girl to move a single step. Some days, wobbly and willowy and unable to stand on her own, my daughter didn't look like the kind of person who would ever hold herself upright and walk. But eventually her hands knew by heart their role of holding onto a bar.

And then Rachel graduated Fiona from the plastic toy with wheels to the sleek blue metallic walker.

And then Fiona took steps with it on her own. She rammed into walls and doorways like a bumper car. Every few seconds we had to redirect the wheels.

And then Rachel unlocked the wheels from a fixed position so Fiona could steer, but this meant the walker wobbled all around. And we had to hunch over it and help Fiona direct it. And each of these phases took months and months.

But then one Sunday, in the dead of winter, with a foot of snow on the ground, Fiona navigated by herself through the church door. She turned left down the church's accessible ramp. She pivoted a hundred and eighty degrees around the ramp's elbow and then walked the pathway to the street. I followed a few feet behind. Her sister was several feet ahead. The pathway was surrounded by walls of snow as high as my children. I stopped. I snapped a photo. For the first time since becoming a mother, I was leaving a building without a person in my arms. And my joy took the form of twenty geese in my chest, mid-flight.

Fiona was screaming inconsolably, and neither Justin nor I knew why because she had no words to tell us why. I took her to her doctor. He examined her body, tried to read its language. When he looked inside her ear, he found the answer. It was her third ear infection that month. I asked the doctor if we should see an immunologist. I told him what the geneticist had told me: that if a kid with WHS keeps getting sick, she should see an immunologist.

But the doctor always liked to find his own answers. "Let me check something," he said, and came back with a navy encyclopedia-size book. He called it a bible and showed me the cover. In the title, I read the word "malformations." I tried to pretend I didn't read that word. That was a part of my grief—not just the word "malformation," but the pretending.

"Everything is in this book," the doctor said. I knew he didn't mean every answer to every question; I knew we wouldn't find in this book, say, the architecture of butterfly wings or the precise locations of our souls. It was supposed to contain every *malfor-mation*. I nodded, holding Fiona, who was weeping and red-eyed and wanting sleep.

He flipped to the index. He paused, turned pages. "W-E?" he spelled, searching for her syndrome.

"W-O," I spelled back.

"Huh," he said, disappointed. "It's not here." He mumbled to himself, almost sadly, "It's too rare."

The loneliness created a significant chunk of my grief. On Martha's Vineyard, between the seventeenth and nineteenth centuries, there were so many deaf people due to a recessively inherited gene that most hearing folks spoke both English and sign language. Because of this, the deaf Vineyarders were, according to disability scholars Jessica Scheer and Nora Ellen Groce, "well-integrated into community life. . . . What to us today would be considered a substantial handicap was reframed as a normal human variation." Or, to use the words of a hearing woman in her eighties: " 'Oh, those people weren't handicapped. They were just deaf.' "

You will always grieve the child you didn't have, a mother told me when I first learned of Fiona's syndrome. It was both a warning and a membership card. *Welcome, New Mother, to the Country Club of Eternal Grief.* She might have been right about the grief, but she was wrong about the reason. I no longer yearned for a different kid. I yearned for a club with more members. Then my daughter's body would have been reframed as a variation to include, rather than an anomaly to scratch a head at. Instead, I lived in a world in which scientists strove to make gene-edited CRISPR babies. One first target of erasure? A gene for deafness.

The doctor was undaunted. He got out his laptop. He found a description of the syndrome online. I'd read it a dozen times: *Dysmorphic features. Short stature. Mental retardation.*

"Bone abnormalities!" he said enthusiastically, like he was shouting *Bingo!* I actually liked this doctor.

But the website said nothing about immune systems. He closed his laptop, discouraged. I felt sad for him, and I felt sad for me. He wanted medical literature to prove what I'd already told him: kids with WHS should see an immunologist if they get sick a lot. I waited patiently for the doctor to realize this. He decided to make a referral to an immunologist.

This was also part of the grief—I often knew more than the doctor.

He looked at Fiona. Her eyes were glassy from the fever, red from the tears. She was still on my lap, curving into my body, needing pain relief and rest.

"She's really special," he said, like it was both a fact and a fortune. Like it was a statistic and a song.

"I know," I said. "She's got a bright light in her eyes."

"Not today," he said, standing up, and called in a prescription.

There were no bad guys here. The absence of bad guys was part of the grief.

And then one day she was shoveling chili into her mouth, all on her own. Gobs of spicy black beans and ground beef and salsa, a half-teaspoon at a time. Sometimes the spoonful landed just left of her mouth and sometimes it landed right, but when it got into her mouth, she clamped down on it and ripped the spoon away in full-fledged drama, as if to say, "Ta-da!" Chili crept into a goatee, and she was 100 percent delighted with her autonomy. Just like that, the kid who might never have fed herself could feed herself. We took a video and plastered it across the sky for all to see.

When Fiona's preschool teachers introduced shapes, we unmasked words on her talker like *Oval* and *Circle* and *Square*. When they introduced the weekly calendar, we unmasked *Monday* and *Tuesday* and *Wednesday*. I could tell that her class of three-year-olds had begun talking about their feelings because the words *Happy* and *Sad* and *Tired* were suddenly accessible. What had once been a black space was now lit with expressive potential.

One afternoon, her teacher told me about an activity: she'd asked the kids their favorite color, and she'd invited them to answer with the classroom's shared iPad. One by one, Fiona's classmates approached a device that looked just like Fiona's talker. They each "spoke" a favorite color. After seeing her peers model their answers, Fiona "spoke" hers (purple).

As I listened to the teacher describe this activity, my joy wanted to pour out of me in the form of tears. Not only did this activity normalize Fiona's talker, and not only did it use Fiona's peers (rather than just her teachers) as models, it also promoted everyone's early literacy—because each icon on the app was represented with both a picture and a word. Fiona's teacher had found a way that my daughter's learning and her peers' learning enhanced each other.

Instead of sobbing and spitting out, *I'm forever indebted to your commitment to inclusion*, I just smiled and said, "That's awesome!"

Often the joy was not the flip side of a coin, not in contrast to what was once lacking. Often it stood all on its own—a sun in a living room, radiating a trillion watts.

This was the light in Fiona's face when she saw a hat.

She had over a dozen. A straw fedora. A floral bucket hat. A straw bolero with a teal ribbon. A navy-and-white-gingham summer hat. A black wool beret. A denim baseball hat, gifted from Lauren, her 4p- friend. A fuchsia ski cap. A raspberry-sequined beret. A winter hat that looked like the face of a penguin wearing, on its head, another winter hat. When she saw one of these lying around, her face lit up in unbridled glee. "Ha!" she cried, meaning *hat*, and put it on, or thrust it in my face so I could put it on. "Ha!" she exclaimed when it was on someone's head, and she touched it and smiled like this sole garment was all the universe needed to be made right.

Pharmaceutical companies would pay billions to bottle this joy.

Six months after steering out of church alone, she no longer needed the walker. She toddled on her own. She slapped her right foot down, and her left foot followed pigeon-toed, afterthought more than intention. She sometimes held her arms out for balance, slightly Frankenstein-style, plowing toward whatever she wanted. On a November day, a few months into her second year of preschool, she wanted the swings.

We weren't even through the gate of the playground when I heard a woman cry out, "Look how tiny that girl is!" I turned my head and saw a heavyset woman in her fifties seated at a picnic table with a fifty-something man and a boy. The woman was staring in our direction.

I stared back at the woman. I did it as armor. I did it to protect my kid. *Don't objectify my girl*, my staring tried to say. In stores and on the street, people sometimes looked at Fiona because she was adorable and magnetic and thrilled by life. And people sometimes looked at her because she was making noises like "ah, ah" and doing the Frankenstein-arm thing.

The woman looked away. We got to the bucket swings, and I lifted both kids into a swing and pushed.

"Whee," said Petra.

Fiona grinned and signed, "More."

The family at the picnic table came to the swings too. The man pushed the boy while the woman observed. Petra and Fiona and I talked, which meant Petra formed full sentences and Fiona made subtly different vowel sounds that stood for specific words, and we communicated great meanings in this way.

But I felt something. The woman was staring again. Mouth agape. Eyes concerned.

"Hello," I said.

She said hello back and turned away.

"Your hat fell off, Q-ball," the man said, and laughed. The boy laughed too.

"Don't call him that," the woman snipped. The boy was bald.

"Friday we go to Albany to check your bone marrow," the man said to the boy.

My heart sank for them, and I thought of that quote. How did it go? Be kind? Everyone you meet is fighting a battle you can't see?

The sun was setting. The night before, we'd turned back the clocks. The woman said she hated how dark it was getting so soon. I pulled the kids out of the bucket seats and tried to corral them toward the car. Petra got distracted by the monkey bars she couldn't reach, and Fiona plopped down and raked her hands through the wood chips. I found myself near the woman, who was looking at her grandson on the swings.

"He just beat cancer," she said quietly.

"I notice you mentioned Albany Medical Center. We sometimes go there too." I was trying to find common ground. I was trying to say, *It's okay that these bodies we live in are not always the promises we'd wished for. Life is full beneath this cracked porcelain. Inside this tender flesh.* Or something like that. But the woman just looked confused.

I felt like I owed her something. An equal sharing. I looked at Fiona and said, "She has a chromosomal syndrome."

Without a beat, the woman asked, "How do they cure that?"

The word "cure" was a bomb. For so many people, disability needs to be fixed in order for it to finish its story. *He just beat cancer.* Her boy had won. This woman wanted to know, how would my girl find her victory?

Fiona walked up to my legs and pushed on them. "Ah, ah," she cried, meaning she wanted me to pick her up.

"No," I said to the woman, and lifted my daughter's twenty pounds. "They don't cure it. It's how she was designed." I tried for positivity in this last sentence, but it was laced with irritation. I was tired from daylight savings, and I was tired from waking with Fiona many times a night, and I was tired from years of conversations like these, where I tried earnestly to become the living counterargument to people's beliefs that my girl needed fixing. That a life with disability was a lesser, a pitiful life. That the right trajectory of the story was to become un-disabled. I was tired of trying to show the opposite by example.

Carrying Fiona, I walked away from the woman. Petra was toddling beside me.

"Well, how do they treat it then?" the woman cried out. She was now a good fifteen yards away.

"Um," I said, still walking. "They don't treat it."

"She's so skinny!" the woman called to me.

She was far enough away that when I said this last sentence, I had to yell it. I yelled it upward, over my shoulder, toward the woman, into the sky: "It's how she was designed," I cried—to the air, to the dusk, to the trees, to everywhere.

Words that, based on frequency of use, we needed to add to Fiona's talker the year she turned four:

high-five
cheers

umeboshi (Japanese pickled plum)
Bob Marley
zerbert

We returned to the old neurologist, the one we used to see before trying Dr. Let's-Talk-Euthanasia. This neurologist nightly prayed an ancient prayer of Christian monks, and Justin and he usually geeked out over liturgy and the intersections of spirituality and science.

"What's the definition of a human being?" the neurologist asked.

"Better question," Justin said. "What is a person? What is a *who*? Any answer needs to include the spirit and the soul."

"It's a big debate in scientific circles," the neurologist said. "Some people want to define a human being as an organism with forty-six chromosomes. But you can already see the problem with that, can't you? A person with Down syndrome wouldn't qualify."

Fiona and Petra were toddling around the examining room. I nodded, half in intellectual connection, half in gratitude that this doctor skated around the edges of disability advocacy.

The neurologist moved to practical matters. He explained that people with WHS tended to have delayed myelination. "Do you know what that is?" he asked.

I shook my head no.

He leapt out of his chair. "Well then, let me get you a brain!" He grabbed a fake brain, split the hemispheres apart, then touched them back together. "You know how a brain is made of white matter and gray matter? The white matter is the myelin, a fatty substance that wraps around the nerves. Myelin speeds up electrical impulses in the brain. It helps information travel more quickly between one nerve cell and another. A brain with less myelin will send information more slowly. Fiona's MRI showed she has less myelin than typical kids. That's why it takes her longer to learn things."

I nodded. I loved the neurologist's factual, neutral tone. He was devoid of pity or problematizing. He was full of enthusiasm for imparting facts.

But it was when the neurologist asked the nurse for Fiona's weight and height stats that I wanted to cheer. She told him Fiona's size, and at first I expected him to respond with worry. Instead, he looked at the nurse and exclaimed, "You see! Her DNA *wants* her to be small!"

Then the neurologist asked to see the rescue medicine that Dr. Let's-Talk-Euthanasia had prescribed if Fiona had a seizure that wouldn't stop. I handed the plastic syringe to him. The neurologist examined the dosage. He got quiet. He asked if we'd given this medicine yet. I said no, we hadn't needed to.

When he spoke again, his tone was somber and low. "This could be enough to stop her breathing."

The point of life isn't to avoid all suffering. It's not to "be happy." Contrary to what Singer and Dawkins argue, a better life is not one that steers clear of the most pain, managing to arrive at the end with the eulogy, *He had it easy*, or *She was the least scathed person I know*. This belief in the virtue of the "happy" and suffering-free life sterilizes and shrinks us, minimizing what makes us most beautifully human: our tenderness, our vulnerability, the profundity of our capacity for heartache, the risks of which deliver us into immense joy.

The point of this human life, I believe, is love. And the ridiculous and brave and risky act of love turns my heart into taffy, stretches it across the broad spectrum of human feeling. My daughter has given me a thousand portraits of grief and a thousand portraits of joy. I hurt, I long, I exalt, I rejoice. Loving my daughter tenderizes me, makes me more human. And yes, my chest sometimes aches from this work. But the ache in my chest is a cousin of joy.

Chapter Fifteen

⌒

The day Justin and I sent Fiona into a typical public kinder-garten classroom, she walked—nay, sauntered—across the threshold. It was August, and she was attending kinder-camp, a two-day orientation for incoming kindergarteners. She wore that straw fedora on her head and carried her foam-blue-covered talker in one hand. Her other hand swung boldly in a way that rivaled RuPaul on the runway. She had the height of a two-year-old and the confidence of a Cool Kid.

My camera caught her from behind: narrow, spindly body mid-step among posters of ABCs. My kid: immersed in the potential of literacy. I felt the grip on my diaphragm as I held back tears, and it wasn't exactly—or only—for those sentimental reasons any parent weeps over their kindergartener. Caught inside myself was the ineffable sensation of a single moment holding eternity. Or at least a single moment holding the past hundred years.

At the turn of the century, there was a pandemic of fear about the so-called feeble-minded. Thanks to Sir Galton and eugenics, people with intellectual disabilities were accused of higher rates of crime, sexual promiscuity, prostitution, and alcoholism. Pamphlets were distributed across the country, warning the public about the supposed dangers of the feeble-minded. A 1914 article from *The American Journal of Nursing* titled "The Menace of the Feeble-Minded" estimated that two-thirds of feeble-minded people were, as the writer said, "at large." The article's argument echoed the sentiment of the country: feeble-minded people were not fit for citizenship. They needed to be rounded up and segregated in institutions; otherwise they'd procreate, increase their numbers, and corrupt society. Between 1904 and 1923, the number of "feeble-minded" people in institutions almost tripled. The overcrowded and underfunded institutions became "schools" in name alone.

One of these institutions was Pennhurst State School and Hospital, just under an hour's drive from my hometown. In 1968, NBC entered it with cameras. The network's viewers saw close-ups of thighs narrower than knees, of wrists tied to bars, of ankles shackled to beds, of adults rocking themselves in front of windows, and of adults lying fetal and naked in cage-size cribs. Members of the Pennsylvania Association for Retarded Citizens, or PARC, went to lawyer Thomas K. Gilhool, whose own brother had spent years in Pennhurst. His brother had called it "Jailhouse Rock." What could PARC do about places like Pennhurst? With Gilhool as prosecutor, PARC made an unexpected move: they decided to sue, not Pennhurst (at least not yet) but the state—for its failure to educate its citizens.

Pennsylvania and other states permitted schools to refuse students whom they deemed "uneducable" or "untrainable" or who had "not attained a mental age of five years." In the 1972 case

PARC v. Commonwealth of Pennsylvania, the list of plaintiffs is chilling and profound. Some were residents of Pennhurst. All were American citizens, legally denied an education. It's easy to imagine my daughter among them, not only because of her diagnosis but because of geography. In the decade that the lawsuit was filed, I was slated to attend the very schools PARC was suing.

The results of the case were definitive: Pennsylvania's law barring certain kids from school was deemed unconstitutional. Within the next year, more than thirty similar suits were filed across the country. In response, Congress passed the Education for All Handicapped Children Act, which eventually was renamed IDEA, a law guaranteeing all disabled students the right to a "free and appropriate public education."

And this—all of this—is why I choked up at the kindergarten door as Fiona headed to kinder-camp.

Not just because my girl was "growing up."

Not just because Fiona was leaving my side and would soon begin full-day elementary school.

I choked on tears because Fiona's body in that classroom— her diminutive, anomalous body holding a talker and standing among posters of the alphabet—was political. With my phone's camera, I captured my fedora-wearing, sauntering, twenty-one-pound kindergartener, claiming her rightful place in what would have been prohibited just decades earlier.

She was nonverbal. She was easily knocked over by kids twice her weight. She walked (in gray or pink Converse sneakers) but wavered and sometimes fell. Steps were higher than her knees.

She used her talker, but intermittently, and only one or two words at a time. ("George," she'd say of a classmate at school, but did George eat with her, or shove her, or wear a hilarious hat? I had no idea.) She would need help in the bathroom. She would need help getting into chairs. She would need help eating and drinking. She would need help holding a pencil and possibly sometimes a fork. She'd need help. How do you entrust a school with a child like Fiona, who, if something went horribly wrong, would not be able to tell you?

You do three things. You prepare the school professionals as best you can. You tune your instincts keenly to their responses, sussing out whether they seem competent and respectful of your kid. And then, if your instincts approve, you let go.

One week before school, I tried a different strategy: channeling all my stress into a ten-dollar purchase. I found myself in our local big-box chain store, standing in the aisle of back-to-school supplies, sweating the food-carry options for a solid thirty minutes. I pulled a black vinyl lunch bag off the shelf only to reject it; picked up a pink lunchbox and refused that one too. With aggressive strips of Velcro and daunting snaps and zippers, they seemed like angry, impenetrable fortresses to my girl's fingers, destined to keep her hungry.

While I deliberated the lunchbox decision like it was a permanent interstate move, Fiona refused to care. "Pink?" I asked. "Plaid?" She kept running away. "Eee-yah!" she squealed, toddling toward the cough syrup, arms flailing in ecstatic rebellion. Petra had her own agenda: removing every princess-themed lunchbox off the shelf and declaring it hers. I finally settled on a rainbow tie-dye-printed vinyl bag that Fiona approved of.

In truth, Justin and I had begun the work of preparing Fiona's future school in April. We'd sat down at a long table with Fiona's current preschool teacher, current preschool therapists, future kindergarten teachers, future therapists, the assistant director of special education, and the elementary-school principal. Over ten people gathered at that table to discuss how a kid like Fiona would be included in a public school.

It's not that the lives of kids with disabilities were perfectly dandy after 1975. Five years after Congress passed the Education for All Handicapped Children Act, a coalition embarked on a six-month investigation and declared the situation "a national disgrace." The coalition found the plight of many students' lives unchanged. "Today . . . more than 71,500 children in institutions or special schools receive totally segregated programming . . . 900 handicapped students in the San Francisco area identified as needing individualized education programs (IEPs) do not have them; more than 200 mentally retarded children in Texas institutions are provided no education at all; and black students across the country are placed in classes for the educable mentally retarded at almost three times the rate for white students." When President Ford signed the 1975 bill into law, he predicted this outcome, writing, "This bill promises more than the Federal Government can deliver."

The promise of the law relies on willingness, competency, advocacy, resources, and goodwill—a tall order. So I was under no impression that "inclusion" would be a breeze for my daughter. As Supreme Court Justice Thurgood Marshall said in a statement about the rights of the intellectually disabled: "Prejudice, once let loose, is not easily cabined."

By the time I'd reached the spring meeting, I'd already read a mammoth book outlining Fiona's rights. My fellow WHS parents often described their interactions with schools as "battles" or "fights," so information was my sword. For a shield, I distributed a handout featuring full-color photos. Top left was Fiona in her straw fedora, sitting in a bucket swing and smiling. Bottom right was Fiona in thoughtful side-glance, holding up a large red crayon, wearing that ski cap of a penguin wearing a ski cap. *I color for long periods of time,* the handout read. The first-person was deliberate. *I love music and can clap to the rhythm. . . . I make specific requests with my talker and know where a lot of words are. . . . I am very social and like to say hello to people in public places.* The not-so-subtle goal was simple: paint a portrait of my daughter's wholeness, of her full personhood. Remember the history. Subvert any person's tendency, conscious or otherwise, to view my girl as "broken" or less-than. Insist that every adult at that table sees her as fully human.

White parents of typical kids are mostly freed from the burden of this kind of work. Parents of black and brown children are not. Double that, a parent of a black or brown kid with a disability. (In fact, it's an example of my white privilege that while pregnant, I never once thought a professional would question the inherent humanity of my kid.) As Taylor Harris writes in *Catapult* about her son's IEP meetings, "I'm never just advocating for an undiagnosed child whom several teachers have found puzzling and whose challenges don't follow any script; I'm also a black mother advocating for my black son in a room full of people who don't look like us."

Contrary to the experiences of so many parents, though, nothing in that April meeting resembled a battle. No one gave me an impression other than utter respect and enthusiasm for my girl. They read my handout with care. They listened carefully to Fiona's preschool teachers, who had brought their own full-color photos and outlined my daughter's strengths. What followed was a meeting where thoughtful educators who knew Fiona well helped new educators understand her. What emerged was a plan that inspired confidence: Fiona would learn in a typical classroom alongside her peers, with an aide for support. She would receive ample occupational, physical, and speech therapy each week, including ninety minutes of speech support a day. And half of those speech services would be in the classroom, so Fiona could practice using her talker and burgeoning speech in relevant social settings. If four years ago Vermont had impressed me with its early-intervention program, it doubled down in its public school setting.

But that had been months earlier. What did it look like for such a "minority body" (as Elizabeth Barnes calls it) to learn in a building of six grades where no one looked or behaved like her? We were days away from kindergarten, and I possessed a pile of latent anxiety and an insultingly insufficient tie-dye rainbow lunch bag.

Justin and I sat down with the new teachers one more time to iron out last-minute details. They still had as many questions as we did. Where was the best place for her to sit? they wondered. Could she sit on the benches at the cafeteria? Due to low tone at her core, I told them probably not. Someone made a note to get her a special chair for the end of a table.

Could they have at least one other similar chair, I asked, at the end of another table, so that the chair wouldn't be stigmatized? I watched heads nod around the table. Someone made a note to get a second chair.

Would she bring lunch or order it from the school? the principal asked.

I was about to say we'd pack it.

"It's free!" the principal said with a megawatt smile. "School lunch is free for all kids!"

The speech therapist, Tracy, a high-energy woman with impressively perfect enunciation, lit up at the idea of Fiona ordering her lunch. She sat tall in her chair. "If she gets school lunch," she said, "she would order it at the beginning of the day. This would give Fiona the perfect opportunity to use her talker!"

It was decided—Fiona would order school lunch. My lunch bag woes were chucked into the trash.

What about classroom chairs? Bathroom accommodations? The playground swings? For over an hour, nine adults collaborated on how to make a typical public elementary school as accessible as possible for the body that housed my kid.

Based on the anecdotes across the country, and based on the history, this thoughtful deliberation about how to include a person like Fiona is in no way universal. I spent the bulk of the meeting torn between my heart's desire to cry in gratitude and my head's desire to hold it together. I wanted to kiss each person in the room and say *thank you thank you*. To think, a few decades before me, parents had none of this. To think, they heard instead, "Your child is uneducable," or "Your child hasn't reached a mental age of five." To think, they heard: Your child isn't worth an education.

Instead, what we heard was, *Your daughter has every right to swing on the playground in a way that is safe and fun for her, so why don't we acquire a bucket swing and attach it to our swing set, just for her.*

On the first day, my girl picked out a *Yo Gabba Gabba* T-shirt and navy shorts. "Ha," she said, tapping her head, meaning *hat*. We let her choose between the navy plaid sun hat and the straw fedora. She went with the fedora. We tied hot-pink Converse high-tops around her plastic ankle braces. She put on her miniature backpack: it couldn't even fit a standard folder, and yet it covered her entire back. She gripped her foam-blue-covered talker and, standing beneath a birch tree, she smiled widely for the camera. *Kindergarten* read my handwriting on a piece of paper, which she'd smashed to her belly.

I sent the photo to my mother. She wouldn't tell me until a year later that it made her cry with fear. How could we trust a school with a kid like Fiona?

The doors to Fiona's public school were flanked by eager greeters. The megawatt-smiling principal stood on the left side of the entry, along with the special educator. "Hi, Fiona!" the principal practically sang. On the other side of the entry stood Fiona's speech therapist, Tracy. In a flared, knee-length dress, she knelt to the ground and showed Fiona an iPad. It was opened to Fiona's communication system. The speech therapist hit an icon. The device said, "Good morning." With infectious cheer, with every consonant annunciated, the speech therapist repeated, "Good morning, Fiona!"

Fiona giggled, head down, and said *hah-m*. Her version of hi. With one hand on the railing and the other in Justin's hand, she summited the three steps to the school's back door and went inside. I trailed a few paces behind.

"How is she?" asked the principal.

"Fine," I said, nodding.

"Or more importantly," she added with a laugh, "how's Mom?"

My eyes filled. I felt the inner scramble to collect myself. "Don't ask me that," I said, and the principal put a hand on my back.

Why all the sentimentality around kindergarten? I'd always wondered this, and now I knew: it marked a kid's first step into their own public life, separate from yours. They would meet people you didn't know. Learn lessons (good or bad) you never taught them. Run up against conflicts you might not even know about, let alone help them navigate. Make choices you could do nothing to prevent. *There you go, kid. We gave you all the words we thought you'd need, and more. We gave you love and a hat and orthotics and string cheese and a brief pep talk.* ("Fiona," I'd said before we'd gotten into the car, "if your teachers don't understand you . . . use your talker. Okay?")

I wasn't sad. I was overwhelmed: with hope and fear, love and ache. How do you let go of a kid like Fiona? Four pounds, twelve ounces was the weight of her beginning. Her onyx eyes were, back then, the Magic 8-Balls of my one million questions, offering only their cryptic replies. *Better not tell you now. Ask again later.* Will you, child, learn to walk? Will you learn to talk? Will you live past three? Will you always need me?

The answers had come, one by one. Yes, yes, yes, and probably yes.

And I'd wondered this too: How would my heart meet your deep need, pour into it like a pitcher tries to fill a lake?

Time had answered that one: bit by bit, spoonful by spoonful, cheese stick by cheese stick, giggle by giggle, seizure-second by seizure-second, ambulance ride by recovery by joke by prayer by song.

And now I asked: How would I let other people pour into your deep need? How could I trust that the world would catch you, child? How could I let you go? You, the child who teeters. You, the child who can't yet speak your name. You, the child who, at birth, had eyes lit with something bright as ember, and yet the assessing doctor couldn't see it.

Before I could answer, she was walking down the long hallway, away from me.

But the answer presented itself as the same easy and impossible solution that raising Fiona had always required. It's the answer that perhaps raising any child requires, but that Fiona has gifted with unique adamancy: Breathe, love, let go.

Off you go, kid.

Go, kid, go.

An hour later, six grades of kids sat in rows on a gymnasium floor. Parents sat in folding chairs behind them. I held the heft of three-year-old Petra on my lap. The principal welcomed everyone "back to school" and then asked all faculty and staff to introduce themselves. The speech therapist spoke toward the end, and she had her iPad tucked under her arm.

"Good morning, everybody," she said to the one hundred kids. She had an infectiously cheerful way of speaking. "I'm going to show you three ways to say 'good morning.' We can use our words to say 'good morning.'" Her eyes were wide, and her vowels were wider as she articulated every syllable. She demonstrated the ASL signs for *good* and *morning*. "We can use sign language." She brought the iPad from under her arm and touched it, lighting up the screen. The grid of rectangles that comprised Fiona's communication system was displayed before the entire school. The speech therapist hit an icon, and Fiona's program spoke. *Good morning.* "And we can use technology. Over the next few weeks, I'm going to visit all of your classes and talk to you about using technology to speak."

My chest bloomed. In her preface to *The History of Special Education*, Margaret Winzer writes, "The way that children are trained and schooled is a crucial demonstration of the way that they are perceived and treated in a given society." On Fiona's first day of elementary school, I saw that my girl would be treated much differently than the intellectually disabled kids in my eighties elementary school, the ones sequestered in that unseen wing. Where did that architecture get me? In my first year of parenting Fiona, the ableism I had to excise from myself was a shock. I held to my breast, to my heart, the kind of human being who had been historically shut out. Becoming a mother is already a rupturing event—an apocalypse of the heart, an undoing and a redoing of your world. In loving Fiona, my heart broke open.

There was a certain kind of agony in this—one for which I'm eternally grateful.

By introducing the entire school to Fiona's communication system, the speech therapist was saying far more than *good morning*. She was saying: Fiona's form of communication is as valid as any other. And this, of course, was a way of saying: Fiona is a valued member of the community. In greeting the entire school with Fiona's app, the speech therapist laid the first plank in a bridge connecting my girl to her new community members.

At three o'clock, Fiona returned to me happy and unfazed. When I tucked her into bed that night, here's what I couldn't possibly know:

That within months of this moment, she'd begin mastering her ABCs. That in a year she'd start identifying sight words.

That in that first year, her gross motor confidence would climb; she'd refuse "special" chairs, join her peers on the cafeteria benches, and learn to pump herself on a standard swing—even before her always-ahead sister. The bucket swing, attached just for her, would come down.

That in first grade, she'd hike a half-mile uphill with her class.

That in the winters, she'd attempt cross-country skiing during gym, where she'd learn in the snow what she already knew on regular ground: the art of falling over.

That on field day, she'd run legs of relay races (modified for her), play water games (modified for her), and soar down a massive slip-and-slide, squealing manically and getting soaked. Tracy, her speech therapist, would volunteer to slide down with her.

That in the company of typical, talking peers, my daughter's verbal language would explode. Within a year and a half, she'd be speaking in simple sentences.

That in first grade, after five years of me writing essays about her, she'd "write" (as dictated to Tracy) her first essay about me: *My mom likes hats. I likes hats. My mom eats ham. I eat ham. My mom does yoga with me. I love my mom.*

That by second grade, her talker would become purely augmentative, clarifying words we couldn't decipher. Currently, *Petra* and *ketchup* sound uncannily close.

That she'd walk the halls of the school like she owned them, swinging her arm wildly with her saunter, asking everyone she passed, including the principal, "What are you doing?" ("Um," the principal would reply, feeling strangely beholden to my confident-ass kid. "Going to a meeting? Is that okay?")

On her first day of kindergarten, I couldn't know any of this—just as I couldn't know that on the day I learned of my daughter's diagnosis, I was being handed a gift. *I suspect she has a syndrome of some kind,* the pediatrician had said as she'd placed my daughter's seven pounds in my arms. Fiona was always a gift, of course. But so was that suspect thing, that syndrome. It had looked at the time like *something wrong.* How could I have known? How could we ever know that the dull spoon jabbing at our hearts isn't always an attack? Sometimes it's a tenderizer, softening us into a stranger, truer way of being human.

Epilogue

Fiona, age seven, sits at the dining table with Petra and two houseguests: a forty-year-old monk and the monk's sixteen-year-old son. The latter are Justin's friends. My mother, also visiting, stands beside Fiona with a mug of coffee in hand.

"Sit right here!" Fiona tells my mom. My kid has the command of a chirpy drill sergeant, and she points to the seat beside her. How could my mother refuse? She sits next to her granddaughter.

"Mom!" she calls out. I look at her. "Me toast!" She points to her chest.

"You want toast?" I ask. I'm heading into the kitchen.

"Yes, pease!" she shouts. She *shouts*.

I bring back the toast. Fiona is gulping water from a cup when I set it down. Over the years, her eyes have darkened from Tahoe blue to deep blue-gray. "Genk-yoo," she says. *Thank you.*

These days, she thanks me for everything. Two days ago, she thanked me for removing a sandy-blond strand of hair from her plate of eggs and toast. The hair—hers—lingered in the air, barely visible between my fingers, and *Genk-yoo*, she said as I let it drop to the floor. Then she ate the eggs and toast all on her own. She thanked me last week when I popped popcorn for her. I scooped it into a bowl and gave it to her while she and Petra watched a movie, and she crunched for fifteen minutes before calling from the living room, "Genk-yoo, Mom, kah-corn." *Thank you, Mom, for the popcorn.* She thanked me yesterday when, after I positioned her on the pink Minnie Mouse toilet seat that slides over the regular white toilet seat, I realized her body wasn't quite aligned with the hole. I lifted her twenty-five pounds and scooted her closer to the edge. "Genk yoo," she said, which in that instance I think meant, *Thank you, Mom, for making sure my butt-hole aligns with the loo.* She does not thank me when I brush her hair. She screams, cries bullets, repeats like a shrill, panicked mantra, *All done? All done?* But she says, *Genk-yoo, Mom, kaka* (chocolate), and *Genk-yoo, Mom, bobbie* (Barbie), and *Genk-yoo, Mom, book to read to me.*

It's remarkably gratifying, all these thank-yous, especially after the million spoonfuls of pureed food and the thousands of hours driving to some specialist or researching IEP goals or sweating scoliosis curves. *Genk-yoo, Mom, banket to seep* (blanket to sleep).

"Does anyone want a napkin?" I ask on this weekend morning. I'm holding a stack. Justin is frying bacon in the kitchen. With three houseguests, the two of us are in full-on hosting mode.

Fiona grabs the stack of napkins from my hand. She lets them drop in her puddle of egg yolk, then picks them up and starts divvying them out.

"Grand-mummm . . . ," she says, her voice upturning at the

end of the name, and gives my mom a napkin. "Ketch-ahhh . . ." She offers one to Petra.

This is when something I read a thousand years ago comes back to me. When I first started researching Fiona's syndrome online, parent after parent offered versions of: *Your child will teach you not to take the little things for granted.* Parents shared this as though it were bona fide encouragement. Alongside it, they sometimes posted videos of their kid taking first steps at age seven or forming first consonants at five or finally, at age three, fisting a rattle. The video footage was often grainy. In one, an eight-year-old plodded across a living room floor with a walker, and the parents cheered and/or cried. The camera shook in someone's hand.

I was a new mother. I had a sleeping baby upstairs. The message was clear: *Steps, if they happen, will be huge. Talking will be a triumph. Every milestone will be a lottery prize you had no reason to believe you'd receive.*

A part of me was vicariously thrilled for the parents—and their kids. But there was another part—not the whole of me, as mothering can reveal all the ways the self is fractioned—but a part of me that did not like this adage. Take nothing for granted? I didn't want to shout *victory!* over what, for other kids, were givens. I didn't want happiness to come from something that seemed, at the time, sad.

This morning, watching Fiona at brunch, I remembered not just the sentiment—*she teaches me not to take the little things for granted*—but my old way of hearing it. I was wrong. There's nothing sad about it.

Elton John bangs away on a piano, made tinny through someone's cell phone speaker. Fiona bops in her chair to the beat. Elton belts, "I'm still standing," and Fiona offers backup right on time, "Yeah! Yeah! Yeah!"

It bears repeating that some doctors told parents of kids like Fiona that their child would have little to no *quality of life.*

"I yike this song!" she says—nay, she exalts! She cheers! She points to the cell phone as ketchup goatees her chin.

I want to say, *Hear that?! Listen to that. Listen to all that language.* I want to look at the guests, the grinning monk and his quiet teenage son, and say, *Watch that too! Watch the fine motor coordination, as my girl sloppily scatters the napkins and yet still manages to hand each one of you a single square of tissue!*

But nobody pauses. Our new guests just met Fiona. They have no idea how long it took her to drink from a sippy cup. How hard it was for her to graduate to a straw. Today she will require nobody to syringe water into her mouth, drop by drop, to keep her hydrated. Our guests have no idea that they are sitting among a thousand feats contained within the anomalous body of my kid, who is in this moment over the moon about brunch with Sir Elton and guests.

"What's your name?" my mother asks, sipping coffee from her mug.

Fiona's answer is certain. "Grandmum." She giggles like someone's just jabbed fingers at her ribs.

"Then what's *my* name?" my mother asks.

"See-ohna," she says. The *F* is one of her last remaining sounds to master. She grins. She's totally tickled with herself.

This winter, Justin gave a sermon about the practice of "giving things up" for Lent. Wearing a robe and chasuble, he stood at the pulpit and talked to his parishioners. "It might be chocolate," he said. "And that's a good start, because for some people that hurts." He put his fist into his gut, feigning pain. "Ooh, chocolate, I'm gonna miss that." People laughed in the pews, and Fiona, standing a few feet from the altar, laughed too.

"Kaka," she said, meaning *chocolate*, and he pointed at her in recognition.

"*You* like chocolate!" he said.

"If the giving up doesn't hurt," he told the pews, "then it's not really a surrender. It's not the cross. And the cross is where we're transformed. So maybe you start with chocolate, and then next you give up the belief that you're right in an argument. Ooh, that hurts a little more. And maybe you give up a grudge you have with a family member. That *really* hurts. That's the dark chocolate."

Seven years earlier, I had to give up the kind of child I thought I was supposed to have. Not just the SuperChild. Not just the child who hiked, scythe in hand, the preferred upward slope of the bell curve. I had to give up the child I could assume would outlive me.

I had to give up the child I knew for certain would grow beyond her need for me.

I had to give up a child who would 100 percent walk. Who would 100 percent talk.

Some of these surrenders would come back to me.

But it was a years-long Lent. It brought my first gray hair, yes, and a hundred thousand gifts of light. Maybe we give up so we can more fully receive. Maybe we give up so we receive something better than what our small minds had wanted.

"All done!" Fiona shouts. I push her chair away from the table. She turns her body toward the seat back, grabs hold, and steps down backward like the chair is a ladder. She's worked months on this move. Bits of egg surround her plate, stick to her chair, fall to the floor. If I have any thoughts later when I clean it, the thoughts will be twofold: *kid is a mess!* and *kid eats!* A pain and a triumph, both equally true.

"What's next?" Justin calls from the kitchen. Sir Elton has ceased. Justin's scrolling on his phone, hunting for songs. " 'Electric Avenue'?"

When Fiona exclaims, "Yeah!" it's like someone has asked her if she'd prefer a dose of Christmas.

What follows is a dance party of Fiona's favorites. Reggae has long been back-burnered in favor of pop. Justin plays Deee-Lite's 1990 hit, "Groove Is in the Heart," and Fiona's flushed face smiles unabashedly. Her dance moves are stilted, usually requiring two feet firmly on the ground, but she occasionally kicks her right leg out and steps forward. She totters side to side. She claps—as she always has—to the beat.

Taking nothing for granted doesn't mean one's expectations for happiness fall painfully low. That's what I'd once thought of those weepy, rejoicing parents. I thought they were telling me that my life would be so difficult that I'd take pathetic scraps and call them wins. Through the phantom chunk of Fiona's missing fourth chromosome, I've gotten to see that we all, every day, take the miraculous for granted.

These bodies, with their heartbeats.

These bodies, breathing air.

These three trillion trees on this planet, exhaling oxygen.

This sunlight, spilling across the table.

This water in a pink plastic cup.

And this tongue's ability—if this tongue has this ability—to swallow it.

I will repeat forever and ever: my daughter doesn't exist to teach me things. Her reasons for being on this planet are as mysterious as the reasons any of us find ourselves here—in these particular bodies, among these three trillion trees. But like any parent, my kid has taught me things. And maybe the wording of the adage isn't quite right. Maybe instead of *My daughter teaches me not to take the little things for granted*, the saying might better go: *My daughter teaches me that the things I'd considered quotidian are also miraculous*. Fiona, with her broad grin, has brought me again and again back to awe. I offer a praise-song for fallen napkins, for napkins dripping with egg. I offer a praise-song for *P*-sounds made with *K*s.

Acknowledgments

Thank you to everyone who helped this book come into being.

Like my child, who always seemed to me the results of a conspiring between her spirit and the divine creator, this book's making felt partly out of my hands—a conspiring between forces
unrelated to my tenacious ego. So first, thanks to that Mystery.
Huge gratitude goes to my agent, Anna Knutson Geller, and my
editor, Ginny Smith, who both came knocking on the door of my
email account at precisely the same time. Anna, you are everything
a writer can hope for in an agent: thoughtful, responsive, grounding, trustworthy, savvy, wise. I'm so lucky to have you. Ginny,
thank you for the first nudge and everything else after: the encouragement, the feedback, the sensitivity, and the faith. It's been an
absolute joy to work with you and your right-hand woman, Caro-
line Sydney, whose whip-smart editing made me *ooh* and *aah*.
Thanks to all the folks at Penguin Press, including Darren Haggar.

Thank you to every educator who supported our family, especially Nicole Boice Goulet, Anne Mele, Rachel Wulgemuth, and
Paula Salazar. Thank you, Maureen Nevers, for big visions.

Thank you, Feresha Patel, for being a huge part of our village, and our family. And special gratitude to Tracy Locher, for every syllable and word and sentence.

Thank you to every big-hearted medical professional, particularly Dr. Amy Calhoun, the red-headed geneticist, and the good neurologist.

Thank you to Amanda, Dave, and Lauren Lortz—for your friendship, but also for letting me share your story. Thank you to the 4p- community. Thank you to the grassy knoll and annual meet-ups and late-night Facebook messaging support. Thank you for getting it when no one else could.

Thank you, Vermont moms, who walked alongside me during the tough, odd, beautiful years of raising wee ones. Special thanks to Kay Trafton, Megan Mazza, Kate Cooper, Genevieve Plunkett, and Michelle Wiegers.

Thank you, good people of St. Patrick's and St. Peter's, especially the surrogate grandmothers.

Thank you, Jennifer and Ray Lanier, and Todd Lanier, for all your love and joy and jokes.

Thank you, Kim, Eli, Miles, and Elliott Lesser, for all your love and challah. Thank you especially, Kim, for letting me say what could not be said elsewhere, and for saying the thing that became the ground: *She is beautiful and we love her.*

Thank you, Mom, for all your love and support and visits. I was much better prepared to be Fiona's mother because you raised me.

Thank you to writers and scholars of disability for making work that served as life rafts, especially: Steve Kuusisto, Nancy

Eiesland, Lennard J. Davis, Dana Nieder, Elizabeth Aquino, Gail Heidi Landsman, Emily Rapp Black, Sonya Huber, Jillian Weise, and the late Bill Peace.

Thank you, Southern Vermont College colleagues, especially Daisy Levy and Jennifer Burg, for supporting my attempts to do a daunting trifecta: teach and write and parent.

Thank you, Sarah Menkedick, for launching "SuperBabies Don't Cry" in *Vela* and for your camaraderie thereafter.

Thank you, readers of *Star in Her Eye,* for the kindness and encouragement and grace.

Thank you, You, whose name I'm most certainly forgetting, but whom I will remember as soon as this book goes to print. You served as an integral part of our lives and/or this book and I'm a knucklehead for forgetting you. I owe you a burrito.

Now, for the finale of gratitude. Thank you, Petra and Fiona, for the honor of being your mother. Petra, God bless your strong rock spirit. Fiona, you are a rascal and a delight. I love you both to Infinity and beyond. Now go clear your spot at the table.

And above all: Justin, my best friend, my love, my home, my chronically late and very handsome husband. I love you. Thank you for helping me carve out all the writing hours. Thank you for listening to my ramblings on draft predicaments. Thank you for being game for this whole parenting endeavor. Thank you for saying *yes* to me twenty years ago and every day since. I will never understand what I did to deserve you. I did nothing to deserve you. The gift of your love is the ultimate lesson in grace. Thank you for your love and your laugh and your light and your everything. May our kids someday sleep through the night.

Notes

EPIGRAPH

vii "have planets inside": Stephen Kuusisto, "The Souls of Disabled Folks," *Planet of the Blind*, April 9, 2012, https://stephenkuusisto.com/2012/04 /09/the-souls-of-disabled-folks.

CHAPTER ONE

7 **language of competition:** Virginia Apgar, "A Proposal for a New Method of Evaluation of the Newborn Infant," *Current Researches in Anesthesia and Analgesia* 32, no. 4 (July–August 1953): 260–67.

14 **poster's caption reads:** Gail Heidi Landsman, *Reconstructing Motherhood and Disability in the Age of "Perfect" Babies* (New York: Routledge, 2009), 26.

CHAPTER TWO

25 **"for every effect":** Louise Hay, *Heal Your Body: The Mental Causes for Physical Illness and the Metaphysical Way to Overcome Them* (Carlsbad, CA: Hay House, 1982), 5.

28 *aggravated by stress:* Some italicized quotes from this paragraph are from Heidi Murkoff, *What to Expect When You're Expecting*, 3rd edition (New York: Workman, 2002).

29 **"most common feature":** Landsman, *Reconstructing Motherhood and Disability in the Age of "Perfect" Babies*, 41.

29 **"excellent birth" campaigns:** Teresa Kuan, *Love's Uncertainty: The*

Politics and Ethics of Child Rearing in Contemporary China (Berkeley: University of California Press, 2015): 35.

29 **"new fundamentalist reasoning"**: Celia Dodd, "Planning for a Super-baby," *The Independent*, April 20, 1997, https://www.independent.co.uk /life-style/planning-for-a-superbaby-1268166.html.

29 branch of Nestlé: Nestlé India's Superbabies campaign was hailed by *Forbes* magazine. See Simon Mainwaring, "Nestlé Wins at Social Story-telling by Combining Purpose and Product," *Forbes*, September 9, 2014, https://www.forbes.com/sites/simonmainwaring/2014/09/09/nestle -wins-at-social-storytelling-by-combining-purpose-and-product /#20281bd3faa7.

30 a Japanese study: David Derbyshire, "Why Pregnant Film Fans Should Stick to Happy Movies," *Daily Mail*, March 11, 2010, https://www .dailymail.co.uk/sciencetech/article-1256990/Unborn-babies-respond -mothers-mood-watches-movie-scientists-say.html. For more examples of articles, both popular and scholarly, claiming a woman's emotions affect her baby, see Rachel Glass, "7 Positive and 7 Negative Feelings that Affect an Unborn Baby," *Babygaga*, March 18, 2017, https://www .babygaga.com/7-feelings-that-affect-an-unborn-baby-negatively-and-8 -that-affect-it-positively; Elysia Poggi Davis, Laura M. Glynn, Feizal Waffarn, and Curt A. Sandman, "Prenatal Maternal Stress Programs Infant Stress Regulation," *The Journal of Child Psychology and Psychia-try* 52, no. 2 (February 2011): 119–29; and Michelle Roberts, "Mum's Stress Is Passed to Baby in the Womb," BBC, July 19, 2011, https://www .bbc.com/news/health-14187905.

CHAPTER FOUR

70 Diagnosing doctors were: Landsman, *Reconstructing Motherhood and Disability in the Age of "Perfect" Babies*, 66.

71 *Intent to communicate*: Agatino Battaglia, John C. Carey, and Sarah T. South, "Wolf-Hirschhorn Syndrome," *GeneReviews*, April 29, 2002, https://www.ncbi.nlm.nih.gov/books/NBK1183/.

85 room for not knowing: Pema Chödrön, *When Things Fall Apart: Heart Advice for Difficult Times* (Boston: Shambhala Publications, 1997).

90 *We don't care*: Alison Gopnik, *The Gardener and the Carpenter* (New York: Farrar, Straus, and Giroux, 2017): 87.

CHAPTER FIVE

93 theologians Martin Luther: Chomba Wa Munyi, "Past and Present Perceptions Towards Disability: A Historical Perspective," *Disability Studies Quarterly* 32, no. 2 (2012), dsq-sds.org/article/view/3197/3068.

93 social Darwinists would: Munyi, "Past and Present Perceptions Towards Disability: A Historical Perspective."

93 American public schools: From the 1972 congressional investigation conducted by the Bureau of Education for the Handicapped, which found that 8 million kids needed special education services, but only 3.9 million received an adequate education, and 1.75 million received no education at all. "Individuals with Disabilities Education Act Burden of Proof: On Parents or Schools?," National Council on Disability, August 9, 2005, https://ncd.gov/publications/2005/08092005#executive.

CHAPTER SIX

117 Amelia's mother, Chrissy: Chrissy Rivera, "Brick Walls," Wolfhirschhorn .org, January 12, 2012, http://wolfhirschhorn.org/2012/01/amelia/brick -walls/.

118 journalist Lisa Belkin: Lisa Belkin, "Denying a Transplant to a 'Retarded' Child?" HuffPost, January 16, 2012, https://www.huffpost.com /entry/denying-transplant_b_1207630.

123 *A Literary Companion*: Lynne Barrett and Kristin Kovacic, *Birth: A Literary Companion* (Iowa City: University of Iowa Press, 2002).

CHAPTER SEVEN

142 validated Dave's observation: Chikako Arakawa et al., "Affinity for Music in Wolf-Hirschhorn Syndrome: Two Case Reports," *Pediatric Neurology* 51, no. 4 (October 2014): 550–552.

CHAPTER EIGHT

150 Lennard J. Davis: Lennard J. Davis, "Constructing Normalcy: The Bell Curve, the Novel, and the Invention of the Disabled Body in the Nineteenth Century," *The Disability Studies Reader*, 2nd edition (New York: Routledge, 2006), 3–16.

152 Deborah Deutsch Smith: Deborah Deutsch Smith, *Introduction to Special Education: Making a Difference*, 6th edition (Boston: Allyn & Bacon, 2006): 8.

153 "Everything is our": Soen Nakagawa, "Teisho Day One," *Mahajana*, http://mahajana.net/en/library/texts/teisho-day-one.

154 *Grace laughs in:* Rob Bell, "Jesus H. Christ, Part 7: You Are Already at the Party," The RobCast, episode 216, October 28, 2018.

165 Trees are satisfied: Thomas Merton, *New Seeds of Contemplation* (New York: New Directions, 2007): 29, 31, 32.

167 experts have blamed: Regarding maternal blame for Down syndrome, see Rachel Adams, *Raising Henry: A Memoir of Motherhood, Disability, and Discovery* (New Haven: Yale University Press, 2013): 71; regarding maternal blame for homosexuality, schizophrenia, and autism, see Eula Biss, *On Immunity: An Inoculation* (Minneapolis: Graywolf Press, 2014): 69.

CHAPTER NINE

178 "Despite our best": Thomas Armstrong, "First, Discover Their Strengths," *Educational Leadership* 70, no. 2 (October 2012): 10–16, http://www.ascd.org/publications/educational-leadership/oct12/vol70/num02/First,-Discover-Their-Strengths.aspx.

179 "articulated as 'problems'": Emily A. Nusbaum, Julie Maier, and Jeanne M. Rodriguez, "Capacity or Deficit? An Examination of the Lens that Educators Use to View Student Disability," PEAK Parent Center's *SPEAKout* newsletter, August 15, 2013, https://www.peakparent.org/blog/capacity-or-deficit-examination-lens-educators-use-view-student-disability.

179 limit a child's: Nusbaum, Maier, and Rodriguez, "Capacity or Deficit?"

CHAPTER TWELVE

229 stumbled across Dana: Dana Nieder, "An Open Letter to the Parent of a Child with Speech Delays," *Uncommon Sense*, April 1, 2013, http://niederfamily.blogspot.com/2013/04/an-open-letter-to-parent-of-child-with.html.

230 earliest electronic communication: For images of early electronic communication devices, as well as a brief history, see Gregg C. Vanderheiden, "A Journey Through Early Augmentative Communication and Computer Access," *Journal of Rehabilitation Research and Development* 39, no. 6 (January/December 2002): 39–53, https://www.rehab.research.va.gov/jour/02/39/6/sup/vanderheiden.html.

CHAPTER THIRTEEN

238 a *gravity problem*: Shankar Vedantam, "You 2.0: How Silicon Valley Can Help You Get Unstuck," *Hidden Brain*, NPR, August 28, 2017, https://www.npr.org/templates/transcript/transcript.php?storyId=546716951.

240 "robust communication system": For further AAC support, including what constitutes a robust communication system, I recommend the *PrAACtical AAC* blog at https://www.praacticalaac.org.

245 number of words: Nickee De Leon Huld, "How Many Words Does the Average Person Know?," *Word Counter*, https://wordcounter.io/blog/how-many-words-does-the-average-person-know. (Note: The average number of known, or passive rather than active, words for a native English-speaking twenty-year-old is estimated at forty-two thousand.)

247 "formerly called feeble-minded": Henry H. Goddard, "What Can Public School Do for Subnormal Children?," *Journal of Education* 72, no. 2 (July 1910): 36–37.

248 "the moron type": Joella Straley, "It Took a Eugenicist to Come Up with 'Moron,'" NPR, February 10, 2014, https://www.npr.org/sections/codeswitch/2014/02/10/267561895/it-took-a-eugenicist-to-come-up-with-moron.

248 "is so witless": Greg Eghigian, ed., *From Madness to Mental Health: Psychiatric Disorder and Its Treatment in Western Civilization* (New Brunswick, NJ: Rutgers University, 2010), 74.

CHAPTER FOURTEEN

267 "normal human variation": Jessica Scheer and Nora Ellen Groce, "Impairment as a Human Constant: Cross-Cultural and Historical Perspectives on Variation," *Journal of Social Issues* 44, no. 1 (Spring 1988): 23–37.

267 "people weren't handicapped": Nora Ellen Groce, *Everyone Here Spoke Sign Language* (Cambridge, MA: Harvard University Press, 1985), 5.

267 gene-edited CRISPR babies: Rob Stein, "Scientists Use Gene Editing to Prevent a Form of Deafness in Mice," NPR, December 20, 2017, https://www.npr.org/sections/health-shots/2017/12/20/571208704/scientists-use-gene-editing-to-prevent-a-form-of-deafness-in-mice.

CHAPTER FIFTEEN

278 crime, sexual promiscuity: In his speech "The Burden of Feeble-Mindedness," here's what Walter E. Fernhald, MD, said to the Massa-

chusetts Medical Society in 1912: "The feeble-minded are a parasitic, predatory class, never capable of self-support or of managing their own affairs. . . . They cause unutterable sorrow at home and are a menace and danger to the community." W. E. Fernald, "The Burden of Feeble-Mindedness," *Journal of Psycho-Asthenics* (1913), www.disabilitymuseum. org/dhm/lib/detail.html?id=1208.

278 **Pamphlets were distributed:** My home state's 1908 pamphlet was titled *The Menace of the Feeble Minded in Pennsylvania.* In the state where I became a mother—Ohio—a 1915 pamphlet was titled *The Feeble-Minded: The Hub to Our Wheel of Vice, Crime, and Pauperism.*

278 **1904 and 1923:** Steven Noll, *Feeble-Minded in Our Midst: Institutions for the Mentally Retarded in the South, 1900–1940* (Chapel Hill: University of North Carolina Press, 1995).

278 **two-thirds of feeble-minded:** Lucia L. Jaquith, "The Menace of the Feeble-Minded," *The American Journal of Nursing* 14, no. 4 (January 1914): 268–271.

278 **brother had called:** "Thomas K. Gilhool," Visionary Voices Interview Series, Temple University, Philadelphia, PA, September 28, 2011, http: //www.temple.edu/instituteondisabilities/voices/detailVideo.html?media =006-01.

279 **thirty similar suits:** Kathryn M. Coates, "The Education for All Handicapped Children Act Since 1975," *Marquette Law Review* 69, no. 1 (Fall 1985): 55.

281 **"a national disgrace":** Education Advocates Coalition, "Report by the Education Advocates Coalition on Federal Compliance Activities to Implement the Education for All Handicapped Children Act," April 16, 1980, https://mn.gov/mnddc/parallels2/pdf/80s/80/80-PEA -EAC.pdf.

281 **When President Ford:** "President Gerald R. Ford's Statement on Signing the Education for All Handicapped Children Act of 1975," December 2, 1975, https://www.fordlibrarymuseum.gov/library/speeches /750707.htm.

281 **Justice Thurgood Marshall:** *Cleburne v. Cleburne Living Center,* 473 US 432 (1985).

282 **Taylor Harris writes:** Taylor Harris, "Two Black Parents of an Undiagnosed Child Walk into a Meeting: On Race, Special Education, and Our Son's IEP," *Catapult,* April 17, 2018. https://catapult.co/stories/

column-what-genes-cant-tell-us-education-race-and-our-sons-iep. Harris's book-length memoir is forthcoming from Catapult.

288 Margaret Winzer writes: Margaret Winzer, *The History of Special Education: From Isolation to Integration* (Washington, DC: Gallaudet University Press, 1993), xi.